Literacy, Textbooks and Ideology

Literacy, Textbooks and Ideology:

Postwar Literacy Instruction and the Mythology of Dick and Jane

Allan Luke

 The Falmer Press

(A member of the Taylor & Francis Group)
London, New York and Philadelphia

UK   The Falmer Press, Falmer House, Barcombe, Lewes
East Sussex, BN8 5DL

USA   The Falmer Press, Taylor & Francis Inc., 242 Cherry Street,
Philadelphia, PA 19106-1906

First published in 1988

British Library Cataloguing in Publication Data

Luke, Allan
    Literacy, textbooks and ideology: postwar literacy instruction and the mythology of Dick and Jane.
    1. Literacy—Canada.
    I. Title.
    302.2'0971   LC154.

ISBN 1-85000-318-1
ISBN 1-85000-319-X (Pbk.)

Library of Congress Cataloging-in-Publication Data

Luke, Alan
    Literacy, textbooks, and ideology.
    Bibliography: p.
    Includes indexes.
    1. Literacy—British Columbia—Case studies.   2. Textbooks—British Columbia—Case studies.   3. Education, Elementary—British Columbia—Case studies.   4. Education and state—British Columbia—Case studies.
    I. Title.
    LC154.2.B8L85   1988   372.9711   88-3921
ISBN 1-85000-318-1
ISBN 1-85000-319-X (Pbk.)

Typeset in 11/13 Bembo by
Alresford Typesetting & Design, New Farm Road, Alresford, Hants.

*Printed in Great Britain by
Redwood Burn Limited, Trowbridge, Wiltshire.*

For
Edwin S. Luke
and
Ahlin Wong Luke

Contents

List of Figures

Acknowledgments

Many people have contributed directly and indirectly to the completion of this book. Between 1980 and 1984, Suzanne de Castell and I undertook collaborative research on literacy and schooling: that work and her critical suggestions are reflected here. This text also owes a great deal to Alec McHoul, Carmen Luke and Kieran Egan, who acted as critics and editors on earlier drafts. Richard M. Coe, Paul Delany, Ted Tetsuo Aoki, Pam Gilbert, and Michael Apple provided valuable commentary on particular sections of the work.

The research for this book was supported in part by the Social Sciences and Humanities Research Council of Canada, Simon Fraser University, and James Cook University of North Queensland. Harry Evans, Margarite Cronkite-Weir, Nancy Greer, Eileen Dailly, the British Columbia Ministry of Education, the Canadian High Commission in Canberra, Bob Overgaard and Hugh McPherson generously made documentary and bibliographical materials available.

I would also like to acknowledge the support of Haida Luke, Richard Baldauf, Rhonda Hammer, Kelleen Toohey, Eileen Mallory, Bill Corcoran and Rob Gilbert, and the constructive help of Malcolm Clarkson and Christine Cox of Falmer Press.

I am grateful to the editors of *Teachers College Record* for permission to reprint parts of Chapter 3, an early version of which appeared in vol. 88, no. 5 of that journal. Finally, I would like to acknowledge the cooperation of W.J. Gage, Canada for their permission to reprint pp. 6–7 from William S. Gray and May Hill Arbuthnot's *Fun with Dick and Jane* (Toronto, n.d.), pp. 6–7 from Gray and Arbuthnot's *Our New Friends* (Toronto, n.d.), and the back cover page from Frank Quance's *The Canadian Speller* (Toronto, 1950).

Introduction

The slogan 'back to the basics' is above all an historical locution. The effectiveness and appeal of the rhetoric of the basics movement can be traced to its lack of a concrete historical referent. Whether repeated in newspaper editorial, parent-teacher meeting, political speech or news broadcast, the slogan allows addressees to recall any particular era of schooling that they may care to romanticize. Many reconstruct images of their own schooling: in the period before the permissiveness of the 1960s, we are often told, children attended, complied with school rules unquestioningly, and joined the workforce with a solid background in reading and writing. In the US and the UK the larger mythology of postwar educational efficiency extols an era of Empire, a period when the particular nation state in question asserted greater economic and geopolitical power. Hence, it should come as little surprise that the present rhetoric of educational reform situates 'excellence' of the educational system as a necessary and perhaps sufficient condition for capital expansion, technological innovation, political and even military leadership. One American academic candidly explains that 'the connection from here to there, from schoolhouse to missile strength, is quite clear'.[1] Moreover, neglect of the educational system, one of the recent government reports tells us, is tantamount to national unilateral 'disarmament'.[2]

Since the late 1950s advocates of the human capital rationale have argued that technological progress and economic equality could be socially engineered through expansion and improvement of the school system. The parallels between the Sputnik-era educational debate and that of the present are many: external threats to technological and military superiority are invoked to justify a reconsideration of educational policy and practice. A range of well-financed reforms — upgrading of teacher pay and training, classroom re-emphasis of the basics, renewed stress of applied and scientific studies — have been placed on the state agenda. Yet through its very rhetoric this latest version of the human capital argument, however detailed, subjects the school system to apparent responsibility for such wider social phenomena as crime and immorality, unemployment, and the loss of technological markets and leadership. There may be a kind of poetic justice at work here. For to argue, as many politicians, teachers, academics and others have continued to do, that education is capable of remediating the social and economic problems of industrial and post-industrial capitalism, sets schooling as a potential scapegoat for the ills of that system.

Nowhere is this kind of rhetorical inversion of the promise of modern education more exploited than in debate over declines in literacy standards and instruction. Even among academics, the widespread acceptance of what Harvey Graff has termed the 'literacy myth' continues: universal, increased levels of literacy are viewed as a necessary prerequisite and primary cause of the exercise of manifest destiny, cultural and economic development, equality and political participation.[3] Acceptance of the myth enables its inversion: that decreased levels of literacy are a primary determining factor for a range of social and educational problems. Yet attacks on the schools for declining standards of literacy have been near constant since the nineteenth-century expansion of universal schooling in North America.[4] Generally speaking, the reiteration of such claims appears to be tied more to various kinds of state crises, whether economic or moral, than directly to particular failures or innovations in pedagogy or curriculum. As Habermas has noted, when state, economic and cultural 'steering mechanisms' run awry, high-visibility institutions are immediate and obvious targets for criticism.[5]

I am not here arguing that there may in fact not be a crisis related to reading and writing as cultural practices. The case that the maintenance and spread of illiteracy is one means for the sustained economic disadvantage and political disenfranchisement of particular minority groups is undoubtedly valid, and as yet there is no sign in any post-industrial English-speaking nation of the kind of 'total national mobilization' that would be necessary to begin addressing this problem.[6] Yet perhaps equally disquieting is mounting evidence that even among the nominally literate there are signs of a 'comprehension crisis',[7] that while most students achieve a rudimentary ability to decode written text, many do not develop the capacity to get meaning from text, much less to analyse critically and act upon it. Elsewhere, Suzanne de Castell and I have argued that the parameters of the crisis may be fundamentally misconceived by advocates of the basics and educators alike: the problem may lie in the successful transmission of rudimentary non-critical skills and the correlative diminution of the critical requirements of the social texts of everyday life.[8] If indeed this is the case, the remedies proposed by many recent reports and commissions — more precise, technical approaches to instruction, more efficient state-of-the-art curricular technology, better teacher training in aspects of instructional psychology, increased standardized testing, firmer school discipline and order — may cover a reassertion of literacy training as a form of social control, as a way of deskilling users of text and of precluding critique on the part of students and teachers.

If we pause to track the logic of the basics movement a step further, the hazy image of the past becomes a bit clearer. Some brazenly invoke nineteenth-century standards, oblivious of the fact that the retention rates of nineteenth-century schools, the student population, and the complexity of the curriculum — as well as the actual social functions and uses of literacy in that era — are at the least difficult to compare with their modern counterparts. Others, academics and countless editorial writers,[9] locate current problems in the 1960s and early 1970s. One wonders how long critics will be able to lay blame for contemporary anomalies on the purported permissiveness and pedagogical experimentation of the 1960s when, nearly two decades later, those limited experiments have long since ceased. In Canada and the United States, the traces of counter-cultural education remain primarily in the institutional repetition of the rhetoric of child-centred education. Stated concern for the individual, whole child continues to be used as a rationale for virtually every kind of intervention from special education programmes to minimum competency testing. There is, additionally, a good deal of evidence that in both beginning reading and writing, skills-based, worksheet oriented instruction, weekly spelling lists and the other staples of 1940s and '50s schooling — rather than the pedagogical *laissez-faire* hypothesized by critics — continue to constitute the core of basic literacy training.[10]

Perhaps the round condemnation of the 1960s and the resurrection of the basics, however construed, are part of a more general, mass-cultural nostalgia for Dick and Jane's white picket fence world of postwar America and Canada. We see it in Hollywood's America, in the spate of movies and television reruns about pristine lifestyles and social relations without visible minorities, economic injustice, English as a Second Language, homosexuality and the like. It is a key vision for politicians and preachers of the New Right, which calls for a return to an unsullied community life, based on simple morality, 'natural' social and economic relations,[11] and, of course, the 'basics' in schools and families. Legitimation crises might indeed have their bases in the contradictory grounds of success and failure of the technocratic state. The ethos of technicism, its suspension of normative questions under the auspices of achieved consensus around the need for technological progress and capital expansion, may have generated across the political spectrum a scepticism towards the putatively value neutral stance of the secular state and corporation. Hence, this nostalgia for a past with unambiguous and simple values and economics may result from a perceived need for the restitution of normative grounds.

But were the 1950s an era of simple efficiency, classroom discipline and the basics in schools? It is perhaps best to begin this story at its ending. I first became interested in the basics movement and literacy standards in the early 1970s while I was teaching at secondary and primary schools in Western Canada. At the time, the gloss of 1960s educational and social reform was fading. In the mid 1970s, the British Columbia electorate turned away its first-term social democrat government, which had curtailed standardized achievement testing and year-end provincial examinations, banned corporal punishment and encouraged a range of curricular experiments in fields such as the creative and expressive arts, environmental education, early childhood and special education. The conservative Social Credit party, which had ruled the province throughout the 1950s and '60s in dynastic fashion, was returned to office and the path lay open for successive ministers of education to reinvent the human capital argument. They were encouraged by an emergent New Right: organizations like the 'Genuine Education Movement' garnered widespread support from both working-class and professional constituencies.[12] In concert with fundamentalist groups in rural and suburban areas, they argued that the child centred programmes of the 1960s had failed and a return to the basics was necessary, that hard work, discipline and simple morality, combined with a curricular re-emphasis on business, technical and scientific skills should supplant an over-emphasis on arts and humanities.

Faced with this, the provincial teachers' union, like many of its partner organizations throughout Canada and the US, attacked the agenda of the basics advocates as authoritarian and overly simplistic. Yet unlike those of the 1960s and early '70s, these were not strategic attempts to mark out further the terrain of reform and innovation. Rather they were tactical, defensive moves to amass public support against a resurgent back-to-the-basics movement supported by a business oriented, conservative government. The rhetoric of progressivism was reinvoked: teachers and the opposition party argued that any such return would diminish equality of educational opportunity. The terms of the debate, which continues to this day, would be familiar to US, UK and Australian educators: standards versus equality, traditionalism versus progressivism, applied sciences versus the humanities.

During this period — at school staff meetings, local school board meetings, seminars with researchers, and from parents and politicians — I heard a widely accepted explanation: that the 'pendulum swings' back and forth endlessly in educational policy, and that as surely as it was swinging to the right, it would, sooner or later, return to the left. This metaphor, used to describe shifts in politics, theology, morality, and economics, is a common form of 'rhetorical symmetrization': by burying historical contingencies in purportedly 'natural' swings, real issues, levels and contexts are mystified.[13] I realized then that most of the participants, myself included, had a very limited knowledge of the historical bases for claims of falling standards and of the wider social factors which mediate educational change.

Unfortunately, many of us trained in the blush of the 1960s and '70s were no more aware of the historical issues and forces at work than those whom we saw as our conservative adversaries. We considered ourselves the first generation of innovators. Many believed that child-centred education was a new movement, contraposed against the traditionalists who had educated us in the 1950s. With the continued domination of teacher training by a curious admixture of educational psychology and child-centred humanism, we were not well versed in the histories of the curriculum or of educational ideas: both revisionist educational history and neomarxist educational theory would, somewhat ironically, only come of age in the subsequent, relatively quiescent period which Ira Shor calls the 'conservative restoration'.[14] In short, many of us beginning our teaching careers in the period were convinced that we had invented humanism and progressivism. Compounding this problem, when I queried older colleagues, local school board members and academics I found that even the very recent educational past was shrouded in myth and anecdote, obscured by current political allegiances.

This book is an attempt to demystify that era from the end of World War II to the launch of Sputnik, to examine what counted as literacy in the public elementary schools of British Columbia. I chose British Columbia as the locale of the present study for both pragmatic and practical purposes: the pressing need to address the local debate over standards and practices, and the need to delimit a field of inquiry into a manageable site and set of texts. However, as in current debates, rhetoric and practices cross borders. I am confident that readers will be able to draw parallels with other, more familiar local contexts. This will be particularly easy in many educational jurisdictions because of the complex and ongoing influence of US educational innovations in other English-speaking countries.

This book is about literacy. Specifically, it is an attempt to reconstruct aspects of the experience of becoming literate in a particular institutional setting, in a particular locale. In taking what counted as literacy as my topic, I do not imply that that range of factors beyond the trace of school documents examined here is of negligible significance. My broad assumptions, however, are that how children learn literacy in the formal setting of the school has some constitutive influence on how they might come to see its purposes and uses, and that how a society chooses to initiate youth into a literate culture is at least in part indicative of how it construes the value and potential of textual competence.

This study is by no means a comprehensive account and, like many other contemporary studies of historical curriculum, it entails a series of methodological and material compromises. I had initially set out to study literacy-related standards in the postwar curriculum from elementary to post-secondary levels, only to unearth such a volume of documentary information that I was forced to narrow the field first to elementary schools, then focusing on beginning reading and language arts instruction. It does, however, attempt to situate that history relative to larger questions in the history of literacy and to current debates about literacy teaching.

This book is about textbooks. Because my concern was to capture not only what textbooks said and how they said it, but how various curricular documents might have been used and experienced, my initial choice was to include oral histories. However, after several interviews with people who had worked in education during this period, I began to suspect that oral history would lead to a reproduction of the same problem which was confounding public and professional debate over literacy. My subjects appeared to be reconstructing the past through twenty years of hindsight, mediating their versions of postwar training through current political allegiances and, often, through several decades of teaching experience. From there, I moved towards documentary, textual materials. Of course these included historical textbooks, and the discourse analysis of selected narratives from beginning and intermediate reading textbooks is focal here. But I have integrated commentary from a range of other texts often neglected in curricular studies: these include teachers' guides, teachers' and research journals, ministry curriculum documents, ministry directives to local administrators and teachers, and educational monographs from the period.

Finally, this book is about ideology. Any attempt to reconstruct what counted as literacy in schools must take its lead from developments in the critical sociology of the curriculum and, indeed, my aim here is to establish how a particular selective tradition of school knowledge and competences operated from and expressed ideological assumptions and structures. However, I intended to avoid a more conventional documentary history of the curriculum, and deliberately set out to expose the texts of that particular era to as wide a range of critical perspectives as possible. Hence, approaches from educational theory and history, discourse analysis and semiotics, and literacy studies are used throughout to 'read' the texts of the postwar era. Specifically, the use of the story-grammar approach to the study of texts heretofore has been limited to psychological and linguistic studies of current curricula and Eco's semiotic typology for textual narratives has not been applied to educational texts. Both, I believe, yield considerably greater latitude in the hypothesizing of possible ideological effects of curricula than a more traditional ideological content analysis might have enabled. Additionally, neither the historical construction of a curriculum, nor the scripts of historical teachers' guidebooks have been scrutinized in critical histories of the curriculum. Both are examined here.

In defence of the wide range of materials examined and methods used, I cannot accept the view that any particular text or context can be seen as determining what counted as school knowledge in a given era, nor the linear view of ideology and curriculum therein. Hence, I attempt here to call attention to a variety of historical texts and contexts, rather than attributing a determining or causal role to any one. Because of this, and the methodological complications involved, educational sociologists will no doubt be bothered by the lack of extended discussion of such social theoretic concepts as ideology and hegemony, historians by the provisional consideration of socioeconomic context, language educators and linguists by the selectivity of the discourse analysis of children's reading texts. From the standpoint of their various disciplines, their criticisms are likely to be on solid footing. But despite the inevitable exclusions that such methodological eclecticism made necessary, I would hope that the result provides a broader and richer sense of what counted as literacy in postwar schools than otherwise would have been enabled, and that it augments the range of current methods for examining both historical and contemporary curricula.

This book, then, concerns how we go about teaching children to master the complex technology of reading and writing. What now strikes me about the 'great debate' over literacy is how naive the participants have been and continue to be about the range of social, political and cultural forces which inform both their positions as debators and the classroom practices around which the debate centres. Perhaps educators will see in the study mirror images of current controversies, for I could not help but be amused at how many of our current practices and positions — whether traditionalist or innovative — and, for that matter, how many of the current social, economic and political influences on schooling have their parallels in the postwar period. Without being overly optimistic, I would hope that there remain for us all some lessons in the not so distant past.

Notes and References

1. John H. Best, 'Reforming America's Schools: The High Price of Failure', *Teachers College Record* 86 (1984), 269.
2. National Commission on Excellence in Education, *A Nation at Risk: The Imperative for Educational Reform* (Washington, DC: US Department of Education, 1983); for critical commentary on the rhetoric of this and other national and regional reports on education, see Michael W. Apple, *Teachers and*

Texts: A Political Economy of Class and Gender Relations in Education (London: Routledge and Kegan Paul, 1986), esp. ch. 6; Allan Luke and Suzanne de Castell, 'Educational "Crises" and the Rhetoric of Reform: The Arnold/ Huxley Debate Reconsidered', *Access* 4 (No. 2, 1985), 22–40; Maxine Green, ' "Excellence", Meanings, and Multiplicity', *Teachers College Record* 86 (1984), 283–98; 'Symposium on the Year of the Reports: Responses from the Educational Community', *Harvard Educational Review* 54 (No. 2, 1984), 1–31.

3. See Harvey J. Graff, *The Literacy Myth: Literacy and Social Structure in the Nineteenth-Century City* (New York: Academic Press, 1979); *The Legacies of Literacy: Continuities and Contradictions in Western Culture and Society* (Bloomington: Indiana University Press, 1987); *The Labyrinths of Literacy: Reflections on Literacy Past and Present* (London: Falmer Press, 1987).

4. Ibid.; see also Shirley B. Heath, 'The Functions and Uses of Literacy', in Suzanne de Castell, Allan Luke, and Kieran Egan (eds), *Literacy, Society and Schooling* (Cambridge: Cambridge University Press, 1986), p. 15; Tom Wick, 'The Pursuit of Universal Literacy', *Journal of Communication* 30 (No. 1, 1980), 107–12.

5. Jurgen Habermas, *Legitimation Crisis* (London: Heineman, 1976).

6. See Leslie J. Limage, 'Adult Literacy Policy in Industrialized Countries', in Robert Arnove and Harvey J. Graff (eds), *National Literacy Campaigns: Historical and Comparative Perspectives* (New York: Plenum, 1987), p. 312. See also Carman Hunter and David Harman, *Adult Illiteracy in the United States* (New York: McGraw-Hill, 1979); Jonathan Kozal, *Illiterate America* (New York: Anchor/Doubleday, 1985).

7. Walter H. MacGinitie and Ruth K. MacGinitie, 'Teaching Students Not to Read', in de Castell *et al.* (eds), *Literacy, Society and Schooling*, pp. 256–9.

8. Suzanne de Castell and Allan Luke, 'Literacy Instruction: Technology and Technique', *American Journal of Education* 95 (1987), 413–40.

9. See, for example, Paul Copperman, *The Literacy Hoax* (New York: Morrow, 1979).

10. For commentary on current practices in the teaching of reading, see Richard C. Anderson, Elfrieda H. Hiebert, Judith A. Scott, and Ian A. Wilkinson, *Becoming a Nation of Readers: The Report of the Commission on Reading* (Washington, DC: National Institute of Education, 1984). For descriptions of the teaching of writing, see W.T. Petty and P.J. Finn, 'Classroom Teachers' Reports on Teaching Written Composition', in Shirley Haley-James, *Perspectives on Writing in Grades 1–8* (Urbana, Ill.: National Council for Teachers of English, 1981), pp. 23–7.

11. For a critique of the ideology of biologism implicit in the rhetoric of the New Right, see Steven Rose, R.C. Lewontin, and Leon Kamin, *Not in Our Genes: Biology, Ideology and Human Nature* (Harmondsworth: Penguin, 1984), esp. ch. 1. See also, Frances Fitzgerald, *Cities on a Hill* (New York: Simon and Schuster, 1986), ch. 3.

12. Margaret T. Morgan and Norman Robinson, 'The "Back to the Basics" Movement in Education', *Canadian Journal of Education* 1 (No. 2, 1976), 1–12.

13. Anthony Wilden, *The Imaginary Canadian* (Vancouver: Pulp Press, 1981).

14. Ira Shor, *Culture Wars: School and Society in the Conservative Restoration, 1969–1984* (London: Routledge and Kegan Paul, 1986) provides a contrasting perspective on the aftermath of 'counter-cultural' education.

Chapter 1

Approaches to the Study of Literacy and Curriculum

Despite theoretical developments in curriculum studies, social theory and educational historiography, the contemporary study of curriculum in historical context confronts us with a range of critical options. Certainly the last decade has yielded various theoretical constructions for explaining the role of official school knowledge in the larger processes of cultural and economic reproduction. What remains problematic is the matter of how we are to go about actually reading the artefacts of schooling. Equally important is the problem of how we establish intertextual relationships between the various kinds and levels of historical artefacts of instruction, that is, how — using contemporary theoretical perspectives — the student of the history of the curriculum situates, for example, the students' textbook relative to the administrative memo, departmental syllabus, or teachers' guidebook.

The study of literacy as a subject in the curriculum poses a second stratum of epistemological and methodological problems, for any sociology of knowledge would acknowledge that such a complex social technology as literacy has, even within a given era, a range of possible constructions and definitions. Social historical research most clearly frames the problems of definition which underlie all studies of literacy, whether current or historical: even the most rudimentary definition of literacy, or for that matter, literacy-related pedagogy, reflects and sets a range of epistemic boundaries. Prior to identifying the curriculum in question and its historical context, then, I want in this chapter to situate the present study relative to larger questions in the historical and contemporary study of literacy, then specifying a body of approaches for reading the texts of literacy instruction in British Columbia, 1946–60.

Issues in the Historical Quality of Literacy

World War II, like the previous war, had revealed to educators and policy makers apparent deficiencies in the century-long effort to achieve universal literacy via mass compulsory schooling. Tests administered to US army recruits, reported in the popular press and teachers' journals, apparently indicated high rates of 'functional illiteracy'. In consequence, organizations like UNESCO, the US National Society for the Study of Education, and later the OECD allocated substantial resources for the study of literacy and the establishment and expansion of literacy programmes in both developed and developing countries.[1] Yet the spate of postwar studies, proposals and programmes — highlighted by leading American reading researcher William S. Gray's involvement with UNESCO[2] — begged fundamental questions about the functions and uses of literacy in modern society. In the headlong rush to achieve universal literacy, many researchers, educational administrators, and teachers tended to presuppose as nonproblematic the collective and individual benefits of literacy.

The historical development and social consequences of literacy, then, remained a relatively minor concern of educational researchers in this postwar era, who in the main were preoccupied with curricular research and programme development tasks. In Canada, however, several major interdisciplinary works addressed these contentious matters: first, economist Harold A. Innis's *The Bias of Communication*,[3] explored the historical effects of particular information technologies on cultural, economic, and political organization. A decade later, literary critic Marshall McLuhan, drawing liberally from Innis's work, speculated on the cultural and cognitive effects of literacy in *The Gutenberg Galaxy*.[4] In Britain, Richard Hoggart, founder of the Centre for Contemporary Cultural Studies at Birmingham University and later director of UNESCO, published *The Uses of Literacy*,[5] an exploration of the relationship of literacy to schooling, mass culture and social class. Finally, Goody's *Literacy in Traditional Societies*[6] opened the study of literacy to a range of social scientific methods. Examining cross-historical and cross-cultural data on literacy, Goody and Watt supported the McLuhan/Innis hypothesis regarding social, cognitive and cultural effects intrinsic to the development of literacy in a given culture.[7] Citing historical, anthropological and literary exemplars, they hypothesized that the advent of literacy was a primary factor in the evolution of various social, economic and cultural phenomena, including scientific thought, the organization of religious practices, bureaucratic and central record keeping, and the development of commerce.[8]

Since Goody and Watt's work, and contemporaneous demographic research,[9] social historians and anthropologists have amassed extensive data on the actual historical distribution of literacy in the West since antiquity. Historical research undertaken in Sweden, France, Britain, the United States and Western Europe has centred on the task of demystifying literacy.[10] This has involved what social historian Graff calls a 'stripping' process: a separation of historical 'literacy myths', alleged moral, political, social and economic attributes of literacy, from actual historical concomitants and effects.[11]

Social historians used the tools of demographic and sociological analysis, as against narrative approaches, to isolate the spread of literacy among the general populace. This task required the surmounting of a major methodological problem: the specification of historically valid criteria of literacy. Having discarded accounts which presupposed the unquestioned moral and cultural value of literacy, and sceptical of conventional criteria offered by educational research (e.g., levels of school achievement, examination and test results), social historians had to generate an alternative standard by which to judge retrospectively who was 'literate'.[12] Graff and Cressy, following earlier work by Lockridge on colonial New England, turned to census figures and signatures on legal documents in an attempt to ascertain the distribution of literacy in nineteenth-century Upper Canada and sixteenth- and seventeenth-century England respectively.[13] These and other analyses succeeded in showing that the extent and importance of literacy had been overestimated and, moreover, that literacy in and of itself may have not been a prime historical agent of social and economic development, and political participation. Speaking of the social efects of literacy in Elizabethan and Stuart England, Cressy comments that:

> Literacy is associated with independence, political alertness, superior information, rationality, modernity and a host of equally desirable accomplishments. . . . We should not assume that people were wiser or more in control of their environment just because they had become literate. . . . The skill could be squandered, used to rot the mind as well as inform it.[14]

The fallacious equation of literacy with sociocultural progress — still prominent in the literature on national development, language planning and language education — Graff labels the 'modernization paradigm'.[15]

Yet this social historical scholarship was itself based on a methodological leap of faith: in their move to isolate literacy as an empirically verifiable phenomenon, social historians of necessity tended towards a reductionist definition of the functions and uses of a complex historical technology. Hence much of their research is premised on a narrowly quantitative interpretation of what counted as literacy in given cultures, in particular historical epochs (e.g., the ability to sign legal documents). This methodological reduction in turn yielded the insight that operant criteria, and formal and informal settings for the acquisition and use of literacy, have varied widely according to time, place, and sociocultural context.

Surveying the historical data, Resnick and Resnick note that literacy campaigns in nation states have typically specified divergent criteria for both 'levels' (quantity) and 'kinds' (quality) of literacy.[16] One implication of this historical relativist position is that the specification of levels of adequate competence in reading and writing and of adequate distribution of those different levels within a given populace involves normative decisions regarding who should actually possess literate competence, and to what ends differential kinds and levels of literate competence should function within a given social context. The historical record, moreover, indicates that those secular and non-secular figures charged by the state, church and other institutions with the institutional disbursement of literate competence have been situated in a prescriptive social role.[17] In fact, in some instances the assumption of responsibility for literacy training by formal state authorities and institutions led to apparent declines in literate competence among the general populace.[18] In his analysis of Victorian educational reforms undertaken in the name of industrial progress, Richard Johnson has argued that 'it is difficult to see how a process that often involved deskilling and the destruction of a previously literate workforce can have produced, by main economic force, an educational revolution'.[19]

Social historians seem acutely aware that their quantitative research has generated a range of questions regarding the historical quality of literacy. The task of collating diverse quantitative data yielded by social historical research is well under way, and levels and spread of basic literacy having been established, the task at hand is to detail more exactly matters of historical quality of literacy.[20] For example, in a site like postwar British Columbia census data enables the specification of levels of 'functional illiteracy' among the adult population at roughly 6.76 per cent, judging by census data on the completion of five years of formal education.[21] Yet criteria used for the interpretation of census data vary: the US National Census appraises levels of literacy in terms of the completion of six years of formal schooling; a recent OECD study indicated that approximately 20 per cent of Canadians were functionally illiterate, not having completed nine years of formal schooling.[22] To compound the problem further, organizations like UNESCO have changed criteria for literacy on a near-continuous basis.[23]

What remains moot is the kind of literacy 'completion of grade five' or, for that matter, 'ability to sign one's name on legal documents' entailed.

Generally speaking, data on historical quantity beget a myriad of questions regarding historical quality. Could the literate 'appreciate' a work of literature? Could they demonstrate 'adequate' proficiency at oral reading? Or 'comprehend' an unfamiliar text? Could they read and write adequately and appropriately to conduct daily social and economic tasks? Crucial here is an acknowledgment that modern data on literacy and illiteracy which use educational achievement as a criterion measure are based upon assumptions about formal and informal practices and standards for the teaching and learning of literacy in institutional settings like the school.

Both social historical research and UNESCO-type studies of educational policy and language planning which rely upon quantitative criterion measures of literacy, then, have returned researchers full circle back to questions of culturally and historically specific literate conventions and educational standards. The detailing of the quality of literacy in contemporary societies has been taken up in recent years by educational ethnographers and social psychologists.[24] Notably, Heath's *Ways with Words*[25] is a model of how ethnographic enquiry can provide a detailed description of context-specific functions and uses of literacy shared by members of a community. Heath's participant observation study details actual literate and oral competence in pre-school linguistic socialization, school-based formal instruction, and out-of-school social and economic contexts. Her findings question many of the assumptions about literacy taken for granted by researchers and educators: that a strict divide can be drawn between oral and literate subcultures; that the industrial workplace necessarily demands higher levels of literacy; that the school is the major institutional support for the acquisition and use of literacy.

One of Heath's most telling findings regards the apparent lack of complementarity between school-based literacy activities and community uses. The popular and academic association of schooling with literacy, which we have seen underlies most large-scale demographic studies, would appear to be a significant aspect of the modern literacy myth. Not only do commentators continue to assume that literacy in itself will yield economic progress and social equality, but as well, many continue to confuse the complex effects and relationships of schooling and literacy. In their fieldwork with the West African Vai, Scribner and Cole examined literacy in three languages, acquired in distinct and autonomous formal and informal settings.[26] Using survey instruments and ethnographic observation, they established the actual spread and significance of literacy in the life of the community. Their qualitative data were augmented with quantitative data from tests developed in the field to measure levels of literate competence, cognitive and linguistic ability. Multivariate analysis enabled the identification of significant relationships between cognition, social competence and literacy in each of the three languages. Scribner and Cole found that the kinds and levels of cognitive and social consequences of literacy in Vai, Arabic and English were mediated by the contexts of acquisition and contexts of subsequent use.

In all, this work signals that the case for intrinsic and universal 'social and cognitive effects' of literate competence may in fact be based on a conflation of the effects of schooling as a socialization and educational process with the effects of literacy *per se*.[27] Scribner and Cole point out that research in developmental psychology, anthropology and other disciplines has been premised on the belief that literacy is 'likely to have the same . . . consequences in all cultures irrespective of the context of use or of the social institutions in which literacy is embedded'.[28] Complementing Heath's research, their analysis underlines the need for a re-evaluation of researchers' and educators' presuppositions regarding literacy's transferability to and ultimate social and cognitive effects in real sociocultural contexts.

A further implication of their identification of distinct effects and competences yielded by differentially acquired and used literacies is that what counts as literacy in modern cultures may be lodged within the prescriptive agendas of social institutions (e.g., school, family, community, religious organization, workplace) which transmit and demand literacy. For instance, Scribner and Cole found that learning to read in Arabic for religious purposes entails very different cognitive consequences and discursive practices than learning to read in English for specialized educational purposes. Heath's review of cross-cultural studies corroborates this general point, showing that the actual acquisition and use of literacy seem to be contingent upon systems of 'institutional supports' which transmit, reinforce and require literate competences.[29]

For my present purposes, these studies of the quality of literacy in modern settings suggest that two particular sociocultural contexts bear further investigation: contexts of use in everyday life *and* institutional contexts geared for the teaching and learning of literacy. The latter are the focus of this study. Since the Protestant Reformation, Western nation states typically have used formal schooling systems as the means for regulating and norming access to, competence with, and understanding of text. This legacy exists intact today: in an atmosphere of seemingly perpetual literacy crises, the citizenry of industrial and post-industrial nations holds the institutions of mass compulsory public education responsible for the provision of competence in reading and writing.

The tenacity of the literacy myth, intertwined with human capital arguments about schooling, is remarkable: the widened distribution of various forms of literacy — whether 'minimum competence' with text or the kinds of literacy now seen as imperative with electronic information media — is generally associated in the discourse of educational policy with an array of social effects, varying from the production of 'highly skilled human capital',[30] to economic and racial equality,[31] ultimately to less abstract outcomes like 'missile strength'.[32] Clearly, the challenge is not only to examine literacy further as an actual social phenomenon in current terms, but as well to demystify further its historical status in the discourses of educational curriculum and policy.

In 'Towards an Ethnohistory of Writing in American Education',[33] Heath describes the task of historical research on the quality of literacy:

> This approach may be conceived of as research directed toward the formulation of a descriptive theory of writing as a part of the cultural phenomenon of literacy (including both reading and writing) and as a part of larger cultural systems (economic, religious, social). A complete description would include definitions of communities in which writing took place; the types of writing acts, events and situations available to specific community members; norms of writing; and the methods of learning these norms and of having them reinforced.[34]

In recent North American history, the description of contexts of acquisition and the norms they presuppose and attempt to enforce requires the examination of historical curricula. Here Heath is concerned not only with the conventions for learning of textual competence, but also with the making and using of text, locating any such description in terms of economic, religious and social considerations. We might conclude from this that historical practices for the teaching and learning of literacy must be reviewed in the larger context of sociocultural ideologies within which they were embedded.

The determination of historical quality of literacy, then, in part involves the reconstruction of the experience of becoming literate, on the basis of existing textual artefacts. This necessarily must be an educational history which focuses on the texts of mass schooling. But as well it must be a kind of discourse analysis since the primary data are documentary:

> a first step would be collection of artifacts of literacy, descriptions of contexts and uses, and their spatial and temporal distribution within the life of members of the community. The internal style of each artifact and the abilities of those who produce these artifacts should be considered part of this context.[35]

This rereading of the 'internal style' of textual artefacts, to see how it is part of the text's 'context', requires discourse analysis with particular stress on the structure and style of discourse and on intertextual relationships. Additionally, to uncover or generalize about the authors' personal histories, intellectual precursors or intents, the focus of such research should be on 'the abilities of those who produce' text as a criticial part of the historical context of text use and comprehension. Heath proposes to use the analysis of historical and contemporary textual artefacts as a means for understanding and making generalizations about authors and users of text, and about how text became a part of the 'life of members of the community'. Integral to my interest here, then, is an analysis of the status, style, structure and content of texts, how they were produced, by whom, and according to what dominant assumptions about literacy, the literate, and the teaching and learning of literacy.

As for the conditions of 'use' and the 'ability to use' text, a range of questions can be asked:

> How are these artifacts presented to children? What activities and explanations surround their use? Do questions directed to children about these artifacts emphasize the acquisition of labels and descriptions of discrete characteristics of items? Are there links made between these representations and use of their real world equivalents?[36]

Also, the reading of historical artifacts should focus on institutional conditions for the production of texts and on the specialized conditions of use encountered by children in formal (institutional) introductions to textual competence.

In any given era, reading and writing 'like other systems of communication' are 'organized . . . in culture-specific ways and according to certain norms of interpretation'[37] within particular communities of speakers and writers; that is, the writing and reading of a text, whether it be broadsheet or scripture, newspaper or novel, follow a set of codes, of interpretative norms. As a contribution to a more comprehensive history of literacy and to the critical sociology of the curriculum, my aim here is to examine two specific aspects of the quality of literacy in a particular era: the culturally and historically specific norms of reading and writing conveyed through curricular texts, and the institutionally prescribed 'methods of learning these norms and of having them reinforced' as described in teachers' guidebooks, administrative directives and contemporary monographs. Moreover, as Heath further suggests, the insights yielded by this kind of research on texts, their making, use and teaching, might provide a valuable perspective on modern approaches and attitudes towards literacy.

The Selective Tradition of Literary Instruction

Definitions and practices of literacy continually change over time in accordance with changing social and cultural conditions for the acquisition and use of literacy. This is even the case in those societies with long-standing traditions of reading and writing. While oracy can be viewed as an innate species behaviour, the abilities to read and write are acquired through culturally specific, formal and informal systems of pedagogy. Hence, literacy can be considered a 'set of socially organized practices which make use of a symbol system and a technology for producing and disseminating it'.[38] Practices of literacy and the very material form of the technology (e.g., script, typography, teletext) undergo historical evolution, as do attendant sets of educational practices for the teaching of literate competence. Different cultures and subcultures, in different historical epochs, have generated distinct modes for the dissemination of literate competence.[39] But while a technology in theory at least may be neutral, modes of training in the use of a given technology invariably prescribe constraints upon and conventions governing that use.[40]

Practices of literacy instruction are based upon assumptions about the characteristics and development of literate competence, and they correlatively prescribe functions and uses of literacy in a given society. We see this most clearly in current debates about contending approaches to teaching reading, writing and the language arts (e.g., 'whole language' versus 'skills-based' approaches, 'process' versus product orientations and, alas, phonics versus word-recognition methods). Often unbeknownst to participants, within such debates lies a stratum of normative assumptions not only about what is to count as literacy but about the ultimate social purposes and political potential of literacy: whether this be the ethos of, for instance, individual empowerment and personal voice,[41] of basic morality and skill, or of rudimentary 'functional' job skills and the maintenance of an industrial order. And yet, as in many debates over pedagogy, with the demand for face validity and public accountability, the primary grounds for rational justification remain circumscribed within the narrow confines of educational policy and research. Proponents of whole-language or culture-sensitive approaches to literacy, for instance, regardless of their ultimate intents, must justify such approaches in terms of conventional technical indices of educational efficiency (e.g., standardized test scores, grade level achievement, job suitability).

Lost in this rush towards demonstrable outcomes is Paulo Freire's insight that literacy instruction essentially implies an orientation towards the relationship between individuals and the world:

> All educational practice implies a theoretical stance on the
> educator's part. This stance in turn implies — sometimes more,
> sometimes less explicitly — an interpretation of man and the
> world.[42]

Here Freire's general point is that educational practice simultaneously
assumes and prescribes a theoretical position regarding the role of language,
thought and action in human praxis. Through pedagogy the literate learns a
way of theorizing about the world,[43] a set of culturally specific schemata
about what will count as text and what will count as interaction around
text.[44] His specific point, constant throughout his writings on literacy
campaigns in developing countries, is that literacy curricula and instruction
imply an ideological agenda regarding the uses, values and functions of
literacy as a social, political and economic tool. This is after all what any
technology is concerned with: the extension through artifice of
humankind's capacity to transform through labour the natural and social
environment.[45]

From the basic assumption that literacy-related pedagogy by definition
entails the selection of a particular educational ideology which in turn prescribes how the technology should be used, Freire further argues, the
analysis of pedagogy should proceed.

> Teaching . . . must be seen, analysed and understood in this way.
> The critical analyst will discover in the methods and texts used by
> educators and students practical value options which betray a
> philosophy of man, well or poorly outlined, coherent or
> incoherent. Only someone with a mechanistic mentality, which
> Marx would call 'grossly materialistic', could reduce . . . literacy
> learning to a purely technical level.[46]

Freire's reading of the ideological role of literacy instruction in 'empowering' or 'disempowering' particular groups within given societies is
corroborated in many of the aforementioned social historical studies. In
Germany, for example, Luther and Melanchthon's first primers for the
transmission of the word indeed were among the first state-mandated initia-
tions into particular secular and non-secular ideologies via basic literary instruction.[47] Apparently empowering literacy pedagogies can have as their
effect mass socialization into a particular ideological belief system. As
Arnove and Graff comment, in national literacy campaigns 'literacy is
almost never itself an isolated or absolute goal . . . [but] rather part of a
larger process and vehicle for that process', namely 'nation building'.[48] By
contrast, the fifteenth- and sixteenth-century Schwarmer movement, which
bears striking similarities to the modern Freirian approach, was banned by

state authorities as seditious.[49] In this latter case, it would seem that those empowering pedagogies which threatened state stability were opted against by authorities.[50] For a more recent instance, recall the Brazilian government's distressed reaction to the apparent success of Freire's early campaigns.

As for the ideological functions of literacy pedagogy in North American education, Graff establishes that literacy as conceived by nineteenth-century promoters of the Canadian state school system was in effect a cover for a larger ideological agenda: his study argued that mass literacy training, when stripped of its egalitarian gloss and non-secular rhetoric, may have been a vehicle for cultural hegemony.[51] Describing the intents and effects of nineteenth-century American schooling, Soltow and Stevens refer to an 'ideology of literacy' operative within pedagogical models and textbooks.[52] The teaching of literacy through texts like the McGuffey Readers, they maintain, was tied to the transmission of nationalism and Protestant/capitalist values.

This research underlines how modern pedagogy designed for the transmission of literacy, from the founding of state schools in fifteenth-century Germany onwards, has embodied, however implicitly or explicitly, a normative agenda which in the most general terms could be considered ideological. Jenny Cook-Gumperz recently explained that

> We expect literacy to provide not just a technical skill but also a set of prescriptions. . . . Literacy is not just the simple ability to read and write: but by possessing and performing these skills we exercise socially approved and approvable talents: in other words literacy is a socially constructed phenomenon.[53]

But how is ideology expressed in educational curricula in general, and curricula for the teaching of literacy in particular? In what follows, definitions of ideology and its relationship to educationally transmitted knowledge and competence are examined. These in turn will form a base of assumptions from which a critical analysis of literacy-related curricula can proceed.

In their historical analysis, Soltow and Stevens define ideology as a set of 'moral and value prescriptions' of a 'given class', which 'functions by an appeal to moral norms' to deal with 'social and political discontent'.[54] Hence, they see school transmitted ideology as an institutional means for the justification of the legitimacy of 'the implements and technical prescriptions which are to ensure concerted action for the preservation, reform, destruction or reconstruction of a given order'.

> What we term an 'ideology of literacy' had the potential not simply to restrain and control but to communicate to children and adults a code for success when the ways for success were becoming increasingly uncommon.[55]

Graff maintains that 'schools reflect social relations and ideology and serve as key agents of transmission, at once legitimating the social order and assimilating it to their charges'.[56] Hence, he views literacy instruction in nineteenth-century Canadian schools as a 'hegemonic tool', leading to students' 'unwilled and unselfconscious consent' to the direction that 'the predominant group imposes on social life — on morality, principles, and all social relations'.[57] Through the adoption of particular curricular texts and models of pedagogy, school-based literacy instruction became a form of ideological imposition:

> With proper instruction, the dangers of unrestrained literacy, or of illiteracy, could be neutralized; in learning to read, children would be taught the rules of the social order and correct behavior and the principles of economic advancement.[58]

In a more general commentary on literacy and industrialization in the nineteenth-century, Graff further points out that literacy was a means for the enculturation of classes into changed economic conditions, that literacy 'could ease the transition and assimilation of the working class ... to industrial and "modern" social habits, if provided in carefully structured institutions'.[59] The aim of schooling, then, was to promote 'moral, orderly, disciplined, deferential and contented workers'.[60]

The foregoing accounts suggest that literacy instruction in modern North American schools has been ideological inasmuch as it has purveyed and sustained 'false consciousness',[61] a particular world view, belief and value system tied to a delimited body of discursive practices, the dissemination of which served the economic interests of a 'predominant group'.[62] This line of argumentation and analysis follows one conventional neomarxist approach to the study of ideology. *The German Ideology*[63] gave rise to the axiom that the 'ideas of the ruling class are in every epoch the ruling ideas: i.e., the class which is the ruling material force of society is at the same time its ruling intellectual force'.[64] Marx and Engels viewed these ruling ideas, moreover, as 'nothing more than the ideal expression of dominant material relations'. After initial formulations by de Tracy and Napoleon, it was left to Marx and Engels to transform the notion of ideology to refer to the systematic body of thought generated, particularly by intellectuals, in a given era to support the economic domination of particular classes.[65] For them, 'in all ideology men and their circumstances appear upside down as in a *camera obscura*'.[66] Stressing this aspect of *The German Ideology*, Giddens defines ideology as 'the mode in which forms of signification are incorporated within systems of domination so as to sanction their continuance'.[67] Additionally, Giddens's definition points to the location of ideology in cultural forms other than the abstract works of intellectuals, specifically in the linguistic and semiotic products of popular and educational culture.

If the present task is to analyse the ideological functions of educational curricula, though, it is crucial to establish Marx's commentary on the role of intellectuals in the production of ideology: intellectuals undertake divided labour with a distinct socioeconomic function, specifically the provision of a version of social history and collective memory, which purports to be dis-interested but in fact represents the interests of a dominant class. Ideological representation in language and culture, and the particular forms of false and unhappy consciousness that it begets, can be seen to evolve historically according to changes in the economic needs and interests of a ruling class. Hence, in classical marxist theory ideology was construed as part of the cultural 'superstructure' determined by the economic 'base'.

Contemporary marxist theorists from Adorno and Lukács to Althusser have recognized that, with the advent of mass literacy and univeral partici-pation in popular culture, the range of modes of ideological signification extends well beyond abstract academic treatises of bourgeois intellectuals scrutinized by Marx to include texts of mass media and mass education. Over the last two decades, various theoretical frames for the explanation of how schooling transmits ideology have emerged.

Arising out of the mainstream of educational research in the 1970s was Bowles and Gintis's *Schooling in Capitalist America*,[68] the first comprehensive historical account of the relationship of the forms, contents and structures of mass schooling to the economic and political structures of industrial capitalism. By their account, the ideological function of the school was determined by the economic needs of the emerging American economy. Thus, they explain, the individualism and humanism stressed in educational progressivism was overridden by the 'technocratic' orientation of American school administration, curriculum, and assessment. In their view, the meritocratic system functioned efficiently to reproduce class stratification and labour needs in an expanding industrial economy. Modern American schools, they argued, produced labour in 'correspondence' with the economic needs of a capitalist state.

The determination of the character of schooling by its functions within an economic superstructure was argued by many other British and American scholars as well. As the sociology of education emerged from a structural–functionalist paradigm, many attempted to use the base/super-structure distinction as a heuristic for explaining the ideological effects of schooling.[69] Yet Bowles and Gintis's analysis, and attendant theoretical posi-tions, presupposed the efficacy of schooling: that schools were 'black boxes' of cultural and economic reproduction.[70] In other words, the dominant pre-supposition underlying such explanations was that schooling worked in an unmediated, non-contradictory manner.

Is schooling merely an agent for the selective distribution of 'ruling-class ideas', a mere 'superstructural' phenomenon *determined* by ruling-class ideas and interests? Is school-based literacy instruction a form of ideological imposition of a false consciousness determined by economic needs of the state, as implied in much of the historical research? In 'Base and Super-structure in Marxist Cultural Theory',[71] Raymond Williams theoretically reframed the base–superstructure relationship, situating educationally acquired competence and knowledge as a primary mode by which individuals were 'incorporated', often non-coercively, into the suppositions, beliefs and practices of the 'dominant culture'.[72] Arguing against economic determinism, he suggests that

> We have to revalue 'determination' towards the setting of limits and exertion of pressure, and away from a predicted, prefigured and controlled content. We have to revalue 'superstructure' towards a related range of cultural practices, and away from a reflected, reproduced or specifically dependent content. And, crucially, we have to revalue 'the base' away from the notion of a fixed economic or technological abstraction, and towards the specific activities of men in real social and economic relationships.[73]

Accordingly, Williams goes on to argue that ideology is not 'some abstract imposed notion', that 'social and political and cultural ideas and assumptions and habits' are not superstructural manifestations considered as 'the result of specific manipulation' on behalf of economic imperatives.[74] Drawing from the work of Gramsci, he argues that cultural hegemony — 'a whole body of practices and expectations, our assignments of energy, our ordinary under-standing of man and his world' — consists of a set of meanings and values which are 'reciprocally confirming' in experience and practice.[75] The processes of cultural, social and economic reproduction across generations, according to Williams, do not entail a simple imposition of a set of ruling ideas determined by the material, economic interests of a ruling class. 'Dominant culture' can be made, remade and experienced non-coercively, through the willing participation of the very human subjects whose interests it does not serve. Importantly, then, Williams holds that reproduction is a dynamic process, mediated by the actions of human subjects. In his reformu-lation, the notion of ruling-class ideological imposition gives way to an understanding that cultural reproduction may be non-coercive, contradic-tory, and subject to varying kinds and levels of historical mediation.

As for the role of schools, Williams points out that these 'main agencies of the transmission of an effective dominant culture' are now both economic (base) and cultural (superstructure) activities. Schools serve to select knowledges, skills and competences for transmission:

> There is a process which I call the *selective tradition*: that which, within the terms of the effective dominant culture, is always passed off as 'the tradition', 'the significant past'. But always the selectivity is the point: the way in which from a whole possible area of past and present, certain meanings and practices are chosen for emphasis, certain other meanings and practices are neglected and excluded. Even more crucially, some of these meanings and practices are reinterpreted, diluted, or put into forms which support or at least do not contradict other elements of the dominant culture.[76]

Schools, in concert with one's total 'social training' inculcate 'practical definitions and organization of work'. Williams concludes that schools do not simply teach 'an imposed ideology ... the isolable meanings and practices of the ruling class' but rather tolerate a range of forms of knowledge and competence, hence enabling the dominant culture to adapt to (and thereby incorporate) variation and divergence.[77]

The range of trainings selected of course becomes part of the taken for granted assumptions about what constitutes an appropriate education:

> If we look at actual educational systems, we can distinguish ... a major general purpose: that of training the members of a group to the 'social character' or 'pattern of culture' which is dominant in the group and by which the group lives. To the extent that this 'social character' is generally accepted, education towards it will not normally be thought of as one possible training among many, but as a natural training.[78]

It is, Williams observes, typical that while to contemporary observers the organization of education and the selective tradition appears clear enough in the case of past periods, these same observers 'never really believe it about our own', precisely because of the uncritical acceptance of contemporary ideological suppositions as 'natural', or for that matter, 'scientific'.[79]

This theoretical formulation enables a reinvestigation of the ideological character of literacy instruction. If indeed literacy is defined as a historically and culturally specific array of social practices associated with the use of a particular technology, both the selection of the textual corpus to be read and written and the selection of particular competences to be transmitted stand as two historical variables. Models of literacy training selected implicitly or explicitly embody suppositions about the purposes and uses of the technology itself. In the interests of incorporation into a state-mandated dominant culture, pedagogical models authorize selected texts and textual competences, rendering official particular norms for literate behaviour while excluding others. Pedagogies thus forward reading and writing practices, attitudes about what will count as literate expression, appropriate contents and relative authority of genres, principles for the organization of work with this particular technology, sites and locations for its social practice, and understandings of its potential and limits.

A further implication of Williams's argument is that literacy instruction, coded in the formal and informal curricula of the modern school, does not necessarily entail the imposition of a unitary set of ruling-class ideas or elite competences. While schooling may provide some children with access to elite forms of linguistic and cultural capital, it may purvey to others those meanings and practices which are not identifiably elite but nonetheless serve to incorporate individuals into a delimited literate participation in a dominant culture. This is not to imply that texts of literacy instruction do not convey a primary value and belief system to children, a world view replete with versions of right reason, action and thought. But through literacy instruction children differentially gain access to aspects of a total selective tradition, one composed of a range of literary forms and functional genres, ideological contents, and sanctioned ways of reading and writing.

A final implication is that the particular knowledges and competences selected for transmission by the school are not wholly determined by economic factors. This stands as a counterpoint to correspondence theories which view cultural phenomena as determined by economic factors. The recognition of cultural reproduction as a dynamic process undertaken by human subjects, coupled with an understanding of the school as a cultural *and* economic agent, suggests that we cannot disregard the role of historical human subjects in the processes of ideological reproduction, and that the analysis of such practices may reveal historical contradictions (e.g., conflicting means/ends, form/content, theory/practice relationships) and patterns of contestation.

In any given era of the history of education, the selection of knowledges, competences and practices for transmission in school curricula is an ideological process, serving interests of particular classes and forms of social organization. But the resultant corpus of curricular knowledge, while part of the processes by and through which individuals are socialized into a dominant culture, need not be a mirror reflection of ruling-class ideas, imposed in an unmediated and coercive manner. Rather, the processes of cultural incorporation are dynamic, reflecting both continuities and contradictions of that dominant culture and the continual remaking and relegitimation of that culture's plausibility system. Ideology so seen functions reflexively to sanction itself by establishing a total field of signification.

Curricular Criticism and Text Analysis

Translating Williams's and Gramsci's understanding of the hegemonic function of modern schooling into a critique of ideology in curriculum has been the focus of subsequent theorizing and research in the critical sociology of the curriculum.[80] Research in this field critiques curriculum not as ideological reflection but rather as a complex historical dynamic in the transmission and maintenance of a selective tradition.

One of the primary effects of the 'new sociology' of the early 1970s was a reconsideration of principles guiding curriculum theorizing and criticism. Previously dominated by systems management and liberal/humanistic models, curricular research began to explore phenomenology and the sociology of knowledge as bases for the critical analysis of the curriculum.[81] This work had the effect of questioning taken for granted assumptions that curricular content was a neutral and unbiased selection from culture. Yet the notion that curriculum was 'socially constructed' was found wanting by those who argued that this construction was not arbitrary, but tended to act in the interests of particular classes.[82]

Since these initial steps in rendering problematic the classification, framing and transmission of educational knowledge,[83] progressively greater attention has been turned to the class-based ideology in the formal curriculum (e.g., textbooks, examinations, policy documents) and in the hidden curriculum of social relations in classrooms and schools. More recent work in the sociology of the curriculum sets out to describe approaches and methods for research on the ideological function of historical and modern curricula.

In *Ideology and Curriculum*,[84] Michael Apple argues that curricular research should entail the explication of how 'the structuring of knowledge and symbol in our educational institutions is intimately related to the principles of social and cultural control'. He views schools as sites for the maintenance of existing patterns of the control, production and distribution of economic and cultural resources. Like Apple's, Henry Giroux's research agenda begins from what he considers the primary failings of correspondence theories of ideological reproduction (e.g., Althusser, Bowles and Gintis): the stress on the economic, rather than cultural, basis of curricular content and the presumption of the efficacy of modern curricula.[85] Arguing that schools are more than 'ideological reflections of the dominant interests of the wider society', he critiques base/superstructure models as ignoring the reality of 'counter-hegemonic forces' embodied in student and teacher contestation and resistance.[86] In other words, while educational knowledge and pedagogical models are organized on class principles, the process of knowledge transmission is *mediated* by the cultural field of the classroom and human subjects engaged in educational practice at all levels (including curriculum development and research) in a manner which precludes 'determinate effects'. Ideology *per se* then, is not the 'determinate instance of a given mode of production', but rather a factor coded in curriculum which is subsequently mediated by the concrete actions of teachers and students in the classroom.[87]

The necessity of capturing the dialectics of determinism and mediation, imposition and contestation, renders curriculum research at once a comprehensive and highly problematic task. Proposing guidelines, Giroux nonetheless sees the curriculum as an embodiment of a 'dominant rationality' and calls upon scholarship 'to lay bare the ideological and political character' of contemporary and historical curriculum.[88] In order to understand school knowledge as a complex historical dynamic, the task of curricular criticism requires the detailing of the entire field of social and discursive relations, practices and priorities which might be seen to constitute school knowledge.

> This means analysing the way in which domination is concealed at the institutional level. . . . a dominant ideology is inscribed in: (1) the form and content of classroom material; (2) the organization of the school; (3) the daily classroom social relationships; (4) the principles that structure the selection and organization of the curriculum; (5) the attitudes of school staff; and (6) the discourse and practices which appear to have penetrated its logic.[89]

Of course, the latter two exist 'in the practice and consciousness of individuals and social groups who produce and experience their relationship to the world in structures that are only partly of their making'.[90] And one aspect of such an inquiry would involve studies of textbook consumption and use. This area is the focus of ethnomethodological and sociolinguistic research which has begun to track the actual discursive practices with and around textbooks in classrooms.[91] But while these studies and more comprehensive educational ethnographies can begin to capture the plausibility structures, self-understandings, and methods for negotiating meaning of students and teachers,[92] the analysis of *historical* curricula is limited to the study of those recoverable documentary materials which may reveal 'the form and content of classroom materials', the 'principles that structure the selection and organization' of those materials, and the 'daily classroom social relationships' in a given era.

Three distinct domains for the (textual) study of historical curricula, then, can be extrapolated from Apple and Giroux's description of the field: (1) an analysis of the content *and* form of prescribed curricular texts; (2) a detailing of the principles which governed and the economic forces which influenced the construction of those texts; and (3) a reconstruction of the organization of daily classroom social relationships around the text, as evidenced in the recoverable textual guidelines for teaching. In what follows, I want to explore further models and methods for the study of these three domains.

In the last ten years research in curricular criticism has come a good distance towards showing how curricular content has been ideologically biased towards the interests of dominant socioeconomic groups in industrial and post-industrial society.[93] In her study of how American history textbooks have distorted labour history, social issues and socioeconomic change, Jean Anyon describes the findings of critical analyses of curricular content:

> The whole range of curriculum selections favours the interests of the wealthy and powerful. Although presented as unbiased, the historical interpretations provide ideological justification for the activities and prerogatives of these groups and do not legitimize points of view and priorities of groups that compete with these established interests for social acceptance and support.[94]

The principal method of curricular criticism has been, and remains, the juxtaposition of official textbook versions of social reality, social and political relations, history and conceptual categories with revisionist social history and alternative views of social, economic, and political culture. Research procedures generally entail a rendering of explicit ideas, value judgments and statements conveyed in the text, followed by a discrepancy analysis of these data with divergent versions of social reality or history. Secondary methods have involved the analysis of quantitative data on gender and race of authors and characters and the notation of stereotyping.[95] In sum, these studies find that the content of the curriculum is a central component in the 'transmission of class culture as common culture'.[96]

A second, complementary step in the analysis of the ideological character of curriculum lies in the examination of its construction, noting the 'principles that structure the selection and organization of the curriculum',[97] as well as the distinctive economic and cultural forces which moulded its production. Although an exhaustive body of research in curricular history has described the development of technocratic, assembly-line approaches to curriculum development,[98] thus far few content analyses have focused on correlative changes in historical models and conditions of text development and authorship. Anyon's discussion of the role of multi-nationals in the production of history textbooks is a notable exception.[99]

Generally speaking, though, sociological and educational research on 'how ... "legitimate" knowledge [is] made available in schools' has bypassed the study of the actual production of the primary medium of school knowledge: the school textbook[100] Text production is at once a cultural and an economic activity: human subjects are engaged actively in the processes of conceiving, designing and authoring texts, within the economic constraints of the commerce of text publishing and the politics of text adoption. So seen, the textbook is an artefact of human expression *and* an economic commodity. As Apple notes, the 'unpacking' of the 'social relations of production' of curricula, and 'the conceptual apparatus that lies behind them' has escaped critical analysis.[101] His proposal for a political economy of text publishing, which entails specifying the commercial and political constraints on text construction, is based on the presupposition that the textbook, and hence educational knowledge, is a cultural product like any other, a commodity for consumption. As cultural products, textbooks are written and produced by particular historical interpretive communities: groups of academics, teachers and curriculum developers operating from paradigmatic assumptions about teaching and learning, and the specific domains of knowledge and competence to be transmitted. The crucial aspect of authorship does not feature prominently on Apple's agenda, despite its emphasis on the construction of curriculum as a conceptual and cultural activity. Accordingly, we might surmise that to capture the making of text as part of its historical context, the social, economic and authorial relations for the production of textbooks can be examined.

Apple thus turns to the detailing of the social organization of text production, as well as critique of the actual content of texts, as a means for explaining how textual curriculum serves as an inscription of ideology. Selection and authorship have been constrained historically by economic influences on the production and consumption of curriculum, as well as by the prevailing belief systems of individuals involved in the writing of curriculum regarding the character of the knowledge and competence to be taught, and the most effective or edifying way of teaching it. Indeed, the critique of curricular form and content would not be complete without a review of the 'series of socially organized labours through which knowledge is made'.[102] Consequently, the present study examines not just the curricular text and underlying assumptions about the world, learning and the learner, but also how that text was constructed in the first place, the 'social organization of meaning production'.[103]

A third focus of curricular research concerns the social relations of classrooms and schools within and through which the curricular text is taught, the synchronic social contexts which mediate access to the text. In Anyon's case study of social class and school knowledge, she confirms a crucial hypothesis of hegemony theory: that the information coded in the text in and of itself is not necessarily that which children bring away from the experience of schooling.[104] Anyon describes children's differential responses to and senses of the same text, showing how instructional mediation, children's background knowledge and acquired epistemic assumptions are contingent factors in how texts are perceived as authoritative sources and, ultimately, in how they are understood. If indeed the discursive practices of classroom instruction, the variables of student and teacher background knowledge, and the communicative characteristics of the school as a site of discourse remake the experience of the text, then it is quite tenable that readings of text content alone are not accurate representations of ideology and school knowledge. Analyses of curricula, then, must consider the 'curriculum in use', that is, the social relations which serve to reconstitute the stated textual curriculum into actual experienced school knowledge.[105]

Working from a textual trace, we can describe this social organization of classroom interaction through the study of the 'technical form' of modern curriculum.[106] Apple's analysis of science textbook instructional guidelines and more recent analysis of the technology of basal reading series signal how curricular form — the adjunct materials, worksheets, teachers' guides, and so forth — can lead to the intentional structuring of classroom lessons and intersubjective relations.[107] That is, the comprehensive technical structure of the modern curriculum, which exceeds the text to include metatextual guidelines on how to structure social practices and interaction around it, may mediate what students do with that curricular text — embodying a hidden curriculum of social relations, of attitudes towards the text, and of knowledge and competences ostensibly being taught. While it cannot be presumed that teachers in the past adhered to teachers' guides and departmental directives any more than the total efficacy of the curriculum can be presupposed, an examination of that text may reveal the underlying assumptions and principles of the curriculum and the particular social practices, espistemological positions, and literate competences that the curriculum set out to teach.

I have briefly outlined three approaches to the critique of historical curricula: notation through a thematic and factual discrepancy analysis of overt ideological content (text content); the analysis of the making of the school text (text construction); and examination of curricular guides and adjunct materials to see how the technical form of curriculum may have led to a parallel organization of knowledge and interaction in the classroom (text use). But is this all that the study of curricular form entails, the examination of the conceptual and physical structure of curriculum? Or might the analysis of the form and content of classroom materials refer as well to the linguistic and literary form within and through which ideology is inscribed?

A major pitfall of research in the sociology of the curriculum has been its willingness to accept text form as a mere adjunct means for the delivery of ideological content: the former described in terms of dominant meta-phors, images, or key words; the latter described in terms of the sum total of values, beliefs, and ideas which might be seen to constitute a false consciousness. For much content analysis presumes that text mirrors or reflects a particular ideological position, which in turn can be connected to specific class interests. This is an interpolation, and in the case of post-corres-pondence theory critiques a somewhat ironic one, of a base/superstructure model, for it is predicated on the possibility of a one-to-one identification of school knowledge with textually represented ideas of the dominant classes. Even those critics who have recognized that the ideology encoded in curricular texts may reflect the internally contradictory character of a dominant culture have tended to neglect the need for a more complex model of text analysis, one that does not suppose that texts are simply read-able, literal representations of 'someone else's' version of social reality, objective knowledge and human relations. For texts do not always mean or communicate what they say. Perhaps more importantly, we need to look further at how literary and linguistic forms of textual expression convey particular ideological messages and create particular ideological effects. Literacy instruction, as noted, sets out to generate or induce certain social practices and norms. To explicate these, more exacting models of text/discourse analysis are necessary.

Without access to actual classrooms and children, historical research must turn its focus to the text itself, building models for the analysis of what particular kinds of texts pragmatically set out to do to readers, and of how curricular texts projected ideal student readers. In his discussion of the relationship between ideology and language, Williams argues that the linguistic sign exists both by virtue of 'the relations of the people who are actually using it' and by virtue of the 'relation between formal element and meaning (its internal structure)'.[108] Following this line of reasoning, texts of a particular selective tradition bear analysis in terms of the social relations within which they are embedded, in terms of social relations portrayed *and* in terms of their internal structures.

To this Phillip Wexler adds that while a critical sociology of curriculum has demonstrated 'how the representation of events is partial and class-based . . . the selective "bias" of selective historical representation is itself the product of a conceptual apparatus that operates within the text'.[109] Clearly, curricular criticism requires not only content analysis, the analysis of text authorship and production, the analysis of the social relations of readership in the classroom, but furthermore a coherent consideration of textual form. It is essential to consider further *how* texts structure author/reader relations, and how rhetorical and semantic structure establishes particular ideological messages and effects. For that, the present study turns to research on the discourse analysis of narratives.

Text Grammars and Ideology

Reviewing the contributions of rhetoric, linguistics, psychology, artificial intelligence, and other disciplines to contemporary models of text analysis, Meyer and Rice argue that no particular model is more accurate than another — rather, various models have been developed for the analysis of particular genres of text (e.g., narrative, journalistic prose, novels) with particular research tasks in mind.[110] In what follows, I want to identify directions for a discourse analysis of curricular narratives, noting the basic principles of story-grammar analysis and forwarding a composite model as appropriate for the study of historical children's literature and basal readers. I first examine the role of connected prose discourse in the representation of culture-specific plans, beliefs and actions through the exercise by the author of particular literary discourse options. I then turn to the use of story grammars to analyse ideological form and content of children's narratives.

Teun Van Dijk maintains that there are three primary levels for analysis of the structure of text: the micropropositional, macropropositional, and top-level.[111] He proceeds from the assumption that a narrow focus on syntactic structure at the level of the sentence, as in traditional descriptive linguistics, fails to identify the rule systems which inhere in larger discourse structures. The micropropositional level of analysis is undertaken at the level of the sentence. Generally, Halliday and Hasan's system for the notation of intersentential and lexical cohesion is forwarded as an exemplar of this kind of analysis.[112] Macropropositional analysis attempts to specify the logical and rhetorical relations between sentences and attendant concepts.[113]

> Macrostructures are structures which relate the non-linear objectual structures and the linear textual structures. Macrostructures allow for the production and analysis of texts. The analysis leads to possible interpretations, distinguishing content, context and communicative force.[114]

Macropropositional analysis thus enables the reconstruction of the non-linear fictional structures and contexts portrayed in the narrative, through the graphing of text propositions in the temporal order they appear.[115] Finally, 'top level' analysis entails the identification and comparative analysis of rhetorical patterns of identifiable genres such as stories, essays or scientific articles.[116]

'Story grammar', 'story schema', and 'story mapping' models have been forwarded for the analysis of macropropositions in narratives. The aim of this research is to chart the major propositional components, the 'constituent structure', of narrative discourse.[117] For the study of children's reading narratives, educational researchers have found the story-grammar approach most effective.

> A story grammar is analogous to a sentence grammar, in that each is composed of a set of rules which describes the possible structures of a class of items which can be called well-formed stories or sentences. In principle, a story grammar is generative, that is, it can produce structural descriptions of stories which never have been told but would be considered to be acceptable stories. In practice, the rules are more often used to describe the organization of a particular story under consideration.[118]

The parsing of the grammar of a story reveals particular syntactic rules and patterns, transformations of which inform the structure of that story. Stories, then, are seen to be comprised of syntactic structures and semantic content; as in individual sentences, semantic/ideational content is expressed within and through particular syntactic relationships which exist at a propositional level.[119] Adopting a schema-theoretic perspective which conceptualizes reading as a reciprocal interaction between the reader's schemata and the grammars coded in the text, researchers have been able to investigate which structures of children's narratives achieve varying degrees of 'goodness of fit' with particular readers' background knowledge.[120]

The different models for the examination of connected discourse vary greatly in both research purposes and in the degrees of comprehensiveness of detail they yield. Much of the research on children's narratives has taken its lead from studies by Rumelhart and others on readers' capacities to comprehend, understand and summarize brief stories. Rumelhart has proposed what he calls a 'problem-solving schema' for stories:

> Casual observation suggests a surprisingly simple motif underlying a remarkable number of brief stories. . . . This motif involves what I call *problem solving episodes*. Such stories have roughly the following structure: First, something happens to the protagonist of the story that sets up a goal for him to accomplish. Then the remainder of the story is a description of the protagonist's problem-solving behavior as he seeks to accomplish his goal. The problem solving behavior itself is usually well structured.[121]

Rumelhart develops a system of graphic representation which enables the detailing of 'sets of embedded goals' or 'goal stacks'. The 'rewrite rules' of this model yield a 'story tree', which breaks down stories into categories of 'episode', 'causes', 'tries' and 'outcomes'. These categories enable us to differentiate 'important parts of a story and the details of the story'.[122]

Drawing upon the work of Rumelhart, [123] Stein and Glenn propose a simplified model for the examination of basic narratives.[124] Their story grammar, used for the analysis of basal reading texts and children's literature narratives, identifies several key rewrite components: *setting* identifies background information on characters and location; *episode* includes an *initiating event, response*, and *attempt* to reach the goal stipulated within and through the initiating event; these represented actions in turn lead to *consequences* or *reactions*. Most children's stories lose some of their coherence if they omit an aspect of this basic grammar.

The Stein–Glenn model, like Rumelhart's, presupposes that stories situate a series of goal-seeking actions undertaken by personae within a particular social setting and context. These actions in turn generally lead to a set of consequences within the particular setting. The model readily accommodates the 'stacking' of multiple goals, attempts, and consequences (as well as sub-goals, sub-attempts and sub-consequences) which may occur in basic narratives, while yielding a simpler, more prosaic rewrite than Rumelhart's model. This model is particularly well suited for the study of ideology in basal reader narratives because of its simplicity and flexibility. Many narratives featured in elementary school instruction do not feature highly complex embeddings of motives and contexts and hence do not require the complexity of the Rumelhart story tree. Additionally, the Stein–Glenn model yields a prose paraphrase of the narrative and thus readily facilitates the identification of relationships between the syntax of story structure and the semantic content of portrayed patterns of motivation, action and belief.

This use of the Stein–Glenn model for curricular critique does diverge considerably from more conventional applications of story-grammar analysis. In most educational research the purpose of grammatical representation of a story is to enable predictions about the relative salience and comprehensibility of a text.[125] Researchers like Rumelhart, Kintsch, Mandler and Johnson, Stein and Trabasso, and others have set as their task the prediction of recall based on differential structures:

> the usual procedure is to apply the story grammar to a given story passage. Thus, the components of the passage are identified according to their position and role in the story. This makes it possible to compare stories with respect to their structure, regardless of the content of the story.[126]

Typically psychological and linguistic research on text structure has not tended to view ideological content *per se*, the actual values, morals, concepts which instantiate the story schema, as problematic for story-grammar analysis. And it is not surprising that most reading researchers tend to omit due consideration of those sociolinguistic, semiotic and literary models of discourse analysis which expressly set out to deal with ideological content.[127]

There are, however, contrasting views on the importance of content, and ideology, as an organizing principle both in the comprehension and in the construction of texts. For the analysis of textual macrostructures not only allows for the prediction of recall, but as well enables the analysis of content and the forecasting of possible interpretations and communicative force.[128] For his part, Van Dijk argues that content itself may provide a key principle for the organization of macropropositions.[129] In the axiological content, manifest in the text's 'frame', the researcher may be able to identify the 'explanatory component of linear and global coherence'.[130] For it is this content/frame, accessible only by means of possession of a parallel 'conceptual structure in semantic memory', which stands as a text's 'organizational principle'. Through the frame or 'gist', author and reader are able to relate a number of 'general but culture dependent' concepts into a semantic 'unit'.

> Convention and experience somehow form a unit which may be actualized in various cognitive tasks, such as language production and comprehension, perception, action and problem solving.[131]

Here Van Dijk points to the relationship between the story grammar and the 'culture dependent' background knowledge (of experience and concepts, of social and discourse conventions) lodged in the long–term semantic memories of authors and readers. In more recent work, Van Dijk has begun exploring the ideological schemata of news reportage and the social class and ethnic specificity of the production and comprehension of particular discourse formats like racist jokes and anecdotes.[132]

The comprehension of oral and textual language presupposes the reader's ability to construct a possible world of intentions, actions, and motivations, on the basis of particular linguistic, in this case textual, information. In an interactive model of text processing, readers use background knowledge and contextual information to posit those world structures expressed or implied in a text. The details of these possible worlds, and how they might be different from those readily accessible in semantic memory, however, depend on how the text structures and projects these worlds:

> when specified, the possible world deviates in systematic directions from the ordinary or common world. Sentences are means of stipulating possible worlds. It is the text which specifies how the possible world is to be taken. Sentences, in these contexts, may be considered as recipes for building possible worlds.[133]

Stories can be seen both to pressupose in their structure and project to the reader through that structure particular fictitious realities which by definition are to some degree discrepant from authors' and readers' actual lived realities.

> A story is set in a false communicational setting, and it creates a false reality in the reader's mind. The sentences of the story play a double role. They connect the real world in which the reader exists and the imaginary world in which the communication takes place. These sentences exist in this world as printed letters. They are sentences materialized in this world. As such they exert the objective function on the reader's consciousness. And it is due to this objective function that the story creates a false reality in the reader's consciousness.[134]

The use of the term 'false' is perhaps misleading here, for stories generate a version of reality other than that lived by the reader. They do this, in a manner reminiscent of Eliot's poetic 'objective correlative', through their style and structure.

These fictitious realities portrayed by textual micro- and macro-structures are in turn social selections. Regarding the construction of text, Gunther Kress argues that the work of Van Dijk, Halliday, Hasan and others marks a shift from 'narrow concerns with syntactic structure to a concern with socially significant linguistic units and to questions about their interrelation with, provenance in and utter imbrication in social structures'.[135] Text he defines as 'material forms of the expression and interplay of the social category of discourse'.[136] Of the rule systems governing the structuring of texts, Kress further maintains that

> Whereas sentences can be shown to be formed on the basis of knowledge of grammatical rules, texts arise on the basis of knowledge of rules and of exigencies which are first and foremost social in their nature — and in their functions and effects. . . . That is to say, the ability to construct texts, alone or in conjunction with others, is seen to arise in response to social demands, which reflect the circumstances in which speakers and writers are placed, as well as their social needs and attentions.[137]

Hence, the construction of text is a socially constrained and embedded activity. Those socially derived rules for the organization and structure of discourse, in turn, may be explicitly linked with the ideological practices of authors and speakers:

> Language is an instrument of control and communication. Linguistic form allows significance to be conveyed and distorted. In this way hearers can be both manipulated and informed, preferably

manipulated while they suppose they are being informed. Language is ideological in another, more political, sense of that word: it involves systematic distortion in the service of class interest.[138]

How, then, do story grammars yield ideological meanings? Clearly, their comprehension requires culturally and/or social class specific background knowledge. Surveying research findings on the comprehension of variable prose structures, Bruce notes the kind of socially constrained and acquired background knowledge one needs in order to recognize and interpret a content frame.

> One needs to know how certain social actions are typically carried out (e.g., giving often involves a physical transfer) and what the preconditions and outcomes of actions are. One also needs knowledge of the normative behaviors associated with social actions and situations, and knowledge of social situations and roles people take. One needs the ability to distinguish one's beliefs from one's beliefs about another's beliefs; also, the ability to handle possibly inconsistent data about the beliefs and plans of others. Finally, one needs knowledge of social action patterns, that is, the sequences of action that typically occur.[139]

Stories can be viewed as structural codings of normative, potentially ideological information, which rely upon knowledge of culturally and subculturally specific patterns of social action, situations, motivation, behaviours and beliefs for their comprehension, and may convey and teach an understanding of those patterns.[140] Story-grammar analysis, accordingly, can underline the patterns of social action and interaction which texts both presuppose and teach.

Not only are the world views conveyed in narrative culturally specific, but as well, attendant discourse structures and conventions are indigenous to particular selective narrative traditions. Oral traditions, for example, tend to have highly conventionalized characters who undertake expected patterns of goal seeking action: e.g., the coyote in American Indian stories, the spider in West African folk tales.[141] Oral story traditions, moreover, may prescribe fixed linguistic forms for these portrayals which storytellers and audiences expect and accept.

Modern literate cultures and (ethnic and social class) subcultures have varying protocols, discourse conventions and structures for what will count as a story.[142] Generally speaking, authors of narratives within the Western tradition — while adhering to conventional event structures like those described by story grammarians — will exercise specific discourse options to achieve particular effects. Brewer's survey of the conventions of Western written stories indicates that authors of written narratives do not tend to be as constrained to 'fixed linguistic forms' as those in oral traditions.[143] For example, 'even the most formulaic genres' do not have such conventionalized openings as oral stories. While 'number and order of introduction of characters does not appear to be a frequently conventionalized aspect of written stories', the 'types of characters generally are'.[144] Ironically, Brewer notes of literary prose, this conventionalizing often involves distinguishing of a particular character from 'society's general stereotypes' through the ascription of an unusual or unique characteristic. Similarly, Western written traditions do not appear to be conventionalized strictly in terms of resolutions, epilogues, closings, and narratorial roles. Variation in written stories thus tends to occur on the level of discourse structure:

> In comparing the Western written story to the oral story it appears that the written story shows less conventionalization with respect to number of story elements and the fixed location of story elements, although it does have much conventionalized content (i.e., types of setting, characters, events and resolutions). In written stories discourse organization tends to replace repetition as a device for producing affect.[145]

Several crucial points about the culturally specific properties of stories in the Western literary tradition are apparent here. The lack of micropropositional linguistic conventionalization runs hand in hand with authors' tendency to exercise a good deal of independence in their selection and arrangement of macropropositional story elements. Brewer refers to these as the 'discourse options' that may be exercised, depending on affective and ideational intent: the author may vary story elements (e.g., opening, resolution, epilogue, narratorial role) in terms of 'presence/absence', 'explicitness', 'type', and 'discourse order'.[146] While not tied to the fixed linguistic forms of an oral storytelling tradition, authors of written stories nonetheless are constrained by 'conventionalized content'. Their latitude, then, exists primarily through their literary reworking of the organization of the text, as expressed in terms of the exercise of discourse options.

Options are selected to produce particular ideational and affective responses. For example, narratorial presence or absence can underline the didactic element of the story, invoking a narrator's reality as distinct from that of the characters, reinforcing or undercutting the particular rules and parameters of a specific fictitious reality and so forth. These stylistic and conventional variations are intentional attempts by the author/storyteller to induce in the reader/listener specific effects.[147] To speak of narratives as culturally specific, then, refers to conventions governing both the content *and* form of stories. All stories, in this dual sense, reflect a selective tradition exercised by authors. And certainly this is the case with curricular texts:

> Ideologies tell a story . . . . At the centre . . . of the ensemble of texts which compose a story. . . . educated language forms a totality of discourses within which each subject draws upon the ideological field of the culture in order, on the one hand, to legitimate and advance its own standing and membership, and, on the other, to realize some recognizable version of its own ideal speech forms and exchanges.[148]

What counts as appropriate or legitimate goalseeking action in narrative may vary greatly across cultures, social classes, and subcultures. Story grammar analysis enables the detailed identification of ideological content in curriculum as a series of represented, structured, and perhaps repeated episodes, settings, plans, actions and interactions (e.g., a pattern of children's play or work) rather than as discrete bits, themes, ideas, or composite images. This seems particularly imperative in light of Williams's enjoinder that the process of cultural incorporation involves the systematic socialization of children into a coherent 'whole body of practices and expectations', including 'assignments of energy' and 'ordinary understanding of man and his world'.[149] Story-grammar analysis thus can demonstrate how specific syntactic structures, discourse options, and stylistic conventions have been structured to communicate particular conventional semantic messages and to evoke particular responses.

But does the plotting of story grammars just offer a more comprehensive means of drafting ideological content as a total world view? What of the possible interpretations, communicative force and norms of interpretation conveyed by and through literacy instruction? Certainly, as noted, children learn what is to count as a story/text and what is to count as appropriate action within texts. But as well they learn what to do with texts and, Barthes adds, 'what can be oppressive in our teaching is not, finally, the knowledge or the culture it conveys, but the discursive forms through which we propose them'.[150] Texts are structural and pragmatic devices and the reading of a text depends as much on how the structure of that text has stipulated its own interpretations, as on the pragmatic accidents of the readers' social situation and background knowledge.

Regarding the particular ideological effects of particular narrative structures, semiologist Umberto Eco examines popular and literary texts' structure to argue that how text is structured effectively prescribes the ideal conditions and constrains the real conditions for its interpretation.[151] Using a typology for 'open' and 'closed' texts, Eco argues that the total semantic structure of a text tends to generate distinct kinds of readership. Analysing the 'structure of the fabula', he points out how the exercise of particular discourse options in the organization of the story can enhance and preclude certain kinds and levels of interpretation. While the structures of open texts beget a range of possible interpretations, those of closed texts tend to delimit and constrain readers to a narrow set of interpretative options. In the absence of actual accounts of historical readers of particular kinds of texts, Eco's theoretical typology enables us to construct models of possible ideo-logical and literary effects of particular narrative structures, reconstructing the 'role of the reader' implicitly prescribed by text structure.

I have in this chapter proposed a three-tiered agenda for the study of ideology in historical curriculum for the teaching of literacy. It involves an examination of the conditions of authorship, theoretical assumptions and economic imperatives behind the making of the curriculum; an analysis of the ideological content and structure of curricular texts; and a description of those adjunct texts designed to set out the conditions for the teaching of curricular texts. Yet I have also indicated that the selective tradition of school knowledge does not just entail the selection of particular contents. Authorship of curriculum as well entails the selection of discourse structures and stylistic conventions with which to communicate ideological content. Accordingly, a story-grammar analysis format will be used as the basis for the discussion of particular narrative structures and literary conventions used to portray values, motive structures, social relations, character types and so forth. Finally, using Eco's typology of open and closed texts the present study will model norms of interpretation and literacy conveyed and pre-scribed by text structures.

First, however, we turn to identify the texts in question and to locate them in a particular historical context: the schools of postwar British Columbia.

Notes and References

1. Tom Wick, 'The Pursuit of Universal Literacy', *Journal of Communication* 30 (No. 1, 1980), 107–12; Leslie Limage, 'Adult Literacy Policy in Industrialized Countries', in Robert Arnove and Harvey Graff (eds), *National Literacy Campaigns: Historical and Comparative Perspectives* (New York: Plenum, 1987), pp. 293–313.
2. William S. Gray, *The Teaching of Reading and Writing* (Paris: UNESCO, 1956).
3. Harold A. Innis, *The Bias of Communication* (Toronto: University of Toronto Press, 1951). For critical commentary on Innis's work, see also William H. Melody, Liora R. Salter and Paul Heyer (eds), *Culture, Communication and Dependency: The Tradition of H.A. Innis* (Norwood, N.J.: Ablex, 1981).

4. Marshall McLuhan, *The Gutenberg Galaxy* (Toronto: University of Toronto Press, 1962).
5. Richard Hoggart, *The Uses of Literacy* (Harmondsworth: Penguin, 1958).
6. Jack Goody (ed.), *Literacy in Traditional Societies* (Cambridge: Cambridge University Press, 1968).
7. Jack Goody and Ian Watt, 'The Consequences of Literacy', in Goody (ed.), *Literacy in Traditional Societies*, pp. 27–68.
8. Ibid.; see also Jack Goody, *The Logic of Writing and the Organization of Society* (Cambridge: Cambridge University Press, 1986).
9. See, for example, Roger Schofield, 'The Measurement of Literacy in Pre-Industrial England', in Goody (ed.), *Literacy in Traditional Societies*, pp. 311–25.
10. For exemplary studies of literacy in various historical contexts, see Harvey J. Graff (ed.), *Literacy and Social Development in the West* (Cambridge: Cambridge University Press, 1981).
11. Harvey J. Graff, 'Literacy in History', Address to the History of Education Society, Vancouver, 1983.
12. Harvey J. Graff, 'The Legacies of Literacy', in Suzanne de Castell, Allan Luke and Kieran Egan (eds), *Literacy, Society and Schooling* (Cambridge: Cambridge University Press, 1986), pp. 61–86.
13. Harvey J. Graff, *The Literacy Myth: Literacy and Social Structure in the Nineteenth Century City* (New York: Academic Press, 1979); David Cressy, *Literacy and the Social Order: Reading and Writing in Tudor and Stuart England* (Cambridge: Cambridge University Press, 1980); Kenneth A. Lockridge, *Literacy in Colonial New England* (New York: Norton, 1974).
14. Cressy, *Literacy and the Social Order*, p. 189.
15. Harvey J. Graff, 'Reflections on the History of Literacy', *Humanities and Society* 4 (1981), 303–33; see also *The Labyrinths of Literacy: Reflections on Literacy Past and Present* (London: Falmer Press, 1987).
16. Daniel P. Resnick and Lauren B. Resnick, 'The Nature of Literacy: An Historical Exploration', *Harvard Educational Review* 47 (1977), 370–85.
17. Gerald Strauss, *Luther's House of Learning: Indoctrination of the Young in the German Reformation* (Baltimore: Johns Hopkins University Press, 1978).
18. See Graff, 'Legacies of Literacy'; Richard Johnson, 'Notes on the Schooling of the English Working Class, 1780–1850', in Roger Dale, Geoff Esland, and Madeline MacDonald (eds), *Schooling and Capitalism* (London: Routledge and Kegan Paul, 1976), pp. 44–54.
19. Ibid., p. 49.
20. Graff, *Labyrinths of Literacy*, ch. 11.
21. Coolie Verner, 'Adult Illiteracy in British Columbia', *Journal of the Faculty of Education of the University of British Columbia* 10 (1964), 100.
22. Labour Canada, *Education and Working Canadians* (Ottawa: Ministry of Labour, 1979).
23. Egil Johansson, 'Literacy Campaigns in Sweden', in Arnove and Graff (eds), *National Literacy Campaigns*, p. 70.
24. See, for example, John F. Szwed, 'The Ethnography of Literacy', in Marcia F. Whiteman (ed.), *Variation in Writing: Functional and Linguistic-Cultural Differences* (Hillsdale, N.J.: Erlbaum, 1981), pp. 13–23.
25. Shirley B. Heath, *Ways with Words: Language, Life and Work in Classrooms and Communities* (Cambridge: Cambridge University Press, 1983).

26. Sylvia Scribner and Michael Cole, *The Psychology of Literacy* (Cambridge, Mass.: Harvard University Press, 1981).

27. See Gordon Wells, *Learning through Interaction* (Cambridge: Cambridge University Press, 1981), ch. 7, for a reevaluation of the relationship between literate competence and schooling. See also Brian V. Street, *Literacy in Theory and Practice* (Cambridge: Cambridge University Press, 1984), chs. 1 and 2, for a discussion of the larger question of the social and cognitive effects of literacy.

28. Sylvia Scribner and Michael Cole, 'Literacy without Schooling: Testing for Intellectual Effects', *Harvard Educational Review* 48 (1978), 452.

29. Shirley B. Heath, 'Critical Factors in Literacy Development', in de Castell *et al.* (eds), *Literacy, Society and Schooling*, pp. 209–32.

30. Task Force on Education for Economic Growth, *A Comprehensive Plan to Improve Our Nation's Schools* (Denver: Education Committee of the States, 1983), p. 13.

31. Twentieth Century Fund Task Force on Federal Elementary and Secondary Education Policy, *Making the Grade* (New York: Twentieth Century Fund, 1983).

32. John H. Best, 'Reforming America's Schools: The High Price of Failure', *Teachers College Record* 86 (1984), 269.

33. Shirley B. Heath, 'Towards an Ethnohistory of Writing in American Education', in Whiteman (ed.) *Variation in Writing*, pp. 25–45.

34. Ibid., p. 27.

35. Shirley B. Heath, 'Ethnography in Education: Defining the Essentials', in Perry Gilmore and Alan A. Glatthorn (eds), *Children In and Out of School: Ethnography and Education* (Washington, D.C.: Center for Applied Linguistics, 1982), p. 47.

36. Ibid.

37. Heath, 'Towards an Ethnohistory of Writing in American Education', p. 27.

38. Scribner and Cole, *The Psychology of Literacy*, p. 236.

39. See Heath, 'Critical Factors in Literacy Development'; Sylvia Scribner, 'Literacy in Three Metaphors', in Nancy L. Stein (ed.), *Literacy in American Schools* (Chicago: University of Chicago Press, 1986), pp. 7–22.

40. Jacques Ellul, 'The Power of Technique and the Ethics of Non-Power', in Kathleen Woodward (ed.), *The Myths of Information: Technology and Postindustrial Culture* (Madison: Coda Press, 1980), pp. 242–7.

41. See Pam Gilbert, 'Authorship in the Writing Classroom: A Critical Comment', in Suzanne de Castell, Allan Luke and Carmen Luke (eds), *Language, Authority and Criticism: Readings on the School Textbook* (London: Falmer Press, forthcoming/1988); *Writing, Schooling and Deconstruction: From Voice to Text in the Classroom* (London: Routledge and Kegan Paul, forthcoming/1988), esp. ch. 2.

42. Paulo Freire, 'The Adult Literacy Process as Cultural Action for Freedom', *Harvard Educational Review* 40 (1970), 205.

43. Paulo Freire, *Pedagogy of the Oppressed* (New York: Herder and Herder, 1973); cf. Michael Cole and Peg Griffin, 'A Sociohistorical Approach to Remediation', in de Castell *et al.* (eds), *Literacy, Society and Schooling*, p. 126.

44. For further discussion of how formal classroom interaction may reconstitute what is to count as text knowledge, see James L. Heap, 'Discourse in the Production of Classroom Knowledge', *Curriculum Inquiry* 15 (1985), 245–79;

Educational Review 49 (1979), 379.

95. See, for example, Alan Wald, 'Hegemony and Literary Tradition in the United States', in de Castell *et al.* (eds), *Language, Authority and Criticism*; Rowland Lorimer and Margaret Long, 'Sex-Role Stereotyping in Elementary Readers', *Interchange* 10 (No. 2, 1980), 35–45; M.J. Croghan and P.P. Croghan, *Role Models in Readers: A Sociological Analysis* (Washington, D.C.: University Press of America, 1981).

96. Phillip Wexler, 'Structure, Text and Subject: A Critical Sociology of School Knowledge', in Michael W. Apple (ed.), *Cultural and Economic Reproduction in Education* (London: Routledge and Kegan Paul, 1982), p. 279. For a further review, see Joel Taxel, 'Children's Literature: Perspectives from the Sociology of School Knowledge', in de Castell *et al.* (eds), *Language, Authority and Criticism.*

97. Giroux, *Ideology, Culture and the Process of Schooling*, p. 22.

98. See, for example, Lawrence Cremin, 'Curriculum Making in the United States', *Teachers College Record* 73 (1971), 207–20; David Hamilton, 'Making Sense of Curriculum Evaluation: Continuities and Discontinuities in an Educational Idea', in Lee Schulmann (ed.), *Review of Research in Education 5* (Itasca, Ill.: F.E. Peacock, 1977), pp. 318–47.

99. Anyon, 'Ideology and United States History Textbooks'.

100. Michael W. Apple, 'The Political Economy of Text Publishing', *Educational Theory* 34 (1984), 309; see also, *Teachers and Texts: A Political Economy of Class and Gender Relations in Education* (London: Routledge and Kegan Paul, 1986), ch. 4.

101. Apple, 'The Political Economy of Text Publishing', 307.

102. Ibid.

103. Wexler, 'Structure, Text and Subject', p. 281.

104. Jean Anyon, 'Social Class and School Knowledge', *Curriculum Inquiry* 11 (1981), 3–42.

105. Carmen Luke, Suzanne de Castell and Allan Luke, 'Beyond Criticism: The Authority of the School Text', *Curriculum Inquiry* 13 (1983), 111–27.

106. Michael W. Apple, 'Curricular Form and the Logic of Technical Control: Building the Possessive Individual', in Apple (ed.), *Cultural and Economic Reproduction in Education*, pp. 247–74.

107. Ibid.; Suzanne de Castell and Allan Luke, 'Literacy Instruction: Technology and Technique', *American Journal of Education* 95 (1987), 412–40.

108. Williams, *Marxism and Literature*, p. 39.

109. Wexler, 'Structure, Text and Subject', p. 287.

110. Bonnie J.F. Meyer and G. Elizabeth Rice, 'The Structure of Text', in P. David Pearson (ed.), *Handbook of Reading Research* (London: Longman, 1984), p. 321.

111. Ibid.; Teun A. Van Dijk, 'Relevance Assignment in Discourse Comprehension', *Discourse Processes* 2 (1979), 113–26.

112. See M.A.K. Halliday and Ruqaiya Hasan, *Cohesion in English* (London: Longman, 1976).

113. Teun A. Van Dijk and Walter Kintsch, *Strategies of Discourse Processing* (New York: Academic Press, 1983).

114. Thomas T. Ballmer, 'Macrostructures', in Teun A. Van Dijk (ed.), *Pragmatics of Language and Literature* (Amsterdam: North Holland Publishing, 1976), p. 2.

115. See William F. Brewer and Edward H. Lichtenstein, *Event Schemas, Story Schemas and Story Grammars.* Technical Report No. 197. (Urbana, Ill.: Center for the Study of Reading, 1980), p. 3.
116. Meyer and Rice, 'The Structure of Text', pp. 327–8.
117. David E. Rumelhart, 'Understanding and Summarizing Brief Stories', in David LaBerge and S. Jay Samuels (eds), *Basic Processes in Reading: Perception and Comprehension* (Hillsdale, N.J.: Erlbaum, 1977), p. 277.
118. Meyer and Rice, 'The Structure of Text', p. 338.
119. Dolores Durkin, 'What is the Value of the New Interest in Reading Comprehension?' in Albert J. Harris and Edward R. Sipay (eds), *Readings on Reading Instruction* (London: Longman, 1983), p. 253.
120. See, for example, Richard C. Anderson and P. David Pearson, 'A Schema-Theoretic View of Reading Comprehension', in Pearson (ed.), *Handbook of Reading Research,* pp. 244–92.
121. Rumelhart, 'Understanding and Summarizing Basic Stories', p. 268.
122. Ibid., p. 278.
123. See, for example, David E. Rumelhart, 'Schemata: The Building Blocks of Cognition', in Rand J. Spiro, Bertram C. Bruce and William F. Brewer (eds), *Theoretical Issues in Reading Comprehension* (Hillsdale, N.J.: Erlbaum, 1980), pp. 33–58; see also Jean M. Mandler and N.S. Johnson, 'Remembrance of Things Parsed: Story Structure and Recall', *Cognitive Psychology* 9 (1977), 111–51; Richard C. Anderson, Rand J. Spiro and Mark C. Anderson, 'Schemata as Scaffolding for the Representation of Information in Connected Discourse', *American Educational Research Journal* 15 (1978), 433–40.
124. Nancy L. Stein and C.G. Glenn, 'An Analysis of Story Comprehension in Elementary School Children', in Roy L. Freedle (ed.), *New Directions in Discourse Processing, Vol. 2* (Hillsdale, N.J.: Erlbaum, 1979), pp. 53–120; cf. Nancy L. Stein and Thomas T. Trabasso, *What's in a Story: An Approach to Comprehension and Instruction.* Technical Report No. 200. (Urbana, Ill.: Center for the Study of Reading, 1981); M.T. Niezworski, Nancy L. Stein and Thomas T. Trabasso, *Story Structure versus Control Effects on Children's Recall and Evaluative Inferences.* Technical Report No. 129. (Urbana, Ill.: Center for the Study of Reading, 1979).
125. Bertram C. Bruce, 'Plans and Social Actions', in Spiro *et al.* (eds), *Theoretical Issues in Reading Comprehension,* p. 375.
126. Meyer and Rice, 'The Structure of Text', p. 340.
127. See, for example, Michel Pecheux and C. Fuchs, 'Language, Ideology and Discourse Analysis', *Praxis* 6 (1982), 3–20; Gunther Kress and Bob Hodge, *Language as Ideology* (London: Routledge and Kegan Paul, 1979); Roland Barthes, 'Introduction to the Structural Analysis of Narrative', in Stephen Heath (ed.), *Image-Music-Text* (London: Fontana, 1977), pp. 79–124; cf. Diane Macdonnell, *Theories of Discourse* (Oxford: Basil Blackwell, 1986); Gunther Kress, 'The Social Production of Language: History and Structures of Domination'', *Journal of Pragmatics* (forthcoming/1989).
128. Ballmer, 'Macrostructures', p. 2.
129. Teun A. Van Dijk, *Text and Context* (London: Longman, 1977).
130. Ibid., p. 159.
131. Ibid., p. 210.
132. Teun A. Van Dijk, 'Discourse Analysis: Its Development and Application to

The war succeeded in propelling Canada's westernmost province out of the doldrums of economic depression and led to an unprecedented increase in employment: British Columbia's primary resources were at a premium on the world market and war-related manufacturing flourished.[2] Strategically positioned on the Pacific coast, Vancouver and Victoria as well were the sites of rapidly growing tertiary service sectors. Shipbuilding and port facilities required immediate expansion, while airplane and munitions manufacture began in the Fraser Valley. This economic activity thrust the province into yet another upswing in the boom and bust economic cycle characteristic of a resource-based economy which is reliant on the needs of other industrial markets.[3] With postwar population growth typical of Western Canadian provinces — birth rates and European migration rose markedly — this economic development would sustain the provincial economy and indirectly, postwar educational expansion, well into the 1950s.

Chief Superintendent of Schools H.B. King, with Liberal Education Minister G.M. Weir one of the principal architects of Progressive modernization, noted the effect of the war on public expectations of education:

> The war . . . caused people to realize the place of education as fundamental to the working of democracy and as an agency for developing those attitudes and ideals which must permeate nations if they are to live together in a peaceful way.[4]

Following Dewey, these self-styled progressive educators looked to schooling as a potential source of cultural continuity, economic development and political security. Yet the immediate effect of the war was to curtail the programme of curricular and administrative modernization begun in the interwar years by Weir, King and others.[5] In 1941, Weir commented that 'during the war we will be obliged to mark time'.[6] School funding had decreased as public monies were directed towards the war effort; school construction was halted, textbook supplies dwindled, and a long overdue increase in teacher pay was postponed. Declining enrolment reflected the lower birthrates of the Depression.[7] Although the public school system was in a holding pattern, on this occasion it was to be used for, in Weir's words, 'the careful planning and study of our reconstruction'.[8] By 1945, Weir had ordered the reorganization of the province's 650 school districts into seventy-four larger administrative units for purposes of fiscal rationalization.[9] And by 1951 the progressive elementary curriculum introduced in the interwar years had been updated through the adoption of the latest American textbooks.[10]

The Americanization of the curriculum, then, was well underway. As early as the 1930s, King had sought to deflect Conservative scepticism towards the reform movement by describing progressivism as an equally British development; in his 1935 report on school finance and administration, he called upon the likes of John Maynard Keynes to testify on behalf of progressive reform in Britain.[11] He and Weir both had successfully defended their programme against Conservative accusations that socialist propaganda had infiltrated the curriculum.[12] Of course, the degree to which daily school practice became more 'child-centred' both in the US and British Columbia as the result of such reforms has been questioned.[13] However, the rhetoric of progressivism — equality with industrial and state development through scientifically verifiable efficiency — had been adopted wholeheartedly by King, Weir and their colleagues. Moreover, as we will see, the use of state of the art textbooks and the implementation of a comprehensive US-style standardized testing and tracking system were but two signs of actual implementation of the meritocracy.[14] Literacy figured significantly in this overall agenda, which posited schooling, in Weir's words, as 'justifiable for the protection of the state against the evils of ignorance and illiteracy, the seedbed of anarchy and communism'.[15] In the immediate postwar era, though, King and Weir seemed caught in the paradox of centralized imposition of progressive principles based on educators' readings of the individual child and community.

The immediate problem for educational planners and curriculum developers was the severe shortage of trained teachers wrought by wartime enlistment and industry. As provincial normal school enrolments decreased by a third,[16] an administrator of the Victoria Summer School appraised the situation:

> The war has taken young men from teaching to the armed forces and war industry. . . . Young women are going where they can make more money than in teaching or where they feel they can render more effective service.[17]

In spite of the adoption of the 'New Pedagogy' and the 'socialized recitation' in provincial Normal Schools and colleges, then, the Department was forced to employ many teachers with minimal, if any professional training.

The war also provided the catalyst for fears about declining standards of literacy throughout North America. C.B. Conway, the leading psychometrician in the province, like many researchers and administrators, was wary of the effects of the war on standards of literacy. He invoked the spectre of mass illiteracy as a recurring historical consequence of global war. Conway recalled the World War I-era US Army Alpha and Beta intelligence testing undertaken by Yerkes, which had revealed unexpected levels of illiteracy among the products of US public schools.[18] Speaking to the Victoria Summer School teachers in training, Conway commented that

'Army tests reveal many people to be illiterate because their schools and homeland were ravaged by the war of 1914–18 and its aftermath.'[19] The logic of Conway's argument is somewhat difficult to follow, inasmuch as he did not specify whose Army tests and, indeed, neither the Canadian nor US Army had tested Western Europeans after World War I.

Yet further to this there was no definitive data on declining provincial school achievement in literacy to justify such alarm. Before his 1945 retirement, King defended the existing curriculum, maintaining that 'the better education of the recruit enables him to grasp quickly the increasingly technical features of military training'.[20] His comments came in the wake of province-wide achievement testing run by Conway: the administration of the *Public School Achievement Tests in Reading* had revealed that 'the medium of the typical British Columbia student is, in reading comprehension, one half year in advance of his American counterpart'.[21] King, Conway and their colleagues in the provincial capital of Victoria seemed satisfied that the psychologically based approaches to elementary reading and language arts instruction instituted in the interwar years were yielding positive results. Not coincidentally, they frequently used subcontracted versions of US developed and normed tests, like Lewis Terman and colleagues' *Stanford Reading Achievement Test*: in some cases, a new title page was printed for the British Columbia version.[22] This use of US tests enabled the comparison of Canadian and US norms.

Indeed much of the alarm expressed by public and educators over allegedly declining levels of literacy seems to have been based on United States Department of Defense data, widely quoted in the Canadian press and provincial teachers' journals. In the *British Columbia Teacher*, Stringfellow Barr, president of St John's College in the eastern US, was quoted as follows:

> The war is showing up a failure that had already become a graver and graver threat to the institutions of a free people. Our army now reports that many college men cannot analyse or interpret a paragraph of plain English and know what is in it.[23]

Barr further noted that college students made 'very sorry officer material' and were the products of the 'breakdown in liberal education'. In the same article, the president of Harvard University was quoted at length for the edification of provincial teachers:

> From all studies ... we hear complaints of the average Harvard graduate unable to write either correctly or fluidly. ... An educational system which cannot teach the young to write their mother tongue fluidly after fifteen or sixteen years of schooling, cannot keep pace with the needs of the war, nor the needs of peace. Nor

can it keep pace with the needs of professors, nor of business, nor of industry, nor of a free press.[24]

A recurring justification for the improvement of the teaching of reading and writing was apparent: literacy was seen as requisite for the 'needs of business and industry' and the preservation of social institutions. Emerging in this postwar debate, then, was a synthesis of the rhetoric of literacy crises with a seminal version of the human–capital argument.

The misapplication of US data to the Canadian educational context continued after the war. Irving Graham, an instructor with the Provincial Normal School in Calgary, assessed for British Columbia teachers 'the kind of education we have been administering to our pupils in the last ten to fifteen years'.[25] He too cited US sources:

> Twenty eight out of every thousand men are rejected because they are too badly trained to pass the simplist literacy tests. . . . Many high school and college graduates are . . . weak in the clear and simple use of the English Language.[26]

Graham concluded that the current educational system was 'not Progressive, not occupational, nor social, nor scientific'. In the atmosphere of heightened expectations for the public school system, the inevitable comparisons of American and Canadian standards and achievement, often invoked by those educational officials responsible for reform, contributed to the perceptions of crisis.

Some sceptics argued that 'true' progressivism had never been effectively implemented. A Richmond high-school teacher explained that

> The institution of Progressive Education was accompanied by a general overhaul of the courses of study. Formalism was given a gleeful chuckle. . . . In some limited areas, a progressive school board, an intelligent inspector, a forceful principal, or an irrepressible teacher may have done much to further progressive outlook and practice. Most schools, however, are bound . . . by the formal cramming methods best suited to examination results.[27]

Liberal Senator Gerry McGeer, former Mayor of Vancouver, agreed.

> We have in our educational institutions the means of creating a literate people. We have advanced to the point where every child is not only provided with a free education but is compelled to accept that education, and yet we fail and fail lamentably.[28]

McGeer, a leading Liberal party spokesperson and long-time advocate of Weir's programme of modernization, was not alone among provincial politicians who expressed displeasure with the educational system. Yet while his urbane protestations focused on the need for a 'truly Progressive' integration of the curriculum with community life, other more right-wing members of the legislative assembly called for a return to the 'three Rs of the Little Red Schoolhouse'. Conservative Coalition member W.J. Johnson commented in the legislature on the Department's postwar planners:

> I get a letter now and then from some of those well educated chaps and if they didn't have good typists I'd never be able to understand them, because I can never make out the signature.[29]

The *ad hominem* tenor of Johnson's attack notwithstanding, it is significant that even in this era of relative consensus on the direction of the public system, there remained regular invocations of 'the basics' and the '3 Rs'. Regardless of whether they accurately reflected the sentiments of his rural constituents, Johnson's comments were reported in the *Vancouver Sun* under the headline '3 R's Needed in Schools'. Then, as now, literacy crises made good press. And apparently, educational authorities were caught in a twin-jawed trap: accused by progressives — and this group would have to include the socialist Cooperative Commonwealth Federation (CCF), British Columbia's second most powerful party — of not being progressive enough, and attacked by Conservatives and later by the Social Credit movement as too permissive and socialist in orientation.

But was there any real justification for charges of declining standards in literacy? Under Conway's direction, the Department of Education had amassed a volume of psychometric data which, as noted, confirmed that elementary achievement in reading appeared on the whole superior to that of American students. However, King found fault with the teaching of literacy in the secondary schools:

> In reading the situation is not so satisfactory. . . . 23 per cent were below the modest California standard for grade X. This not inconsiderable body of students is not well equipped to deal with the . . . material . . . they encounter in their high school studies.[30]

These results King attributed to teachers' lack of understanding of researched approaches to the teaching of reading, and to a preoccupation with 'literary aesthetics':

> Until recently it was not understood that a programme of reading development should be carried on in all high school grades. . . . Teachers were untrained in the techniques of reading development, and taught as they had themselves been taught.[31]

Provincial authorities saw classical, literature-based approaches to English teaching as the last bastion of non-scientific traditionalism. King located the key to successful teaching in knowledge of psychological 'experiments, research and investigations' occurring in the 'growing science' of education: teacher professional 'competence' required knowledge of the 'current stream of educational literature' emerging from American and Canadian universities.[32] Certainly, as we will see, emergent educational science had begun to assert a major impact on the teaching of reading.

By the postwar era, Conway and colleagues had deployed as comprehensive a standardized testing system as could be found in Canada, providing annual results of IQ, reading and literacy-related tests. Yet the publication of test results alone could not silence reactionary criticism of the progressive, avowedly scientific approach to basic and advanced literacy instruction. In an era of increasingly militant anti-communism, the populist government of W.A.C. Bennett had replaced the Liberal/Conservative coalition. With the emergence of a rural based, free-enterprise government which drew strong support from the both farmers and the middle class, the last vestiges of the interwar New Deal government which had introduced educational progressivism were swept away.[33] Effectively red baiting the CCF, Bennett's Social Credit Party was elected in its own right in 1953.

Schooling had been made a central issue by Social Credit in the run up to the election when member J.A. Reid attacked 'immoral textbooks', arguing that insidious socialist influences were at work in the curriculum. Reid, secretary of the legislature's Social Welfare and Education Committee, attacked an 'Effective Living' coursebook as an immoral form of sex education, calling it 'Effective Loving'.[34] He was joined in his criticism by Social Credit Education Minister Tilly Rolston, who spoke in the legislature of the need for a return to the 'little red schoolhouse': she promised to correct the 'lopsided viewpoint' of the Department of Education curriculum committee by including more 'practical people'. Her call for the basics complemented her overall agenda for the reform of public schooling. Rolston set out in her brief tenure to eliminate what she perceived as the immorality and lack of discipline which accompanied neglect of the '3Rs'.[35] Such trends as permissiveness, sex education, and socialist influence were to be rooted from the system.

The move to the right was supported by some members of the local press and furthered by academics' complaints about the products of the system. In 1953 the *Vancouver Province* ran an editorial entitled 'Get Closer to Three R's'. The editors argued that the 'pendulum had swung too far' towards a progressive model which gave 'less emphasis on the three R's and more on giving boys and girls well-rounded personalities that would integrate them into society and ensure them happier lives'.[36] Quoting Social

Credit MLA Lydia Arsens, the editorial further noted that the previous generation was thoroughly 'dissatisfied with current methods':

> Those of us who are a bit shy about admitting our ages can remember when the three R's were the cornerstone of education. Reading, writing and arithmetic were dinned into our heads until we were thoroughly fed up with them. But at that, most of us could at least read, write and tot up a column of figures with pretty fair facility.[37]

The editors concluded by encouraging Rolston to press on with reform and 'to replace some of the educators on the [Departmental curriculum] committee with representatives of the business community'.

The credibility of this populist call for the basics was enhanced by claims from university academics that incoming students 'can't spell or write grammatically'. Under a front-page banner headline which read 'Second R Needed at UBC', M.W. Steinberg, co-chairman of the University of British Columbia's first year English programme, argued that 'we have to spend almost all the first year teaching students simple grammar and even then most of them can't handle the language'.[38] This crisis he attributed to the 'lack of discipline in teaching'. But Steinberg also argued that class sizes needed to be smaller and teachers better qualified.

Indeed the postwar 'baby boom' and increased immigration from Europe had led to an unprecedented rapid growth of the public school system in British Columbia. Between 1947 and 1953, enrolment jumped by more than fifty per cent from 137,827 to 210,744 students.[39] By the end of the 1950s, the total enrolment would reach 292,403 students.[40] The largest growth of course was in elementary schools, with over 65,000 new students entering between 1947 and 1953.

Despite these shifts in partisan politics and the retirements in the civil service which inevitably accompany redirection of educational policy, the progressive orientation of the Department of Education — in stated policy at least — remained intact during this period. Weir's electoral demise had come in 1946, yet the Liberal party had maintained control of the education portfolio in successive coalition governments until Rolston's ascendance in 1951. More importantly, key civil service posts were passed on to those who had apprenticed as inspectors under King and Weir's departing mandate to 'direct the practical application' of progressive reform.[41] The postwar educational progressives had to contend with rapidly escalating costs and, from the early 1950s on, the Social Credit government. As Rolston's and Arsens' comments amply illustrate, standards and practices of schooling in general, and basic literacy in particular, became major public issues.

It was in this historical context, then, that postwar administrators undertook to update and further implement the reforms initially introduced before and during the war. In stated policy, the Department of Education remained committed to 'scientific' approaches to curriculum and instruction, with a Deweyian 'child-centred' pedagogical philosophy. And, with formal establishment in 1946 of a Research and Standards Branch under Conway's direction, standardized testing was expanded to monitor achievement throughout the newly created 74 provincial school districts.[42]

This total approach to the modernization of education fitted nicely with a postwar belief in scientific progress and potentially unlimited economic development. However, strong counter-positions were expressed in provincial politics and the popular press: a scepticism towards the tenets of modern (American) education, a rumour that progressive education was an incipient form of socialism, and a staunch belief in the 'basics', however defined. According to Cremin, this early 1950s critique of progressivism, epitomized in the satire of *Auntie Mame*, was widespread throughout the US as well.[43] In British Columbia this trend was particularly strong in those rural and resource areas where economic prosperity stood side by side with traditional community and religious values.

The Basics Lost?

Throughout the 1950s complaints centred on the need for a return to traditional standards and classical curricula, wider teaching of phonics, and greater attention to the study of quality literature. In an extremely influential and popular book, *So Little for the Mind*, classicist Hilda Neatby argued that

> this excessive appeal with 'interest', this consequent concern with the modern, the familiar and the simple in theory, combined with a multiplication of methods and techniques, is responsible for the well known fact that up to the end of intermediate or junior high school stage many Canadian pupils cannot read.[44]

Neatby's reading of postwar curriculum guides and textbooks had convinced her that Canadian schools were neglecting the Arnoldian liberal arts and, in so doing, were weakening both the moral fibre of children and the educational excellence of schools: 'anti-cultural', 'revolutionary', 'pseudo-scientific', and 'materialist', progressivism had spawned an 'age without standards'.[45] In particular she singled out the derogation of literacy, with its high cultural association with literature study, into the 'art of communication', a trend in curriculum documents which reflected the influence of Mead and Dewey's social psychology. Noting the laments of businessmen and academics, Neatby claimed that

Intellectual leaders of the future literally cannot read, write, or think. They are good at word recognition, but to 'read, mark, learn and inwardly digest' even simple material is beyond them. They can write, and often type, but too often they cannot construct a grammatical sentence. They emit platitudes, but they can neither explain nor defend them.[46]

Neatby's criticism, then, located the failure of the American science of pedagogy, of the 'industrial techniques' of educational psychology,[47] in terms of a lack of reverence to the longstanding traditions of the humanities and liberal arts. Her comments caused a storm of controversy and received considerable support from fellow academics and the general public. Many provincial teachers dismissed her criticism as reactionary. In a letter to the editor of the *British Columbia Teacher*, a teacher describes their collective response:

Evidently, whenever any aspect of the system of education we administer is under fire, the view is expressed for us by our professional magazine — 'Close Ranks!' The late controversy over the writings of Dr Neatby is a case in point . . . it must be recognized that this lady brought serious charges, and brought them sincerely and honestly. They were never answered . . . point by point, and refuted. Rather they were buried under a mass of shameful invective and then ignored.[48]

Rudolf Flesch's iconoclastic critique, *Why Johnny Can't Read*,[49] took an opposite tact, a direct attack on the expertise of the reading/instructional psychology community. He argued that scientific evidence could be marshalled to demonstrate the efficacy of phonics instruction and implied, not so subtly, that reading researchers had collaborated to hide this evidence in order to maintain the 'look-say', word recognition approach to beginning reading. With personal criticism of leading reading psychologists David Russell of the University of California and Arthur Gates of Teachers College, Flesch claimed that 'in every single research study ever made phonics was shown to be superior to the word method'.[50]

Flesch, who had completed a doctorate at Teachers College, was as skeptical as Neatby of the postwar educational establishment, 'the educators in their teachers colleges and publishing offices [who] think up all these fancy ideas'.[51] But he attempted to distance himself from the general red-baiting attack on 'progressive-liberal minded' educators.

Mind you, I am not one of those people who call them un-American or left-wingers or Communist fellow travelers. All I am saying is that their theories are wrong and that the application of those theories has done untold harm to our younger generation.[52]

Though dismissed in provincial teachers' journals as 'incorrect' and full of 'loopholes',[53] Flesch's attack was read and reported widely. The notion that there was scientific proof that the schools induced 'Johnny's' reading failure had entered the public domain.

In retrospect, we can see that both attacks were moot, given the conflicting data on the *actual* implementation of progressive pedagogy throughout North America in general, and British Columbia in particular.[54] However, both generated a good deal of support and commentary in British Columbia and throughout English-Canada: the teachers' journals and newspaper letters to the editor columns were filled with accusation and counter-accusation. What is of interest here is that the critiques, as in current debates over educational reform, were mounted from divergent positions: the problem with schooling in general, and the teaching of literacy in particular was seen alternately as one of too much modern educational science, or too little.

The postwar context of the curriculum thus was one of polarization and acrimony. At least in sites like British Columbia, the issues of standards and practices were not ones which reflected pastoral harmony and broad consensus, as many subsequent commentaries have suggested. In the midst of this, the advocates of progressivism, though admitting some teacher intransigence in the form of entrenched traditionalism, continued to speak on behalf of the virtues of American scientific approaches to curriculum. To mark the success of child-centred practices, they cited psychometric data culled from their burgeoning testing programmes, often comparing Canadian children's achievement with that of their American counterparts.

Yet it would seem that no one was wholly contented with the status quo of literacy instruction. While putting on a brave public face, the likes of King, Weir and later Conway were anxious that the war had delayed modernization and that postwar industry would make greater literate demands on workers. They argued that it was primarily a matter of staying the course, of fully implementing modern pedagogy, the science of testing, and administrative rationalization. They were besieged, however, from several sources: university-based academics periodically complained about standards of literacy of secondary-school graduates; classicists and traditionalists, moreover, coalesced in support of Neatby's book which, like recent words by Adler and Bloom, received considerable editorial support and popular paraphrase. As if this wasn't enough, adding to their problems were the insistent attacks of Flesch and an emergent pro-phonics lobby. Flesch's book went through several printings, and well into the 1960s many parents' groups would embrace phonics as the basics which they believed were omitted.

Additionally, the popular association of progressive education with, at best, political liberalism and, at worst, Moscow-inspired socialism, complicated the picture further. With the shift to the political right in the early 1950s, the basics movement, led by Social Credit ministers and members, came into full flight: calls for a return to non-secular morality, the '3 Rs' and business skills would grace both parliamentary debate and newspaper editorials throughout the decade.

Yet an altogether different picture of the 1950s emerges when we turn to more recent reappraisals. In 1961 Arthur Gates of Teachers College, apparently having survived Flesch's attack, noted that children in 1957 had a half-year advantage in reading ability over comparable children in the 1930s.[55] More recently, Paul Copperman argued that literacy was optimally taught in the 1950s, when educators maintained discipline among students and teachers.[56] He notes that achievement test scores were uniformly high during this period, prior to 'curricular deterioration' and the 'degeneration of authority relations' which ensued in the 1960s. A far more credible source, the 1985 Report of the US National Academy of Education Commission on Reading, argues that 'what was a satisfactory level of literacy in 1950 probably will be marginal by the year 2000'.[57]

How were children taught literacy in postwar British Columbia schools? Having isolated a locale for study, and described the various political, social and cultural forces which may have influenced the curriculum, we turn to a closer examination of the British Columbia elementary reading and language arts curriculum in the 1950s.

The Texts of Elementary Instruction, 1945–60

According to the Provincial Program of Study and lists of prescribed texts issued by the British Columbia Department of Education, British Columbia school children in the 1950s progressed through several basal textbook series.[58] They began to learn to read in the early primary years with the W.J. Gage's Curriculum Foundation basal readers[59] — published in the United States by Scott Foresman and commonly known as the Dick and Jane series — or one of its competitors, similar in structure and content. In the intermediate and late elementary grades, they progressed to J.M. Dent's Canadian Parade readers.[60] This western Canadian reading series provided a matrix for the whole language arts programme, covering such related areas as content area reading skills, grammar, study and reference skills, creative writing and speech. Throughout the elementary grades, these basic reading texts were augmented with the W.J. Gage's Canadian Spellers.[61] For the teaching of all three texts, teachers were provided with voluminous guidelines in the form of Departmental curriculum guides, memos and circulars, teachers' guides, and local, national and American teachers' journals.

It is impossible to ascertain with absolute certainty the extent of use of any of these series for teaching literacy. Using the official Departmental Programmes of Studies and lists of prescribed textbooks as indicators, though, it appears that by the 1950s the Curriculum Foundation series and Canadian Parade readers were the major texts in use, and that the 1947 abandonment of the aging Highroads to Reading[62] series marked a modernization of basic literacy curricula. However, a search of British Columbia curriculum collections, booksellers, secondhand stores, and school attics revealed that series like the Beckley-Cardy Company's Functional Phonetics[63] series of phonics texts and the J.C. Winston Company's Easy Growth in Reading[64] basals were used at least sporadically. Students were issued various grade level versions of the Gage spellers from grades 2–6.

The likely exceptions in this predominant instructional sequence were those children classified as 'slow learners' who lived in areas where an alternate, phonics-based mode of instruction was used. Other children in rural areas where textbooks were in short supply, despite the Department's concerted postwar effort to improve access to universal free textbooks, might have learned to read with the superceded Highroads series.[65]

In the postwar period, then, three principal textbooks series formed the matrix of the elementary school curriculum for the teaching of reading and related literate competences. In what follows, Chapter 3 documents the economic bases and theoretical assumptions underlying the development of the comprehensive curricular technology, the basal reader series, and Chapter 4 features a discourse analysis of exemplary narratives from the Dick and Jane readers which many children used. As a counterpoint to the analysis of these US texts imported into Canada, Chapter 5 focuses on the nationalist response to US curricula and the consequent development and content of the Canadian Parade reading series. Chapter 6 examines the text on how to teach these various textbooks, and the psychometric/bureaucratic machinery developed to enforce the norms of literacy learning in the postwar elementary school.

Notes and References

1. George S. Tomkins, 'Foreign Influences on Curriculum Policy Making and Development in Canada: Some Impressions in Historical and Contemporary Perspective', *Curriculum Inquiry* 11 (1981), 157–66; 'The Moral, Cultural and

Intellectual Foundations of the Canadian Curriculum', in Douglas A. Roberts and John O. Fritz (eds), *Curriculum Canada V: School Subjects Research and Curriculum/Instruction Theory* (Vancouver: Centre for the Study of Curriculum and Instruction, 1984), pp. 1–24; Jean Mann, 'G.M. Weir and H.B. King: Progressive Education or Education for the Progressive State', in J. Donald Wilson and David C. Jones (eds), *Schooling and Society in Twentieth Century British Columbia* (Calgary: Detselig, 1980), pp. 91–138. For a more general, theoretical discussion of progressive orientations to literacy instruction see Suzanne de Castell and Allan Luke, 'Models of Literacy in North American Schools: Social and Historical Conditions and Consequences', in Suzanne de Castell, Allan Luke and Kieran Egan (eds), *Literacy, Society and Schooling* (Cambridge: Cambridge University Press, 1986), pp. 87–109.

2. Margaret Ormsby, *British Columbia: A History* (Toronto: Macmillan, 1962), pp. 481–4.

3. Edwin R. Black, 'British Columbia: The Politics of Exploitation', in Hugh G. Thorburn (ed.), *Party Politics in Canada* (Scarborough: Prentice-Hall Canada, 1972), pp. 225–36.

4. British Columbia Department of Education, *Public Schools Annual Report, 1941–2* (Victoria: Department of Education, 1942), p. D37.

5. The central tenets of Weir's version of progressivism applied to a critique of 'formalism' in British Columbia schools can be found in John H. Putman and George M. Weir, *Survey of the School System* (Victoria: King's Printer, 1925).

6. George M. Weir, 'Retrospect and Prospect in Education', *British Columbia Teacher* 21 (1941), 460.

7. F. Henry Johnson, *A History of Public Education in British Columbia* (Vancouver: University of British Columbia Publications Centre, 1964), p. 123.

8. Weir, 'Retrospect and Prospect in Education', 460.

9. Maxwell A. Cameron, *Report of the Commission of Inquiry into Educational Finance* (Victoria: King's Printer, 1946). Cameron was extremely ill during the preparation of this report, and it is quite likely that Weir was responsible for a good deal of its contents.

10. See British Columbia Department of Education, *Prescribed Textbooks* (Victoria: Department of Education, 1951).

11. H.B. King, *School Finance in British Columbia* (Victoria: King's Printer, 1935); see Mann, 'G.M. Weir and H.B. King', for a critical discussion of King's introduction of the rhetoric of fiscal and pedagogical efficiency into provincial educational policy.

12. Ibid., pp. 111–13.

13. See Neil Sutherland, 'The Triumph of "Formalism": Elementary Schooling in Vancouver from the 1920s to the 1960s', *BC Studies* 69–70 (1986), 175–210, which argues, on the basis of oral histories, that British Columbia urban schools remained traditional despite the popularization of the rhetoric of progressive education by provincial authorities. In a review of inspectors' and researchers' reports for US schools, a similar conclusion is drawn in Arthur Zilversmit, 'The Failure of Progressive Education: 1920–1940', in Lawrence Stone (ed.), *Schooling and Society: Studies in the History of Education* (Baltimore: Johns Hopkins University Press, 1976), pp. 252–63.

14. For a discussion of the meritocratic assumptions of British Columbia reformers, see Mann, 'G.M. Weir and H.B. King'.

15. George M. Weir, *A Survey of Nursing Education in Canada* (Toronto: University of Toronto Press, 1932), p. 478.
16. Johnson, *A History of Public Education in British Columbia*, p. 123.
17. B. Mickleburgh, 'Victoria Summer School Report', *British Columbia Teacher* 22 (1942), 15.
18. For a detailed description of US Army testing programmes during World War I, see Stephen J. Gould, *The Mismeasure of Man* (New York: Norton, 1983), pp. 192–205.
19. Cited in Mickleburgh, 'Victoria Summer School Report', p. 17.
20. British Columbia Department of Education, *Public Schools Annual Report, 1941–2*, p. B32.
21. Ibid., p. B38.
22. See, for example, *British Columbia Primary Reading Test, Form E* (Victoria: Division of Tests, Standards and Research, 1949).
23. Cited in John H. Sutherland, 'Education and War Needs', *British Columbia Teacher* 26 (1946), 183.
24. Cited in ibid.
25. Irving H. Graham, 'The Army Appraises Our Educational System', *British Columbia Teacher* 25 (1945), 57.
26. Ibid.
27. S. Oswald Harries, 'Has Progressive Education Failed?' *British Columbia Teacher* 28 (1948), 147.
28. Gerry McGeer, 'Education and Peace', *British Columbia Teacher* 26 (1946), 113.
29. *Vancouver Sun*, 17 February 1946, p. 23.
30. British Columbia Department of Education, *Public Schools Annual Report, 1944–5* (Victoria: Department of Education, 1945), p. Y35.
31. Ibid.
32. Ibid., p. Y38.
33. Martin Robin, *Pillars of Profit: The Company Province, 1934–1972* (Toronto: McClelland and Stewart, 1973), p. 185.
34. Ibid., p. 179.
35. Ibid.
36. *Vancouver Province*, 28 September 1953, p. 6.
37. Ibid.
38. *Vancouver Province*, 28 March 1952, p. 1.
39. Statistics Canada, *A Century of Education in British Columbia: Statistical Perspectives* (Ottawa: Information Canada, 1971), pp. 129–30.
40. Ibid., p. 129.
41. British Columbia Department of Education, *Public Schools Annual Report, 1945–6* (Victoria: Department of Education, 1946), p. MM35.
42. Clifford B. Conway, 'Centralized Test Programs in Education', *Education* 1 (No. 13, 1956), 49–52.
43. Lawrence Cremin, *The Transformation of the School: Progressivism in American Education, 1896–1957* (New York: Vintage Press, 1961).
44. Hilda Neatby, *So Little for the Mind* (Toronto: Clarke, Irwin, 1953), p. 157.
45. Ibid., pp. 16–19.
46. Ibid., p. 12.
47. Ibid., p. 6.
48. 'Leprechaun', 'Let's Be Honest', *British Columbia Teacher* 36 (1956), 308.

49. Rudolf Flesch, *Why Johnny Can't Read* (New York: Harper and Row, 1955).
50. Ibid., p. 61.
51. Ibid., p. 133.
52. Ibid.
53. 'Review of "Why Johnny Can't Read" ', *British Columbia Teacher* 36 (1956), 211.
54. See Sutherland, 'The Triumph of "Formalism" '; Zilversmit, 'The Failure of Progressive Education'; cf. Harries, 'Has Progressive Education Failed?'.
55. Arthur I. Gates, *Attainment in Elementary Schools, 1957 and 1937* (New York: Teachers College Bureau of Publications, 1961).
56. See Paul Copperman, *The Literacy Hoax* (New York: Morrow, 1979); 'The Decline of Literacy', *Journal of Communication* 30 (No. 1, 1980), 113–22.
57. Richard C. Anderson, Elfrieda H. Hiebert, Judith A. Scott and Ian A. Wilkinson, *Becoming a Nation of Readers: The Report of the Commission on Reading* (Washington, D.C.: National Institute of Education, 1984), p. 3.
58. British Columbia Department of Education, *Programme of Studies for the Elementary Schools* (Victoria: King's Printers, 1947); *Programme of Studies for the Intermediate Grades* (Victoria: Department of Education, 1954); *Prescribed Textbooks*.
59. The Curriculum Foundation readers, by William S. Gray and May Hill Arbuthnot, were published in Chicago by Scott-Foresman from 1935 to 1965. The version of the series used in British Columbia was published in Toronto by W.J. Gage.
60. The Canadian Parade readers, by Donalda Dickie, Belle Rickner, Clara Tyner and T.W. Woodhead, were published in Toronto and Vancouver by J.M. Dent from 1947 to 1957. Woodhead was Principal of Kitsilano Secondary School in Vancouver in the interwar years; Sheila Shopland of the University of British Columbia was series editor.
61. The Canadian Spellers, by Frank Quance, were published in Toronto by W.J. Gage from 1930 to 1950.
62. F.L. Ormond, C.M. Ormond and M.A. Beresford's Highroads to Reading series was published in Toronto by W.J. Gage in 1932.
63. The Functional Phonetics basal series by Anna Cordts was published in Chicago by the Beckley-Cardy Company in 1953.
64. The Easy Growth in Reading basal series by Gertrude Hildreth, Elsie Roy, F.C. Biehl, A.L. Felton and M.J. Henderson was published in Toronto by the John C. Winston Company in 1950.
65. For a description of the expansion of textbook availability in postwar British Columbia, see P.G. Barr, 'The British Columbia Textbook Rental Program', *Education* 2 (No. 8, 1958), 29–31.

Chapter 3

Making the Text:
Genesis of the Modern Basal Reader

When one lacks adequate understanding of the conceptual and economic activity of textbook development and publication, the genesis of the ideological character of children's textbooks may be viewed erroneously as the determinate result of a hidden hand of class or economic agency, historical accident, or authorial genius. As noted in Williams's explanation of ideological production, the process of the selective tradition, whereby class-based knowledges and competences are sanctioned as legitimate school knowledge, is historically dynamic, mediated throughout by the agency of human subjects. This mediation, moreover, may result in contradictions between means and ends, intents and outcomes within the cultural selection progress. The consequent structure and content of the curriculum can be reconsidered as the product of historical processes engaged in by human subjects, rather than as a simple mechanistic reflection of dominant class interests.

What is needed, then, is an account of the making of educational texts which identifies the points of convergence and contradiction between the intellectual labour of text production (conception and authorship) and the economics of publication and distribution (commoditization). An analysis of the conditions and conventions of text production can specify the 'historical complexity of the influences on publishing and its content, readership, and economic reality',[1] focusing on the relationships between dominant paradigms of educational research and curricular development, between authorial conception and mass production. Hence a 'theoretically and politically grounded . . . investigation that follows a curriculum artifact such as a textbook from its writing to its selling (and then to its use)'[2] is undertaken here.

The Curriculum Foundation basal reading textbooks in effect constituted many British Columbian, Canadian and American's first encounter with official, school-based literacy training. In the following overview and critique of the development of the Curriculum Foundation series, I want to identify the dominant assumptions of the authors and publishers of the curriculum regarding literacy, the role of literature in curriculum, and the optimal conditions for learning to read. Further, I want to situate this analysis within a parallel discussion of the emergent early and mid-twentieth-century industrial relationship between publishing, large-scale curriculum development, and corporate financial interests. In concert with the foregoing description of local and regional curricular debates, this should provide an historical context for the more detailed examination of the actual texts children read. What follows, then, is a history of the conceptualization, authorship, and production of one of the most successful basal reading series in the history of publishing: Scott Foresman Company's and W.J. Gage's Curriculum Foundation readers, known to a generation of American and Canadian teachers and students as 'the Dick and Jane readers'.

The Production of the Selective Tradition:
Educational Publishing and Curriculum Development

School textbooks — despite the historical development of an anonymous, authoritative 'textbookese' which succeeds in disguising their subjective and ideological origins[3] — remain commodities, objects produced and consumed by human subjects. The book, like media, music and artwork, is the product of a particular form of labour: the production of aesthetic and expressive artefacts of both elite and mass culture entails the intellectual work of conceptualization and authorship. But books are also actual physical commodities and cultural artefacts,[4] bought and sold in the educational marketplace. Their production involves actual design, printing, marketing and sales.

Textbooks require a specialized form of literate labour within mass culture. Unlike trade texts they have been developed by educators and, particularly since the early twentieth century, by university-based researchers. Although they are produced by large companies and marketed to administrators and consultants representing local, regional and state jurisdictions at professional conventions and meetings, their ultimate consumers of course are those teachers who teach them and those students who read and respond to them. As for their overall social function, textbooks act as the interface between the officially state-adopted and sanctioned knowledge of the culture, and the learner.[5] Like all text, school textbooks remain potentially agents of mass enlightenment and/or social control.[6] Problems in ascertaining what will count as a common culture notwithstanding, textbooks are a specialized means for the ritual introduction of children into a culture's values and knowledge.[7]

The development and marketing of the modern school textbook in the last century has been subject to progressively more industrialized, and systems-oriented approaches to curriculum development[8] *and* to the economies of scale of what has become historically an increasingly monopolized publishing industry.[9] In the US, combined textbook sales rose from $7,400,000 in 1897 to $17,275,000 by 1913. By the end of World War II, sales had risen to $131,000,000.[10]

Beginning in the twentieth century, the influence of applied psychology spread to all sectors of the industrial economy. The rationale of the universal application of scientific inquiry to social and cultural domains in industrial and post-industrial society was, and remains, a technocratic belief in the unbiased, ideological neutrality of science.[11] In the case of education, this rationale was reinforced by Dewey's argument that 'science has familiarized man with the idea of development, taking effect practically in persistent gradual amelioration of the estate of our common humanity'.[12] As noted in Chapter 2, in both Canada and the United States the enthusiasm of progressive educators for scientifically based pedagogies was fuelled by a postwar belief in the prospect of unlimited economic growth and scientific development, even in an outpost of the industrialized world like British Columbia. Certainly, the extension of applied psychology to such practical domains as education, mass media, advertising and marketing is a paradigm case of the progressive advocacy of the application of scientific approaches to the remediation of institutional life. It is also a case in which educational scientists, following Taylorist principles, ignored Dewey's caveat:

> Industry that is empirically controlled forbids constructive applications of intelligence; it depends upon following in an imitative slavish manner. . . . Experimental science means the possibility of using past experiences as the servant, not the master, of mind.[13]

Early twentieth-century psychologists like Wundt's student Hugo Munsterberg, Elton Mayo and others led the way to the scientific assessment of social and industrial needs.[14] While 'scientific management' offered increased output of standardized products through normed and controlled production processes,[15] 'market research' yielded data on consumers' wants and needs, and the new 'science' of advertising played an increasing role in the stipulation of consumer demand. John B. Watson's departure from foundational academic research on behavioural psychology to the greener fields of Madison Avenue in the 1920s exemplified this application of science to early-twentieth-century enterprise.

Since the rise of progressive and scientific approaches to educational practice, curriculum theorizing, making and evaluation has fallen under the auspices of this technocratic rationale. The 'assembly-line' approach to curriculum developed by Charters and Bobbitt at the University of Chicago and the later educational 'needs assessment' and 'goal' formulation advocated by Tyler laid out a wholly scientific rationale for the selection of curricular knowledge. Much of this foundational research for the development of a positivist science of curriculum development and evaluation, moreover, was undertaken during the interwar years with increasing support of private corporate funding.[16] Lawrence Cremin describes this historical application of systems management to curriculum and instruction:

> From the second decade of the twentieth century . . . Taylor's . . . scientific management swept not only industry, but education as well. . . . Its influence is manifest in the work of Franklin Bobbitt and W.W. Charters . . . [who] tended to analogize from the world of the factory to the world of the school, conceiving of the child as the raw material, the ideal adult as the finished product, the teacher as the worker, the supervisor as the foreman, and the curriculum as the process whereby the raw material was converted into the finished product. To the extent that the characteristics of the raw material, the finished product, and the conversion process could be quantitatively deferred, rationally dealt with and objectively appraised, curriculum-making could become a science; to the extent that the workers and the foreman could engage together in the scientific determination and rational pursuit of curriculum objectives, teaching could become an applied science, a form of educational engineering.[17]

The historical end product of this inter- and postwar trend towards the mechanization of curriculum development is the standardized and mass marketed curricular package, replete with teachers' guides, worksheets, guidelines for testing and other adjunct instructional materials, an exemplar of technical form.

These early- to mid-twentieth-century developments in curriculum were concomitant with expansion and growth in the publishing industry in general, and in the marketing of educational products in particular. In *Communications*,[18] Williams explicates the effects of capital expansion on the development of textual and electronic mass-communications media. He argues that the larger (and by definition more heterogeneous) the audience, the more the message is generalized and universalized, diluted of any potentially problematic and thereby unpalatable meanings. The result, Williams claims, is development of a 'synthetic culture, meeting and exploiting the tensions of growth' of the market.[19]

Surveying the status of text publishing in this culture industry, Williams maintains that 'the production of books seems to be undergoing similar changes of ownership to those noted for the Press at the end of the nineteenth century', namely the 'tendency towards combine ownership' and the merger of independents into large media corporations.[20] The result was the subordination of more traditional motives for publishing (e.g., bookcraft, literary and aesthetic merit, political expression, religious conversion) to the 'methods and attitudes of capitalist business'. Williams goes on to argue that 'all the basic purposes of communication — the sharing of human experience — can become subordinated to this drive to sell'. In an increasingly competitive market, he notes, decisions about what will be published and how are concentrated in the hands of fewer and fewer individuals. This 'concentration of ownership' in turn constitutes 'a severe threat to the freedom and diversity of writing'.[21] In a complementary analysis, Nicholas Garnham maintains that the 'increased international competition and the resulting take over of domestic, national publishing companies' is a key step in the 'absorption of the sphere of reproduction into full scale commodity production'.[22] The twentieth-century selective tradition, the very process of cultural reproduction and transmission, has been mediated to an ever greater extent by the economic interests of corporate publishers. Appraising the situation after World War II, Miller noted that 'as more American houses became big and bureaucratized', 'financial terms' had become the 'basic language of the firm'.[23]

Clearly, audience and consumer demand maintains and spurs on modern culture industries like publishing. As with Eco's 'consumer of text', 'hungry' from and for 'redundance', the culture industry creates in its audience a sense of dependency on the continuance of its conventions, codes, and messages.[24] In this manner, market demand is generated and sustained by the accessibility and ease with which cultural products can be consumed. Hence, the need to produce further 'identical' (textual) products is increased: this process whereby 'appeal' is 'manufactured' figures prominently in modern publishing.[25] In the case of educational products, practitioner/consumer wants are generated to reflect pedagogical trends, developments and vogues, which may or may not serve legitimate educational purposes and outcomes. Cultural production and reproduction thus become ideologically and aesthetically nonproblematic processes, and worth comes to be perceived primarily in terms of increased demand. The related consumption does not satisfy 'need', nor does it simply exhaust supply, but conversely generates greater 'wants' for and 'output' of similar, standardized products.

Since the turn of the century era of what Henry Holt, founder of Holt-Rinehart and Winston, called 'the commercialization of literature',[26] modern publishing houses have operated on the basis of a tension between the maximization of profits and editors' perceived cultural and social responsibilities: 'Operations are characterized by a mixture of modern mass-production methods and craft-like procedures.'[27] Book making itself gradually has evolved into 'an industrial craft'.[28] Textbook authors and editors remain, however, members of rhetorical and interpretive communities, which in turn share knowledge and values, political ideologies and economic interests. The development of books is most certainly dictated by editorial behaviour, which reflects market and economic interests, as well as the cultural values and editorial perception of the needs of the market shared by a particular class of modern professionals. In the case of the textbook, editorial behaviour and authorial conception are also shaped by dominant trends in educational research *and* regional educational policies, both of which historically have been far from ideologically and economically disinterested enterprises.

The Best of Intents: William Gray and the Historical Development of the Dick and Jane Basal Readers

By the end of the war, Scott Foresman and Company had become the largest publisher of elementary school, high-school and college textbooks in the United States, having captured nearly one-fifth of the educational market. Of their total sales, some US $20,407,000, elementary school textbooks accounted for 80 per cent.[29] This success was due largely to a series of elementary textbooks under the head editorship of William S. Gray, professor of education at the University of Chicago, first president of the International Reading Association, and perhaps the pre-eminent reading psychologist of the inter- and postwar period.

The connection between Scott Foresman and Gray's best-selling Curriculum Foundation textbooks can be traced back to the nineteenth century. In 1896 E.H. Scott, and W.C. and H. Foresman founded a publishing house which within two years was the only American publisher printing both high-school and elementary textbooks. This was accomplished largely through the purchase of catalogues from other companies.[30] The buying out of financially troubled competitors was an early form of corporate consolidation.[31] Within a year of beginning operation, the Company landed the first in a series of statewide adoptions: Kansas, then Texas, Oklahoma, Oregon and other states. Then as now US textbook adoption was largely decentralized: local and state officials selected texts.[32] As a result sales to those states and large metropolitan school districts that did pursue centralized adoption policies were (and remain) crucial for competing companies like Scott Foresman, Ginn, and the American Book Company.[33]

The increased competition and frequent mergers were not without effects. During this period, the American Book Company was taken to court for corrupt dealings with state officials. Of the effects on the quality of trade and textbooks, Henry Holt wrote in 1905 that 'the more publishers bid against each other stockbrokers do, and the more they market their wares as the soulless articles of ordinary commerce are marketed, the more books become soulless things'.[34]

Among Scott Foresman's first successful series was W.H. Elson's Grammar School readers,[35] which quickly became known as 'the modern McGuffey'. This series, from primer to fourth reader, was an exemplar of the emergent new synthesis of nineteenth- and twentieth-century orientations to literacy instruction. Elson saw himself as the bearer of a long-standing tradition in the development of readers, a tradition which emphasized 'literary values enriched by familiarity with the classics of our literature'.[36] Like E.B. Huey and other early reading experts, Elson believed that moral and cultural edification was an essential element of early literacy training.[37] Primers and readers, he argued, should elevate the 'taste and judgment' of youth. Nevertheless, Elson agreed with progressive-era educators like Gray that 'interesting material is the most important factor in learning to read'.[38]

The selection of literature for the readers indeed reflected this dual conception of the role of the text. Some stories covered topics traditionally included in primers and readers: traditional folk tales and history, nature and science, history and biography, and invention. Others evinced the more civic concerns of progressive education, including transportation and communication, citizenship, industry, adventure, humour, travel and world friendship.[39] In Elson's early readers, then, stories of modern life were set beside more traditional Mother Goose and folk tales. By modern standards, they were sparsely illustrated: about a third of the primer consisted of large two-colour pictures. The fourth reader, for the intermediate grades, was largely printed text, with only thirteen pictures in 320 pages. It included stories by American authors about home and country, fairyland and adventure, nature, American and world heroes.

Elson's Grammar School readers, then, were transitional textbooks between two historical types: the traditional literary texts favoured by the likes of McGuffy, Elson, and Huey, and the later, more lexically and syntactically controlled, more brilliantly illustrated and packaged basal readers of the mid- and late-twentieth century. Canadian publisher Ryerson Press's Highroads to Reading series,[40] used in British Columbia from the 1930s until the 1950s, was a similar transitional type, linking the nineteenth-century

British Columbia Readers and Ontario Readers with the modern basal series.

Yet while a text like McGuffy's was taught with minor revisions for over a hundred years,[41] rapid developments in the fields of curriculum and educational psychology in the early twentieth century accelerated cycles of obsolescence, revision and replacement of textbooks. In an attempt to keep up with near continuous changes in educational theory and research, publishers competed for liaisons with university-based academics. Scott Foresman began the modernization of the Elson readers nine years after Elson's own 1920 revision, when educational psychologist Gray was brought in 'for the purpose of taking advantage of later developments in the field of reading instruction'.[42] The products of this editorial merger of two distinct and in some ways divergent approaches to children's reading texts were the Elson–Gray readers.[43] This series foreshadowed the development of a more scientific, psychologically derived approach to reading instruction. Additionally, it introduced American students and others to Dick, Jane, Sally, Father, Mother, Spot, Puff and an array of what would become archetypes for basal characters. Its publication, moreover, marked the expansion of firms like Scott Foresman into a growing international market: the 1930 edition was copyrighted in, among other English-speaking nations and American colonies, the Phillipines. The series subsequently was licensed to publishers in Canada.

The Elson–Gray readers were part of an integrated editorial strategy and pedagogical conceptualization on the part of the remaining Foresman brother and Gray himself. By 1933 Hugh Foresman's publishing company — E.H. Scott had died in 1928 — was able to offer a striking and comprehensive array of state of the art educational texts, including E.L. Thorndike's *Thorndike-Century Junior Dictionary*,[44] adopted in both the United States and Canada. Reflecting the progressive preoccupation with the integration of language and literacy across a range of curricular subjects, the Elson–Gray Life Reading Service texts were linked under Gray's editorial direction with other existing series. The resultant unified curricular package was marketed as the Curriculum Foundation series. Under various editors the series carried on for over forty years.

This was a major development in modern curricular design and in the marketing of educational textbooks: the provision of books in different curricular fields, all structured for readability and developmental appropriateness under Gray's watchful eye, all correlated with an extremely popular basal reader series. They promised teachers a unified, up-to-date approach to the total elementary curriculum, designed by pre-eminent curriculum experts and psychologists. Moreover, with state adoptions and an emergent international market, it was a brilliant stroke of marketing. The 'piggybacking' of products by publishers under a similar brand name can lead to the development of mass 'product loyalty'.[45] Children, teachers and administrators would feel that they were dealing with a familiar product of proven quality. During the 1930s, Scott Foresman augmented the series with texts in social studies, arithmetic, health, art and science.

The basal series, then, became part of a total cross-curricular package. The readers themselves — two pre-primers, a primer, a first reader and a reader for each of grades 2–6 — were highly innovative. Frequent multiple coloured pictures marked a major advance over Elson's Grammar School Readers. Other innovations followed suit: along with the already common teacher's guide, Gray introduced workbooks and a 'Junior Dictionary' for the readers. These were later augmented with an 'administrator's handbook'. Also available was the Literature and Life series, supplemental secondary reading materials which extended from and complemented the elementary basal series.[46] Sustained sales enabled Scott Foresman to achieve a new standard in production and format: primers in the new series were set in the Century Schoolbook typeface, a specialized type introduced in 1927. Its letters were strongly drawn, with emphatic serifs, aiming at maximal clarity for young readers.[47]

A range of other basals authored by prominent reading psychologists like A.I. Gates and M. Huber marked increased competition between publishers for the basal reader market, which alone constituted a sizeable portion of textbook sales.[48] Few, however, demonstrated the mass appeal and consistent market strength of the Scott Foresman basal series, which stands as one of the most successful textbook series of the mid-century.

In the 1940s Elson and Runkle were replaced by May H. Arbuthnot, who would go on to author a well-known book on reading and children's literature, also published by Scott Foresman.[49] Illustrator M.S. Hurford was replaced by E. Campbell and K. Ward, and the modernization of beginning reading texts was near complete. Under Gray's supervision, primers and readers like *Fun with Dick and Jane* and *Our New Friends* were total curricular creations: *all* stories were either written specifically for the textbook or significantly revised and adapted versions of previously published narratives.

What emerged was an altogether unprecedented genre of literature: the short literary passages consisting of fables and tales of the previous century had been superseded by the lexically, syntactically and semantically controlled texts about modern inter- and postwar life in an industrial democracy. These tales were fabricated solely for the purposes of teaching the 'skills' and 'habits' of reading. The application of scientific theories of reading and linguistic development to the engineering of basal readers completed the shift from traditional literary content. While narrative remained the primary discursive structure of primers and early readers, 'old tales' and poetry were replaced with 'modern fanciful tales'. In the 'Fourth Readers' (about grade 3 level), myths and fables were supplanted by informational reading, stories of everyday life, civic socialization and, of course, silent reading exercises.

Certainly the Curriculum Foundation series led the way for many of the next generation of readers, D.C. Heath's Reading for Interest series, the Ginn Basic Reader series, Silver Burdett's Learning to Read texts, and the American Book Company's Betts Basic Readers.[50] Though varying in approach, these series retained many of the structural characteristics of Gray's basals: teachers' guides, workbooks, related and supplementary series of texts. The scientifically designed and packaged reading series had come of age. In conception, structure and content they were and could only have been the products of an inter- and postwar America that believed that social institutions (e.g., the family, the school, the workplace) were progressing thanks to the application of modern science.

The traditional cultural orientation of nineteenth-century readers had given way to Deweyian concerns of civic relevance and adaptability to environment. Gray spoke of the need for children to judge 'the value and significance of the ideas acquired and, in many cases, the beauty and quality of the language used'.[51] In fact, Gray and other reading psychologists were committed overtly to early reading as a process for the transmission of values and cultural knowledge. As to the nature of those values, their position diverged considerably from that of McGuffy and Elson, who had inherited an understanding of literacy training as moral instruction from the Protestant Reader and New England Primer tradition. The emergent sense of the normative goals of education fit closely with progressive rhetoric: they aimed for, in Gray's words, 'children . . . to mature into efficient citizens, and to cultivate and preserve the democratic heritage which we prize so highly today'.[52] Reading fitted squarely within this normative agenda of social adaptation. In a 1950 interview published for British Columbia teachers, Gray argued that 'there was never a time when reading was more useful in promoting personal development, school progress, and social understanding'.[53] In other words, postwar educational scientists' sense of the end-product of this modern instruction was an 'efficient' citizenry, capable of 'sound judgments' in 'democratic' society. These goals — the creation of a new kind of literate — were to be achieved through a literacy pedagogy conceived as the 'systematic' cultivation of 'habits' and 'skills' of oral and silent, 'work-type' and 'recreational' reading.[54]

The interwar and postwar success of this modern version of the basal reading series, and the correlative emergence of reading psychology as the foundational basis for the educational practice of early literacy training are exemplified in Gray's career. In the early twentieth century, while other psychologists' interest in reading came and went, Gray's concern with research and the teaching of reading was constant. He became arguably the single most influential academic expert on reading in the United States and Canada. Gray personally dominated reading research for a period of over forty years, beginning with his initial published experiments in the 1910s until his death in 1960.

Gray, who had studied educational psychology under E.L. Thorndike at Teachers College from 1912 to 1914 before returning to Chicago to complete his doctorate, influenced the development of every phase of reading research: experimental design, pedagogy, curriculum development, testing, and in the 1950s, functional literacy and language planning. Gray's work on reading with Guy Buswell and Charles Judd at the University of Chicago was highlighted by publication in the 1910s and '20s of major research on silent and oral reading.[55] His standardized paragraphs for the assessment of oral reading remained benchmarks for over forty years. Gray's influence on trends and developments in reading research also is evident in his editorial work: between 1925 and 1932 he contributed a regular 'Summary of Reading Investigations' to the *Elementary School Journal*; between 1932 and 1960 his widely cited summaries appeared in the *Journal of Educational Research*. He is considered a pioneer in research on oral reading; the use of prose passages for the testing of silent reading; the 'diagnosis' and 'treatment' of 'remedial cases in reading'; developmental stage theory of reading acquisition; the extension of systematic reading instruction into the secondary schools; the definition of 'functional literacy'; and, the pre- and in-service training of teachers of literacy.[56] He edited three of the four US National Society for the Study of Education yearbooks on reading between 1912 and 1960 and he wrote one of the first UNESCO postwar reports on literacy.[57]

Gray's first published works on reading appeared in the 1910s, concurrently with research by Thorndike on silent reading, and shortly after work by Huey, Dearborn and others on eye movements and 'reading hygiene'.[58] By the early 1920s many of his fellow psychologists had moved away from a concentration on reading as an object of study. Gray and Gates's mentor was Thorndike, whose early empirical research on recall, recognition in silent reading, and lexical usage had generated the first silent reading tests. Both the Thorndike–McCall reading test and Gray's standardized Oral Reading Paragraphs were used throughout British Columbia and the English-speaking world through the interwar period.[59] Through lexicographical studies and the development of 'word books', Thorndike, Gates and others had succeeded in defining the core vocabulary of basal readers as well.[60] In the post-Elson period virtually every children's reader was constructed in consultation with these word lists. By the 1920s, when Thorndike had established himself as the most prolific and influential educational psychologist since James and Hall, his research and publication interests ran far afield to include IQ testing and the expanding range of social and educational applications of psychology.[61] Many other early reading researchers like Huey, Terman, Pintner had begun to concentrate on more general issues of mental measurement. At Chicago, Judd, whose 1920s work on reading as social experience was often quoted by Gray, had moved into the field of general social psychology pioneered in the US by Mead and Tufts.

This left the field in the hands of two psychologists: Gates of Teachers College and Gray at Chicago. Both Gates and Gray authored basal reading series, developed a range of tests of silent and oral reading, and provided guidelines and suggestions for teachers. Their articles were republished in various British Columbian, Canadian and US teachers' journals, their National Society for the Study of Education yearbooks were quoted in curriculum guides, their work and that of other reading psychologists was referenced in these same journals and guides and, most importantly, their texts and tests were used in elementary school reading instruction.[62] Certainly, in the field of reading education, as well as administration, curriculum design and so forth, trends and developments begun at Teachers College, Chicago, Stanford and other American universities[63] spread across the US and Canada to remake basic instruction in reading and the language arts for several generations of children.

Gray and Gates oversaw the application of reading research to all aspects of the teaching of reading — and by extension but to a lesser extent, writing, oral language, and spelling — in the period from the late 1910s through the 1950s. The 1937 NSSE yearbook on reading, *The Teaching of Reading*, highlighted findings of a committee chaired by Gray. This framing of 'desirable trends in reading' set the stage for the postwar modernization of reading instruction which would follow a wartime hiatus in research, development and implementation. These trends included: increased interest in reading problems; greater recognition of every teacher's responsibility for the teaching of reading; allocation of more time to guidance of reading in different subject areas; a greater concern for reading 'readiness'; increased use of better curricular materials; progress in the organization of reading pedagogy into 'units' which reflected areas of interest; greater emphasis on comprehension; increased recognition of children's varied motives and interests; greater provision for 'individual differences'; wider use of standardized reading tests; and the systematic diagnosis and remediation of problem readers.[64]

This was, in all, a description of the new paradigm of reading and language arts instruction advocated by reading psychologists. It called for an admixture of identifiably humane, 'child centred' practices (e.g., units or projects, teaching for individual difference, early childhood intervention, curricular integration) and scientific approaches to pedagogy (e.g., use of tests, systematic diagnostics and remediation, the use of modern systematic curricula). The extent to which many of these prewar recommendations remained throughout subsequent decades and indeed constitute the matrix of basic assumptions about the teaching of reading today testifies to the significance of this particular paradigm shift towards more technocratic, research-based and empirically derived approaches to curriculum and ins-truction.

At the centre of this scientific approach to literacy was the use of modern curricula like Gray's reading series, which provided the teacher with (textual) guidance in all of the aforementioned areas. Upon what assumptions did Gray and his colleagues develop and design the Dick and Jane series? Gray's was not a wholly mechanistic reading psychology by any means, for he was basically in agreement with Thorndike that reading is 'clear, vigorous and carefully directed thinking'. Citing Thorndike, Gray maintained that 'in effective reading, the mind selects, softens, emphasizes, correlates, and organizes information' according to 'mental set or purpose or demand'.[65] Nor, as noted, was Gray strictly opposed to literary merit in and of itself as a criterion for curricular selection. However, his sense of the kind of literary content which could stimulate such thinking, conceived with Thorndike as a 'reaction' to textual/experiential stimulus, remained acritical. He noted a truism shared by reading psychologists: 'As psy-chologists pointed out long ago, it is not what is presented to a child that promotes growth, but rather his reactions to the ideas acquired.'[66] Far from being a blanket dismissal of the importance of cultural content, Gray's state-ment reflects the Deweyian concern with teaching 'the child not the subject'. He saw in traditionalists' overriding concern with literary quality a failure to consider the validity and value of student 'reactions'. Moreover, while the 'formal' classroom had stressed 'oral interpretation' with 'little adaptation of instruction to meet the varying needs of the pupils', the modern classroom depended upon 'flexible' yet 'carefully planned' and 'systematic' approaches.[67]

Yet Gray's concern with student 'reaction' led to a relativist position on the selection of content for children's texts. In his scepticism of the tra-ditional cultural approaches to reading, Gray, like many of his con-temporaries, had developed a critical blindspot on the matter of literary and ideological content. This is not to imply that Gray had neglected altogether the specification of criteria for selection and development of children's stories. On the contrary, appropriateness could be determined according to how text enhanced the development of reading and general linguistic competence. Drawing from Judd's work in the 1910s at the University of Chicago, Gray held that 'reading was experiencing': the vividness of image and the range of possible meanings showed how text was both 'a process of re-experiencing' and potentially a unique experience itself.[68] To this end, he noted that 'as pupils grow in ability to use familiar experiences in interpreting what they read, they also increase in ability to acquire new experiences through reading'.[69] However mundane by traditional standards, everyday experiences — 'various purposes and needs . . . both in and out of school' — were posited as both the basis for the selection of educational knowledge, and the end of successful pedagogy.

Hence Gray advocated an initial reading experience which reflected 'familiar experience', gradually moving forward to works by 'the author who combines familiar concepts in a form that presents new ideas'. Accordingly, reading was to be taught in conjunction with pedagogically constructed language experiences: field trips, unit study, activities, simulations, role playing, and so forth. Reading texts were to be conceived of as authentic representations of children's lived experiences. By extension, the representation of social reality therein was completely in line with his experiential theories of reading. The aim was to generate in the reader 'a focus, or radix, of interest to which much of his reading relates and which serves as an inner drive or motivating force'.[70] Texts were to be based on the everyday, until the child had the ability to confront through text 'new experiences', tales for instance of 'Eskimo land' and 'Niagara Falls', to cite Gray's own examples.[71]

This concern with the textual representation of the known, the familiar, and the everyday was linked to his particular approach to teaching reading. In a 1955 *Reading Teacher* response to Flesch's popular crusade for phonics, Gray argued that 'contrasting methods' differed mostly in that they 'secured most growth in different aspects of reading'.[72] He contraposed those methods which concentrated on smaller linguistic units (e.g., the 'alphabetic or spelling method', the 'phonic method', the 'syllabic method') with those models which concentrated on meaning (e.g., 'the word method', the 'sentence method', the 'story method', and the 'experience method'). Like Chall over a decade later, he noted that 'the results of studies of the relative merits of teaching beginning reading do not show conclusively which is best'.[73]

Gray clearly had his preference, however. Citing Buswell's research, Gray argued that 'word recognition' would lead to 'word reading': 'an ability to follow the printed lines, to pronounce all the words but to display no vital concern for the content'.[74] What he argued for was a mixture of 'word recognition' (e.g., both whole word and phonics) with other pedagogies which 'cultivate a vital concern for the content and a clear grasp of meaning'.[75] Far from avoiding consideration of content, then, Gray clearly believed in its importance. For 'effective progress would only result from parallel emphasis on meaning and word recognition'.[76] While not against phonics in itself, he, like many of his contemporaries, saw it as only 'means to broader ends' of word recognition and language experience.

Accordingly, the Gray–Arbuthnot readers reflected several basic principles of construction. First, Gray's concern for the representation of the actual language and experiences of beginning readers led him to write and edit texts according to strict controls on lexical selection and syntactic complexity. Each reader, following strict readability guidelines, introduced a limited amount of new words and syntactic structures; the readers for grades 1 to 3 were pitched almost exclusively in dialogue intended to simulate children's oral language. These new words were gleaned from the beginning reader's oral language vocabulary as represented in word lists by Thorndike, Gates, Dolch and others. The Dick and Jane narratives, then, were to be recognizable texts, which required of children the recognition of words already in their oral lexicon. Once established, commonly occurring words were repeated in simplified sentences, versions of direct speech.

Second, Gray and his contemporaries extolled the virtues of high interest, populist texts which provoked thinking and meaning in a wide audience of students. The semantic possibilities of the text, the interpretations and meanings enabled by Dick and Jane narratives, were those that Gray thought children could easily relate to: the texts were not about fairy queens or princes, but about what he and his colleagues considered typical and shared childhood experiences in a nonspecific locale which resembled Lynd and Lynd's Middletown (or, for that matter, the midwestern American community described by Lewis in *Babbitt*). The setting and construction of stories, then, was not intended to be biased or overtly ideological. Rather Gray set out with a stated concern for 'average' and 'slow' children, to ease the transition from preliteracy to literacy by offering texts which were lexically, syntactically and semantically accessible to all. The design of a redundant, recognizable and predictable text was intentional.

The 1960 NSSE Yearbook on Reading solemnly noted Gray's death. In that same year Hugh Foresman, the last of the remaining founders of Scott Foresman, died as well. Yet their shared legacy remained. There was nothing Machiavellian about the standardization of literacy instruction: Gray operated from the best of intents. Regardless of whatever qualms he may have had over Deweyianism,[77] Gray believed in the egalitarian ends of progressive education: the advancement of every child's opportunity to participate 'efficiently' in democratic, industrial capitalism. While the Scott brothers and Hugh Foresman had set as their goal the successful development and marketing of the comprehensive educational product, Gray and his contemporaries had sought to supplant the inflexibility of traditional, rote instruction with the teaching of reading and linguistic competences which they hoped would 'exert an equally potent influence on the understanding, outlook, thinking, and behavior of the child'.[78]

There was, he wrote shortly before his death, an increasing recognition among educators of the 'expanding role of independent, critical reading on the part of all citizens if they are to understand the problems faced in a rapidly changing world, to participate intelligently in the duties of citizenship and to lead rich well-rounded personal lives'.[79] And for this the compulsive, habituated ways of nineteenth-century pedagogy and curricula would not suffice. In its place, a thoroughly scientific approach to literacy teaching was needed, one which emphasized 'psychological background for teaching, including known facts and their implications about human development, individual differences, learning theories, emotional problems, motivation, and the psychology of school subjects including the psychology of reading'.[80] As well, he noted that teachers needed to be aware of 'the social purposes and foundations of education; the role of reading and other mass media in current life; the nature and diversity of the cultural background, personal characteristics, and capabilities of children and youth'.[81]

The Dick and Jane reading series was indeed a mass-produced and standardized product distributed internationally, and in some regional jurisdictions on a near monopoly scale. It became an archetype, a model for dozens of imitators and would-be sales leaders.[82] And it was the product of a series of overlapping educational sciences. This particular exemplary modern basal series is indicative of a central shift in assumptions about children's reading and the teaching of reading towards a systems approach, featuring 'diagnosis' and 'clinical' intervention.[83] The educational psychology of Thorndike, Gates, Gray, Terman and others was an applied science, and the remaking of pedagogy and the experience of schooling was an extension of the application of that science. Enhanced by Charters and Bobbitt's interwar assembly-line model of curriculum development, and the subsequent needs assessment model of Tyler in the postwar period, a wholly scientific orientation to curriculum development *and* instruction *and* assessment had been born. A principal ramification in terms of reading pedagogy was that reading texts should be and could be so designed, and, moreover, that the efficacy of curriculum, pedagogy and actual learning could be verified through the use of standardized tests.

Gray, like King, Conway and the Canadian progressives, would have teachers be reading 'experts', knowledgeable in the ways of instructional psychology. Certainly, the grounds had shifted from the previous century.

And the discourse of applied educational science served the dual function of prescribing a set of practitioner wants while simultaneously, in collaboration with the publishing industry, producing products which ostensibly satisfied these. As a result, in spite of the increasing quantity of reading series on the market, there was a narrowing of the actual diversity of texts/products available for use by teachers, many of whom no doubt would have preferred older, more traditional literary materials. Within this new discourse, literary merit, cultural tradition and Protestant morality no longer stood as central criteria in the development of children's readers. It was now a matter of selecting and adopting appropriate literature on the surface of the curriculum development process only. The development of a reading textbook depended, in this new administrative and institutional regime, on the possession of a theory of reading (e.g., phonics, word recognition, developmental stages, readiness), on the intentional construction of specialized, standardized texts to enhance assessable 'skills', and, of course, on a significant capital investment by the publisher to make and market a total curriculum package. Related, moreover, was a normative sense that the aim of literacy, of the 'personal and social development of youth'[84] as more efficient adaptation to existing social knowledges and organization.

Assessing the modern legacy of the early- and mid-century modernization of curriculum development and pedagogy by educational scientists like Charters and Bobbitt, Gates and Gray, Apple comments that

> systems approaches are not essentially neutral, nor are they performing a 'scientific' function. By tending to cause its users and other publics involved to ignore certain possible fundamental problems with schools as institutions, systems management also acts to generate and channel political sentiments supportive of the existing modes of access to knowledge and power.[85]

These were consensus texts on several levels. Certainly they represented what Gray and Arbuthnot construed as the shared images and messages of democratic life in the '50s. But as well they represented an emergent scientific and professional consensus, an agreement among publishers and researchers that psychologically based pedagogies, and readable, mass-produced and consumed texts would be more efficient at the transmission of literacy (and the accumulation of capital) than the previous generation of traditional, literary readers. Gray, Gates, Russell and others professed to be concerned with literary content, with progressive social values and critical thinking, and with highly motivational pedagogy. Yet their texts remained the products of Thorndike's conception of reading as a 'sarbond' activity, as 'response', *and* of Watson's Madison Avenue (or Scott Foresman's Madison Avenue, to be more precise). The rules of capital expansion, as well as the science of Teachers College and the University of Chicago, helped shape what would count as children's readers, and what would count as reading and language arts instruction. And Gray and Arbuthnot's texts dominated the market for over three decades. The New McGuffy indeed.

Notes and References

1. Michael W. Apple, 'The Culture and Commerce of the Textbook', *Journal of Curriculum Studies* 17 (1985), 152.
2. Michael W. Apple, 'The Political Economy of Text Publishing', *Educational Theory* 34 (1984), 319.
3. See Avon Crismore, 'The Rhetoric of Textbooks: Metadiscourse', *Journal of Curriculum Studies* 16 (1984), 279–96; 'Rhetorical Form, Selection and Use of Textbooks: Case Studies', in Suzanne de Castell, Allan Luke and Carmen Luke (eds), *Language, Authority and Criticism: Readings on the School Textbook* (London: Falmer Press, forthcoming/1988); David R. Olson, 'On the Language and Authority of Textbooks', in de Castell *et al.* (eds), *Language, Authority and Criticism*.
4. See Christopher Caudwell, *Studies and Further Studies in a Dying Culture* (New York: Monthly Review Press, 1971).
5. See Olson, 'On the Language and Authority of Textbooks'; Carmen Luke, Suzanne de Castell and Allan Luke, 'Beyond Criticism: The Authority of the School Textbook', *Curriculum Inquiry* 13 (1983), 111–28.
6. For a discussion of this dual potential of the technology of text, see Jack Goody, *The Domestication of the Savage Mind* (Cambridge: Cambridge University Press, 1977).
7. Olson, 'On the Language and Authority of Textbooks'; see also Peter Freebody and Carolyn Baker, 'Children's First Schoolbooks: Introduction to the Culture of Literacy', *Harvard Educational Review* 55 (1985), 381–98.
8. See Lawrence Cremin, 'Curriculum Making in the United States', *Teachers College Record* 73 (1971), 207–20; David Hamilton, 'Making Sense of Curriculum Evaluation: Continuities and Discontinuities in an Educational Idea', in Lee Schulmann (ed.), *Review of Research in Education 5* (Itasca, Ill.: F.E. Peacock, 1977), pp. 318–47; Herbert M. Kliebard, *The Struggle for the American Curriculum, 1893–1958* (London: Routledge and Kegan Paul, 1986).
9. Apple, 'Culture and Commerce of the Textbook', 153; Rowland Lorimer, 'The Business of Literacy: The Making of the Educational Textbook', in Suzanne de Castell, Allan Luke and Kieran Egan (eds), *Literacy, Society and Schooling* (Cambridge: Cambridge University Press, 1986), pp. 132–44.
10. Charles A. Madison, *Book Publishing in America* (New York: McGraw Hill, 1966), p. 218.
11. See Jurgen Habermas, *Towards a Rational Society* (Boston: Beacon, 1970); *Knowledge and Human Interests* (Boston: Beacon, 1971).
12. John Dewey, *Democracy in Education* (New York: Macmillan, 1910), p. 225.
13. Ibid.
14. For a description of the early twentieth-century application of psychology to the 'functional' domains of social and industrial life, see Edward G. Boring, *A*

History of Experimental Psychology. (New York: Appleton-Century Crofts, 1950), esp. chs 21 and 22; see also Geraldine M. Joncich, *The Sane Positivist: A Biography of Edward L. Thorndike* (Middletown, Conn.: Wesleyan University Press, 1968).

15. Frederick W. Taylor, *Principles of Scientific Management* (New York: Harper, 1911); cf. Harry Braverman, *Labor and Monopoly Capital* (New York: Monthly Review Press, 1974).
16. Hamilton, 'Making Sense of Curriculum Evaluation', p. 327.
17. Cremin, 'Curriculum Making in the United States', 213.
18. Raymond Williams, *Communications* (Oxford: Oxford University Press, 1968).
19. Ibid., p. 33.
20. Ibid., p. 32; see also Raymond Williams, *Towards 2000* (London: Chatto and Windus, 1983), pp. 67–9.
21. Williams, *Communications*, p. 152.
22. Nicholas Garnham, 'Contribution to a Political Economy of Mass Communication', in Richard Collins, James Curran, Nicholas Garnham, Paddy Scannell, Phillip Schlesinger and Colin Sparks (eds), *Media, Culture and Society* (London: Sage, 1986), p. 30.
23. William Miller, *The Book Industry* (New York: Columbia University Press, 1949), p. 32.
24. Umberto Eco, *The Role of the Reader* (Bloomington: Indiana University Press, 1979), esp. ch. 4. See also Max Horkheimer and Theodor Adorno, *Dialectic of Enlightenment* (New York: Herder and Herder, 1972), pp. 120–67.
25. Cf. Lewis Coser, Charles Kadushin and Walter Powell, *Books: The Culture and Commerce of Publishing* (New York: Basic Books, 1982), esp. ch. 3.
26. Madison, *Book Publishing in America*, ch. 3.
27. Coser *et al.*, *Books*, p. 198.
28. Hugh Williamson, *Methods of Book Design* (New Haven, Conn.: Yale University Press, 1983).
29. Madison, *Book Publishing in America*, p. 449.
30. Ibid., p. 246.
31. Coser *et al.*, *Books*, pp. 21–2.
32. For a detailed discussion of the social, legal and political influences on text adoption and censorship, see Stephen Arons, 'Lessons in Law and Conscience: Legal Aspects of Textbook Adoption and Censorship', in de Castell *et al.* (eds), *Language, Authority and Criticism*.
33. See Francis Fitzgerald, *America Revised* (Boston: Little Brown, 1979), ch. 1.
34. Cited in Coser *et al.*, *Books*, p. 18.
35. W.H. Elson's Grammar School readers were published in Chicago by Scott Foresman, 1909–14.
36. Cited in Nila B. Smith, *American Reading Instruction* (Newark, Del.: International Reading Association, 1965), p. 153.
37. See, for example, Edmund B. Huey, *The Psychology and Pedagogy of Reading* (New York: Macmillan, 1908).
38. Cited in Smith, *American Reading Instruction*, p. 153.
39. Ibid.
40. F.L. Ormond, C.M. Ormond and M.A. Beresford's Highroads to Reading series was published in Toronto by W.J. Gage in 1932.
41. By 1920, McGuffy's sales had reached 122,000,000; see Madison, *Book Publishing*

in America, p. 123. For contrasting commentaries on the ideological contents and purposes of early American reading textbooks, see Ruth H. Elson, *Guardians of Tradition* (Lincoln: University of Nebraska Press, 1964); and Lee Soltow and Edward Stevens, *The Rise of Literacy and the Common School in the United States* (Chicago: University of Chicago Press, 1981), ch. 3.

42. Smith, *American Reading Instruction*, 154.
43. The Elson–Gray readers, by William H. Elson, William S. Gray and Lura P. Runkle, were published in Chicago by Scott Foresman, 1930–36.
44. Edward L. Thorndike, *Thorndike-Century Junior Dictionary* (Chicago: Scott Foresman, 1932).
45. See Lorimer, 'The Business of Literacy', 136.
46. See, for example, Edwin Greenlaw (ed.), *Literature and Life* (Chicago: Scott Foresman, 1932).
47. For details on the development of this typeface, see Williamson, *Methods of Book Design*, 132.
48. The Work Play Books series, by Arthur I. Gates and Mirian Huber, was published in New York by Macmillan, 1930.
49. May H. Arbuthnot, *Children and Books* (Chicago: Scott Foresman, 1947).
50. See Paul A. Witty's Reading for Interest series (Boston: D.C. Heath, 1942–55); David A. Russell *et al.*'s Ginn Basic Readers series (Boston: Ginn, 1948–64); Nila B. Smith's Learning to Read series (New York: Silver Burdett, 1940–45); and Emmett A. Betts and Carolyn M. Welch's Betts Basic Readers series (New York: American Book Company, 1948–63).
51. William S. Gray, 'Reading as Experiencing, Thinking and Learning', *California Journal of Elementary Education* 27 (1959), 157.
52. Ibid., 135.
53. William S. Gray, 'Questions about Reading', *British Columbia Teacher* 30 (1950), 316.
54. Ibid.; for exemplary regional curriculum documents that paraphrase these and other of Gray's ideas about reading, see British Columbia Department of Education, *Programme of Studies for the Elementary Schools* (Victoria: King's Printer, 1947); *Programme for the Intermediate Grades* (Victoria: Department of Education, 1954).
55. See, for example, William S. Gray, *Studies of Elementary School Reading through Standardized Tests*. Supplementary Educational Monograph, no. 1. (Chicago: University of Chicago Press, 1917); Charles Judd and Guy Buswell, *Silent Reading: A Study of Various Types* (Chicago: University of Chicago Press, 1922).
56. In addition to Gray's regular research articles and commentaries, see M.A. Burgess *et al.* (eds), *Twentieth Yearbook of the National Society for the Study of Education: Part II, Report of the Society's Committee on Silent Reading* (Chicago: University of Chicago Press, 1921); William S. Gray (ed.), *Twenty-fourth Yearbook of the National Society for the Study of Education: Report of the National Committee on Reading* (Chicago: University of Chicago Press, 1925); William S. Gray, *Summary of Investigations Relating to Reading*. Supplementary Educational Monograph no. 28. (Chicago: University of Chicago Press, 1925); William S. Gray (ed.), *Thirty-sixth Yearbook of the National Society for the Study of Education: The Teaching of Reading* (Chicago: University of Chicago Press, 1937); William S. Gray (ed.), *Forty-seventh Yearbook of the National Society for the Study of Educa-*

tion: Reading in the High School and College (Chicago: University of Chicago Press, 1948); William S. Gray, 'The Role of Teacher Education', in Paul A. Witty (ed.), *Sixtieth Yearbook of the National Society for the Study of Education* (Chicago: University of Chicago Press, 1961).

57. William S. Gray, *The Teaching of Reading and Writing* (Paris: UNESCO, 1956).
58. See, for example, Gray, *Studies of Elementary Reading through Standardized Tests*; *Oral Reading Paragraph Test* (Bloomington: Public School Publishing Co., 1915); cf. Edward L. Thorndike, 'Reading as Reasoning: A Study of Mistakes in Paragraph Reading', *Journal of Educational Psychology* 8 (1917), 323–32; 'The Understanding of Sentences: A Study of Errors in Reading', *Elementary School Journal* 28 (1917), 98–114.
59. Gray, *Oral Reading Paragraph Test*.
60. Edward L. Thorndike, *The Teacher's Word Book* (New York: Teachers College Press, 1921); Arthur I. Gates, *A Reading Vocabulary for the Primary Grades* (New York: Teachers College Press, 1926); cf. Edward L. Thorndike and Irving Lorge, *The Teacher's Word Book of 30,000 Words* (New York: Teachers College Press, 1944).
61. For examples of Thorndike's later ventures into social engineering, policy and issues, see Edward L. Thorndike, *Human Nature and the Social Order* (Cambridge, Mass.: MIT Press, 1969); *Your City* (New York: Harcourt Brace, 1939). For discussion of the ideological implications of Thorndike's work, see Michael W. Apple, *Ideology and Curriculum* (London: Routledge and Kegan Paul, 1979), ch. 4; and Barry M. Franklin, 'Curriculum Thought and Social Meaning: Edward L. Thorndike and the Curriculum Field', *Educational Theory* 26 (1976), 298–309.
62. For examples of the dissemination of Gray's and Gates's work to teachers, see William S. Gray and May H. Arbuthnot, 'Word Analysis in the Intermediate Grades', *British Columbia Schools* 3 (no. 2, 1947), 35–43; William S. Gray, 'What to Do about Reading', *British Columbia Teacher* 28 (1948), 181–4; Arthur I. Gates, 'Improvements in Reading Possible in the Near Future', *The Reading Teacher* 12 (1958), 83–8. See also British Columbia Department of Education, *Programme of Studies for the Elementary Schools*; *Programme for the Intermediate Grades*.
63. See David Tyack and Elizabeth Hansott, *The Managers of Virtue: Public School Leadership in America, 1820–1980* (New York: Basic Books, 1982).
64. Gray, *Thirty-sixth Yearbook of the National Society for the Study of Education*, pp. 5–38.
65. Gray, 'Reading as Experiencing', 142.
66. Ibid., 137.
67. Gray, 'Questions about Reading', 316–17.
68. Gray, 'Reading as Experiencing', 140.
69. Ibid., 142.
70. William S. Gray and B. Rogers, *Maturity in Reading* (Chicago: University of Chicago Press, 1956), 236.
71. Gray, 'Reading as Experiencing', 139.
72. William S. Gray, 'Phonics Versus Other Methods of Teaching Reading', *The Reading Teacher* 9 (1955), 105.
73. Ibid., 104; cf. Jeanne S. Chall, *Learning to Read: The Great Debate* (New York: McGraw Hill, 1967).

74. Gray, 'Phonics Versus Other Methods of Teaching Reading', 105–6; see also, *Preliminary Survey of Methods of Teaching Reading and Writing* (Paris: UNESCO, 1953).
75. Gray, 'Phonics Versus Other Methods of Teaching Reading', 106.
76. Ibid.
77. See June R. Gilstead, 'Commentary: William Gray: First IRA President', *Reading Research Quarterly* 20 (1985), 509–11; cf. Nancy A. Mavrogenes,'More Commentary on William Gray', *Reading Research Quarterly* 21 (1986), 106–7.
78. Gray, 'Reading as Experiencing', 138.
79. Gray, 'Role of Teacher Education', p. 161.
80. Ibid., p. 151.
81. Ibid., p. 161.
82. The Dick and Jane series was published in Canada by W.J. Gage publishers. In other countries, the text was used as a prototype for the development of indigenous basal series. For example, one popular Australian series features 'Dick and Dora' in similarly controlled narratives. 'Spot', the all-American family dog, is replaced suitably by his Australian counterpart 'Digger'.
83. Cf. William S. Gray, 'Summary of Reading Investigations: July 1, 1933 to June 30, 1934', *Journal of Educational Research* 28 (1935), 410.
84. Gray, *Forty-seventh Yearbook of the National Society for the Study of Education*, p. 42.
85. Michael W. Apple, 'The Adequacy of Systems Management Procedures in Education', in R. Smith (ed.), *Regaining Educational Leadership* (New York: John Wiley, 1975), p. 116.

Chapter 4

Reading the Text:
Dick and Jane as Introductions to
Literacy

Were Gray's good intentions realized? The foregoing pointed to historical tensions and contradictions *within* the dominant discourse on literacy between egalitarian goals of Progressive education and evolving industrial orientations to curriculum and educational publishing. Scrutinizing the Curriculum Foundation reading textbooks, several critics of the 1960s and '70s have argued that they conveyed a postwar ideology of individuality and compliance to authority. Zimet sees the shift from more traditional textbooks to the Dick and Jane genre as indicating a movement from the 'inner-directedness' of nineteenth-century life to the 'other-directedness' of twentieth-century industrial culture:

> Contemporary America, as seen through these readers, is an other-directed society in which the individual is not motivated to act by traditional institutional pressures but by others whose requests or demands are respected enough to produce compliance. Individuals enter into relationships for specific reasons, and these relationships are generally controlled by the opinions of others.[1]

Gray and Arbuthnot's texts, seeking a broad audience in a national and international market, distorted the 'pluralistic' character of American society.

> One might conclude from these books that Americans are almost exclusively Caucasian, North European in origin and appearance, and are quite well to do. . . . Religion is rarely mentioned, but Christian religious observance is over-emphasized with no hint of the range or variety of observances found among different religious groups.[2]

In the estimation of liberal and left critics, the texts are blatantly classist, sexist and racist. The gender relations portrayed in these readers, moreover, commonly are cited as archetypal cases of textbook stereotyping.[3]

For their part, child psychologists Bettelheim and Zelan have compared the literary and psychological content of American basals in the 'Dick and Jane tradition' with those of European schools.

> The universal use in the United States of basic texts that are alike in their repetitious emptiness, and of stories that tell only about the most shallow 'fun' activities, makes one wonder whether it is indeed possible to teach reading to modern children by means of texts that are neither condescending to them, nor dull, nor excruciatingly repetitious, nor restricted to the use of a few simple words.[4]

They argue further that traditional fairy tales, children's poetry and novels should 'stimulate and encourage children's imaginations' by providing 'literary images of the world, of nature and of man'.[5] Bettelheim and Zelan conclude that primers and early reading textbooks

> should be able to render in a few sentences three-dimensional, true to life images of people in their struggle with some of life's more serious problems, demonstrating how, through these struggles, people are able to achieve greater clarity about themselves, about their relations to others, about what is required to be able to live a meaningful life.[6]

These assessments, however astute, are based on general impressions of the textbooks in question, and although the Dick and Jane textbooks are often cited as models of postwar American educational ideology, a closer analysis of their textual content and structure has not been undertaken. We now turn to a story-grammar analysis of nine selected narratives from *Fun with Dick and Jane* to establish the relationship between story syntax and semantics, between narrative structure and ideology. My aim here is to indicate how ideological themes and contents are established through the repetition, within and across story grammars, of particular social roles, relationships and intersubjective exchanges. This is followed by a survey of pictorial and lexical content which specifies how the textbooks establish a total fictional reality that in turn acts as an overarching contextual frame for the situating of said roles and actions. Lexical choice, pictorial content, and the role of the narrator are examined to establish how stylistic and literary conventions serve the didactic and pedagogical intent of the narratives: to present an univocal version of postwar childhood.

A further examination of stylistic and literary devices is undertaken to show how this portrayed reality is posited in relation to other possible worlds of the authors, characters and readers. The text analysis concludes with a summary critique of the ideological contents, literary merits, and possible pedagogical effects of the text, using Barthes' concept of the ideological function of modern 'mythologies' in conjunction with Eco's category of the 'closed text'.[7] Further, the use of Eco's categories enables the reconstruction of the particular 'role of the reader' generated by the Dick and Jane texts.

A Story Grammar Analysis of Fun with Dick and Jane

The early primary readers *Fun with Dick and Jane*[8] and *Our New Friends*[9] were designated for first grade reading instruction. Both texts, while composed of distinct stories by eight different authors, were adapted to repeat basic themes, lexicon, syntactic structures, and macropropositional structures across and within successive episodes. *Fun with Dick and Jane*, the grade one primer, comprises thirty-three stories organized into four subsections: 'Family Fun', 'Fun at the Farm', 'Fun with Pets and Toys', and 'Fun with Our Friends'.

The particular set of nine episodes in 'Family Fun', the first series from the first primer, was many six-year-old children's actual first institutional encounter with literacy instruction. In what follows, each episode's basic story grammar is outlined according to a Stein–Glenn model. A running commentary highlighting continuities and discontinuities between story grammar and thematic content ensues.

> *Episode 1 – 'See It Go'*: In the backyard (setting), Dick throws a toy airplane (initiating event); Sally and Jane observe (internal response); the plane goes over the fence beyond the yard; it almost hits Father who, in a business suit, is walking home (consequence); Jane expostulates 'This is not fun for Father' (reaction/didactic reiteration).

Commentary: In this particular passage Dick is the initiator of ensuing action while Sally and Jane are relegated to secondary roles as observers of and commentators on male play. Their conversational description (which enables the teaching of high frequency prepositions: 'Up up! Down down!') narrates the plane's flight. These utterances also form an internal response: readers do not glimpse the thoughts and action plans of the characters, instead they 'see' and hear the characters' observations. Father, who apparently is coming from work or another business engagement (signified here by grey business suit and hat), seems startled when the plane knocks his hat off. It is left to Jane to distill verbally the event into a lesson.

A unique discourse option is exercised throughout this and subsequent episodes. The reaction in the story grammar takes the form of a didactic utterance by a principal character which in turn reframes for other characters and readers the foregoing events: 'This is not fun for Father'. This discourse feature functions as an interpretation *within* the text to restate and reinforce an intended message. It provides simultaneously a dramatic resolution and reconciliation, closing down the narrative and restoring all to their original psychological (and temporal) states. In all, it would seem that this is a parable about children's play running into the adult world with unexpected, if harmless results. It remains nonetheless a didactic tale which teaches the distinction of 'family fun/not fun' in relation to judgments in 'play'.

> *Episode 2 — 'Guess'*: In the house, Dick approaches Mother from behind (setting); she is seated in an easy chair, sewing; Sally and Jane crowd around and Father and Spot enter the room from behind; Dick places his hands over Mother's eyes and asks her to guess who it is (initiating event 1); Mother guesses correctly (internal response 1/attempt 1); Sally verbally confirms (consequence); Father places his hands over Mother's eyes from behind (initiating event 2/reiteration of 1); after verbalizing a process of elimination (internal response 2), Mother guesses correctly (attempt 2); Jane verbally confirms (consequence 2); Sally places her hands over Mother's eyes and Jane asks for a guess (initiating event 3); Mother guesses that it is Jane (internal response/attempt 3); Sally expostulates 'This is fun, Mother can not guess'; Mother guesses Sally (consequence 3); Dick confirms the guess; Mother expostulates 'My family is here. My funny, funny family' (reaction/didactic reiteration).

Commentary: A more complex and structured pattern of intersubjectivity is instantiated in this episode's story grammar. Verbal and behavioural repetition of a pattern of play involves the whole family and this pattern in turn acts as a set of unstated social rules.

But the point of the game is not its rules: there is more to it than this. Dick and Father, who again is pictured in three-piece suit with Spot the family dog nipping at his heels, are the primary initiators of action in this domestic set piece. Mother is carrying out her daily routine. The males' actions are repeated with variations by the other characters. Invariably, Dick and Father initiate the pattern and Jane follows naively; Mother pushes the game along as a physically passive addressee of the family's actions. The schematic structure of repeated actions, designed to enable repetitive recognition and oral recitation of key words and phrases (e.g., 'Guess, guess!',

'Mother can not see.'), has a dramaturgical effect: the reiterated attempt →
consequence → attempt → consequence . . . pattern is self-referential and
self-reinforcing, conveying the need for behavioural modelling, imitation
and practice in play situations.

Yet within the rules of family intersubjectivity novelty is not ruled out
altogether. Baby Sally — a progressive-era Noble Savage — begins to
evince a characteristic of infancy which recurs throughout the series, a
capacity for creative extrapolation within the rule structure of male-
initiated play. In subsequent stories, Sally, the young pre-school child, will
come up with novel approaches, at times indicative of her naïveté of rule
systems and at others showing her (innate?) cunning ability to set up her
elders', and the readers', expectations and reverse them. Her socialization
into rule-bound intersubjectivity is focal throughout this sequence of
episodes. Here it is left to Mother, who verbally interacts with the children
more than Father, to confirm the value of non-violent, interactive play
involving the entire family unit: a 'funny, funny family' indeed.

> *Episode 3 — 'Something for Sally'*: In the house, Father asks Sally
> (setting) to 'find something' in his coat pocket (initiating event).
> Digging into Father's pocket (attempt 1), Sally discovers a red ball
> (consequence 1); Father asks Sally to 'Look in the ball' (reaction
> 1/initiating event 2/reiteration of 1); Sally discovers a blue ball
> within the red (attempt 2/consequence 2/reiteration of 1); Father
> asks Sally to look in the blue ball (reaction 2/initiating event
> 3/reiteration of 1); Sally discovers a yellow ball within the blue ball
> (consequence 3/reiteration of 1); Sally states her intentions to share
> the three balls with Dick and Jane (reaction/didactic reiteration).

Commentary: This particular episode highlights the formal didactic relationship between Father and Baby Sally. Again a male is the initiator of the
incident: Father is introducing Sally to a traditional toy, the object concealed within an object. Lexical and syntactic repetition (e.g., 'Look and
see! See the yellow ball!') is enabled by a story-grammar restatement of a
macropropositional attempt → consequence sequence. The character's
attempts to resolve the cognitive/play problem in turn result in a moral
lesson.

Contrasting with Mother's role in episode two as the recipient of
children's play is Father's verbal and behavioural control over the initiating
event → attempt → consequence sequence. The syntax of father's gestural
cues (e.g., physical distance, hand signals) and linguistic expression (e.g.,
'Find something!', 'Look in the ball') are set in the imperative case. Notable
is his correlative lack of physical contact with Sally: he holds his arm out of
the way so that she can inspect his coat pocket; he leans over her with his

hands on his hips; he sits with his hands clasped in front of him. He of course is garbed in his business suit and tie, even in this casual play setting. Clearly, Father adopts a detached but directive, explicitly pedagogical role (give/take/request/answer), instructing Sally in patterns of play and discovery that involve manual dexterity and thinking.

Emerging is yet another pattern which is mirrored across discrete narratives: the role of female characters in framing verbally the didactic lesson of the story. Although Father is in a clearly authoritative position, again it is a female who reiterates the didactic element of the story with a concluding verbal declaration.

On the literal level of story-grammar consequence, two beneficent pro-social behaviours are conveyed: gift-giving and, as underlined in Sally's reappraisal of her own learning, sharing rather than egocentric hoarding of toys. But at the level of the repeated interactional pattern in the story grammar, this finale acts as a confirmation of a foundational social relation: Father teaches, daughter learns.

> *Episode 4 — 'Do What I Do'*: In the house, Dick jumps (setting) over a play bridge made of blocks and challenges the observing family to 'do what I do' (initiating event 1); Jane, Mother and Father all comply (multiple attempts/subordinate consequences to 1); Sally tries (attempt) and fails, knocking over the bridge (primary consequence to 1); Dick verbally chides Sally, arguing that she, 'a baby', is 'too little' to play (reaction/didactic reiteration 1); Father asks the family to touch their toes, to imitate his behaviour (initiating event 2); all are able to comply (multiple attempts/consequences 2) except Sally (attempt/consequence 2); Father chides Sally as 'too little' to do this (reaction/didactic reiteration 2); Sally asks the family to crawl under a wooden chair (initiating event 3); all fail in their attempts to imitate Sally (attempts/ consequence 3); Sally concludes that all are 'too big' to 'do it' (major reaction/didactic reiteration to 1/2/3).

Commentary: Again, an archetypal play pattern is introduced, one that requires repetition of an intersubjective pattern, that of 'Simon Says', and again, males assume initiating roles. Sally's inability to participate in this particular kind of family play which requires advanced psychomotor development is highlighted. Both male figures take turns at berating her and denigrating her inferior social status, without visible cheer (e.g., Dick: 'No, Sally, you can not play. You are too little. You are a baby.'). Dick gesturally embellishes this utterance, leaning over towards her and pointing his finger at her. Father ('No Sally! You can not do this. You are too little.') proceeds to Sally's turn without the visible smiles of encouragement and verbal approval present in episode three. Nonetheless, Sally turns the tables on her elders and has the last and crowning didactic word.

To this point the only divergent actions in family relations have been initiated by Sally, whose unpredictability is becoming predictable. While others reflect the adequacy of their socialization by carrying through their parts in the causal chains of the story grammar with utter faithfulness and repetitiveness, Sally, the uninitiated, blunders her way through play sequences, characteristically vindicating herself through novelty of action. Yet her immature ego-identity is implied and throughout she refers to herself as 'Sally', excluding a personal pronoun.

By this stage in the initial series, distinctive character traits and associated syntaxes of action are beginning to emerge. Father is involved formally in family play and learning yet seems emotionally detached. Dick is active, somewhat impulsive, and domineering of the female children. Of the female figures, Mother remains on the sidelines while Jane is an omitted, often silent middle child. Sally's verbal and behavioural cleverness is restated in this episode.

> *Episode 5 — 'Father Helps the Family'*: In the house Mother brings Father (setting) a broken wooden chair to fix (initiating event 1); Father changes into work clothes and repairs it (attempt/consequence 1); Jane brings her baby carriage wheel for repair (initiating event 2/reiteration of 1); Father repairs it (attempt/consequence 2); Dick brings his roller skate for repair (initiating event 3); Father repairs it (attempt/consequence 3); Sally brings her ripped dress for repair (initiating event 4/attempt); Father refers her to Mother (reaction/didactic reiteration); Mother sews the ripped dress (consequence 4/subreaction 4).

Commentary: This episode signals the introduction of two new concepts, 'help' and 'work', within a specified division of labour in the home. Again, the story grammar consists of a repetition of an intersubjective exchange, building readers' expectations of similar outcomes and providing maximal opportunities for the repetition of key words and phrases. For the first time, a female initiates the episode, although her problem is not indicative of her ingenuity or control, as in previous and subsequent male-initiated episodes, but rather of her reliance on Father to undertake repair of mechanical objects.

Jane, still extremely passive, imitates Mother's request, impelling Father with the utterance: 'You work for Mother. Can you work for me, too?' As a speech act, this is a direct invocation of Father's responsibility to extend the services provided Mother to other female members of the family. It begets a *pro forma* compliance, which is tentative, stern, and impersonal

(Father: 'We will see.'). In sharp contrast, Dick's request is responded to with a cheerful 'Yes, Dick.'

In each successive case, Father, who finally has shed his business suit for coveralls, complies. The didactic reinforcement of specific service roles in the household concludes with Father somewhat brusquely leaning down and teaching Sally the proper roles within the domestic division of labour (Father: 'I can not help you. Mother can help you.'). Sally's naïveté here emerges as undersocialization. In her attempts to imitate and repeat the model pattern of intersubjectivity, to follow the script of family relations, she has shown her ignorance of the social norms underlying and mediating action within that script.

As if to underscore her compliance with Father's verbal injunction and the sociocultural norm it implies, Mother is depicted in the lower-right-hand corner of the last page sewing Sally's dress. She is silent. And this pictorial sign stands as a narrative coda, a visual didactic reiteration. There is no correlative verbal exchange between her and Sally, or with any of the children. Father has stated and enforced the rules. Clearly, Dick and Jane have learned who does what within the family unit and Sally's socialization into that unit is the focal point of this episode. Within this narrative portrayal of hierarchical roles and interrelationships of the family, Sally (and perhaps the reader as well) is pressed to modify her schematic expectation of typical events and patterns of action.

> *Episode 6 — 'Sally Makes Something'*: In the home (setting), Dick draws boats and cars on a large sheet of paper while Spot and Puff and Sally observe (initiating event 1); Sally observes that Jane is also 'working', drawing a 'big big boat' (attempt 1); Jane corrects Sally and states that she is drawing a house (consequence 1); Sally asks whether Mother and Father are in the house (sub-attempt); Jane responds that Sally, Jane, Spot and Puff are the inhabitants (sub-consequence); Sally draws 'something yellow' on Jane's picture while Dick and Jane observe and asks them to 'guess what it is' (initiating event 2); Jane guesses that it is a ball (attempt); Sally expostulates that it is 'a big, big cookie for Sally' (consequence 2/response).

Commentary: The attempt/consequence structure of this episode's story grammar mirrors Sally's efforts to participate in this work/play situation. This particular episode, the first without explicit adult participation or intervention, takes a different format. Although the narrative begins with the usual focus on Dick, it soon becomes clear that Sally is the initiator; her responses to Dick and Jane's drawings generate further action.

The content of each drawing portrays prototypical 'boys'' and 'girls'' interests. Dick, reflecting the aforementioned division of labour within the home, is concerned with mechanical and technological items, while Jane is clearly interested in domestic matters. Curiously, her ideal possible world (in her drawing) depicts a nuclear family which excludes Father, Dick and Mother, implying her role as surrogate mother for Sally. This role in turn is reflected by her status as teacher within the narrative.

As if on schedule, though, Sally outmanoeuvres the other children, generating the only clear problem to be solved by challenging her siblings to guess at her drawing. Jane's interpretation of Sally's drawing is incorrect; Sally again has baffled the other children, albeit with the absurdity and novelty of her drawing. Clearly, a different kind of macropropositional structure is at work here: the only obstacle in the children's play pattern is generated by Sally's participation. In all, the scene represents the model of quiet play unaided and unstructured by direct parental intervention. It is left to Dick and Jane to incorporate and domesticate Sally into their play patterns, although Dick's involvement gradually declines as the story proceeds. Unlike previous episodes, there is no overt didactic reiteration. Messages regarding children's stereotyped interests are coded in the content of their pictures while norms of play are coded in portrayed social inter-actions and relationships.

Dick is noticeably less rambunctious in an environment free of parental observation. Aggressive and almost exhibitionistic in the presence of adults, Dick here seems to be acquiring the trappings of Father's domestic role — present but quiet, relinquishing of domestic tasks to females. Yet the work/play theme is established at the onset with Dick's initiating utterance 'See me work'; in this sense, Dick's very presence frames the interaction between his sisters. The boundaries between work and play, between adult and child here are blurred intentionally for didactic purposes. In this particular fictional reality they become synonymous entities.

Episode 7 — 'Pretty, Pretty Puff': In the house (setting), Jane is unable to find Sally and seeks Dick's assistance (initiating event); Dick leads Jane inside to find Sally (internal response); they find 'something white' on a child's cushioned chair (attempt 1); they find similar material underneath the bed (attempt 2); they discover Sally under another bed with Puff (consequence)' Sally has powdered Puff, their yellow cat, white and left traces of powder throughout the house (explanation).

Commentary: Here Dick and Jane, without parental supervision, are cast in the role of detectives, simultaneously fulfilling their obligation to monitor their younger sister. Jane, like Mother in previous episodes, is the initiator by default, having recognized Sally's absence. Typically she turns to Dick for assistance and it is Dick who subsequently uncovers all essential clues. Again, the hunting of clues facilitates a lexical and syntactic redundancy ('Can you guess what it is?'): as initiating parts of adjacency pairs, these interrogatives are directed to both fictional personae and student readers. The children employ a deductive method to find Sally who, as usual, is engaged in novel and unconventional play. As in episode six, the lack of adult intervention eliminates the need for an explicit didactic reiteration: messages regarding who does what, how and in what circumstances are again conveyed by the assignment of agency within the story grammar.

> *Episode 8 — 'Jane Helps'*: In the kitchen (setting), Dick declares that 'I can work. I can help Mother' and Jane agrees that she can help too (problem/initiating event); Jane begins setting out dishes for the family, counting out four plates (attempt); the family sits down for dinner but is one setting short (consequence); Dick points out Jane's error and laughs at her, pointing out that she has excluded herself (didactic reiteration); Jane gets a plate for herself (reaction).

Commentary: This episode again highlights the notion of work, in this case helping with domestic chores. Although Dick initiates the event with a loud declaration of intent to 'work' and 'help Mother', he disappears shortly thereafter, leaving Jane to lay out the table. At the actual dinner — Father is again dressed in a double breasted business suit and is the last to be seated — Jane's folly is pointed out once again by Dick, who literally reminds Jane that she is part of the social group: 'Dick laughed and laughed. He said, "Oh Jane! You are funny. You are in this family too." '

In this case, the 'neglected' middle and female child has made a cognitive/social error, counting for all members of the family unit but failing to include herself. In her rehearsal for adult female self-sacrifice and self-effacement she has literally become a selfless domestic worker, one who eradicates her selfhood in and through labour. Like Sally, she refers to herself in the third person (Jane: 'I will get one for Jane too.'), a discursive habit never employed by mature ego-identities like Father and Dick.

Suitably amused, Jane rectifies the error. Jane is being socialized into a subordinate domestic role and again Dick is the one to initiate, mediate and adjudicate the entire affair. Although the notion of helping and miming adults is reiterated, parents are seen but not heard: it is left to Dick to indicate the error of his younger sister's ways, to assume Father's role and to reassure Jane of her social role as domestic helper in the family.

> *Episode 9 — 'A Funny Ride'*: The family is riding in the car, a gray four door sedan, through the generic community (setting); Father declares that 'he wants something for the car' and pulls up to a

service station (initiating event); Sally requests further information (attempt), but Father bids her to wait and see (consequence); a uniformed service station attendant, speaking with Father, puts the car on a hoist while the family observes (initiating event 2); Spot and Puff remain in the car and Tim, Sally's teddy bear, sits on the running board (initiating event 3); while Dick observes the attendant undertaking the repair, Sally pleads with Father to rescue the animals (attempt); with Dick narrating, the car is lowered and Sally rescues her teddy bear (consequence); the family reboards the car and father declares it repaired (reaction); the family drives 'away'.

Commentary: Father is clearly master of the family technology and on this weekend ride, he is captain, garbed in brown business suit and hat. Dick and Spot ride in the front with Father; Mother attends to the cat, stuffed animals and two female children in the back seat. Sally's problem is apparently the result of having dropped her teddy bear on the running board.

Regarding Father's intervention, his problems/conflicts seem to emerge from three primary sources: children, females and technology. Throughout, Mother and Jane are omitted and the focus is on Sally's despair. Dick remains thoroughly preoccupied with the actions of the mechanic and the machinery involved. Again following Father's lead, Dick acts as a surrogate for his Father, narrating the lowering of the car and interpreting the events for both Sally and Spot (e.g., 'Look Sally! See the car coming down.').

The final scene returns Father to the situation. The interesting aspect of this episode is the role exchange which Father and Dick undergo. Both are charged with the male roles of monitoring the repair procedure and, simultaneously allaying the anxieties of Sally. At this stage in his development Dick is aspiring to Father's position in the family.

Summary Comments: These initial nine stories constituted approximately two to three weeks of basic reading and language arts instruction. As such, they provided an introduction to the principal characters and setting, and a linguistic foundation for subsequent stories and textbooks. Subsequent sections in this first primer present a trip to Grandmother and Grandfather's farm, animal and pet stories, and play with other children. Vicariously through the personae of Dick and Jane, student readers are introduced to a range of family rituals: the family meal, household labour, the Sunday drive, a visit to the country, the birthday party and so forth.

A coherent relationship between overt ideological content and story grammar emerges. Each narrative conveys an obvious moral lesson but each is also didactic in a more subtle manner: fundamental patterns are repeated both within and between stories, modelling and typifying behaviours, turns of events, and sequences of action. With the related employment of characters to restate the obvious in didactic reiterations, the text literally interprets itself for the child reader, holds its interpretative uptake in line with its didactic intent, and thereby militates against any aberrant readings. Typically, the principals interpret their experience and the narrative chain of events through an utterance for the (moral) benefit of the other participants, including the child readers.

Consider the following example of this discourse option: Jane receives three baby dolls from Mother and Father, Grandmother and Grandfather. This story, like the others, relies on the conceit of repeated action: first Dick and then Sally secretly communicate to family elders what Jane wants for her birthday. Her reaction within the story grammar is as follows:

'Oh my!' laughed Jane.
'Three new dolls!
Three baby dolls!
I like baby dolls.
I wanted one for my birthday.
Now I have three.
Now I have a big doll family.
Thank you, thank you, thank you.
This is a happy, happy birthday.'[10]

In the reaction component, Jane signals to the reader her assessment of the chain of events. In this particular didactic reiteration, she indicates to the audience (both the assembled family in the story and assembled student readers) how they are to react and how they are to interpret the story ('I like baby dolls . . . This is a happy, happy birthday.'). There is, moreover, a concomitant prescription of social norms for subsequent speech situations (e.g., 'Thank you, thank you, thank you.'). Through this pattern of characterial paraphrase and reiteration at the conclusion of each story, the reader is invited to identify with the characters, to interpret experience as they do, and to mime their verbal graces.

Rarely but occasionally in the early primers the help of an omniscient narrator is required. For example, Sally's venture onto the bus concludes with 'Sally was happy. She said, "Look at me. I am a big, big girl. I can ride up here." ' Here, by describing Sally's psychological state, the narrator collaborates with Sally to provide a full interpretation of the lesson to be extracted from the text. So in the event the reader missed the authors' preferred interpretation of the story, it is restated explicitly by the character. This effect of leading (and thereby constraining) the child reader is also enhanced throughout by the use of the imperative case by the characters (e.g., Sally: [You] 'Look at me!'). The ideological didacticism of the episodes in *Fun with Dick and Jane*, then, is achieved at the level of literal lessons stated by characters, through verbal modelling, and at the level of the story grammar itself, which instantiates patterns of social action and relations. As shown in episode three, 'Guess', the lessons yielded on these different levels while complementary need not be identical: there the overt, reiterated lesson concerns giftgiving and self-centred behaviour, while the covert lesson fixes father/daughter social roles and relations.

As stated by the title, the unifying theme is 'fun and play', represented in various typical settings and locales. But this is a kind of play that goes into the making of 'efficient' citizens, for beneath the veil of play is the rehearsal of adult social roles and relationships. Sally's predictable wit, her creative rule-breaking, is attributed to naïveté, and consequently her socialization into the family unit requires that she be domesticated. This ideological theme correlates with the Deweyian and Meadian maxim that play is not without pedagogical merit and that children learn, develop and grow through creative play, rather than through formal discipline, didactic instruction and hard work.

The lessons of Dick and Jane's universe stand centrally within the curricular goals of 'progressive adaptation' to social environments, and of creative development, the very essence of progressivism restated in Departmental curriculum guides which so rankled postwar classicists like Neatby.[11] The kinds of play portrayed — playing house, playing school, 'Simon says', hide and seek, guessing games, and cooking — are not gratuitous but rather direct preparations for mature social life, mimetic of the syntaxes of action which characterize adulthood. Hence, the adaptation is selective, a kind of conformity to highly conventionalized authority and gender relationships within the family structure: the text displays parallel but altogether differentiated paths to social development for male and female children. Yet do Dick, Jane and Sally, and their friends model authentic development, change and growth throughout?

The answer lies in the inter-narrative structure of the textbooks. Throughout the basal series, the groups of seven to nine stories are in fact autonomous episodes strung together in similar settings with recurring characters, constituting a closed universe of discursive possibilities, social relations and possible actions. What counts as a legitimate social action or linguistic turn within these story grammars tends to fall into identifiable patterns repeated even within the narrow confines of the nine episodes sampled: males initiate action, females respond and observe; small children innovate and experiment but are ultimately initiated into a script of conventionalized roles and expectations. There remain points of thinly concealed disagreement and overt competition in play, and at times Dick's condescension to Sally and Jane verges on becoming gloating and hostile, but within these patterns overt conflict is never portrayed.

Additionally, inter-narrative cohesion is established through the use of the same characters across espisodes and through the repetition of singular attempt → consequence → reaction patterns. Stories have a high rate of lexical cohesion, featuring more repetition than ellipsis: the limited vocabulary is repeated through and across stories, each new story building on vocabulary introduced in previous stories and textbooks. Settings also are carried across episodes: several successive stories begin in the house, at Grandfather's farm, in the larger community.

However, stated inter-narrative macropropositional cohesive ties are altogether absent: throughout the series previous actions and events are not referred to, future events and episodes are not foreshadowed. Each episode, then, essentially operates as an independent (though redundant) story grammar, as a self-contained unit with no stated relation to previous or sub-sequent episodes. Across narratives, basic macropropositional structures are repeated again and again, but *without any explicit reference to each other*. Consider that neither Dick nor Jane would ever say 'this reminds me of yester-day!' Obviously this serves pedagogical purposes, enabling the teaching of a separate story in a distinct, boundaried lesson to be covered within a twenty-to-forty minute time span. But there are concomitant effects: specifically, the familiarity sought by Gray and Arbuthnot is achieved through the repetition of story-grammar macropropositions, sentence-level syntax and vocabulary, without the development of any coherent narrative cross-references.

This text structure *qua* series of unrelated but similar episodes bears significant implications in terms of character development, thematic continuity and narrative temporality. Each story takes up in 'virtual beginning, ignor-ing where the preceding event left off ',[12] and concludes with complete narrative resolution and closure. In each, the setting is established picto-graphically, the initiating event occurs, a familiar and recognizable sequence of caused events ensues towards a resolution, and the lesson, in case the reader has missed it, is paraphrased in a character's didactic reiteration. The anonymity of place is matched by a similar suspension of time: the passage of time between episodes seems non-existent. Dates and times, seasonal change are omitted altogether. This putative cross-contextuality and universality also is constituted through characterization. For without time, characters cannot develop and change either systematically or incre-mentally. The text provides no evidence that, for instance, Baby Sally brings what she has learned from a previous episode to a new one, or that Jane bears a grudge over being repeatedly ignored or dominated. These episodes thus hide their temporality and spatial location through their autonomy from each other.

In all, then, the story grammars in these selected narratives are simple, linear, highly redundant and repetitious. As noted, it is the repetition within and between story grammars of particular social relations and actions — rather than the establishment through explicit connection of temporal, spatial or human relations across the episodes — which unifies the text. This kind of semantic priming of particular patterns of social interaction is paralleled by a high degree of lexical and syntactical repetition. The strict control of lexical content, in conjunction with the provision of pictorial cues throughout, shaped a particular kind of universe: a synthetic culture of children's talk.

The Fictitious Reality of Dick and Jane

The analysis of selected story grammars from *Fun with Dick and Jane* enables the identification of typical ideological content in terms of both the overt lessons stated in the texts, and in terms of the actions and social relations expressed through discourse structure. Yet the total fictitious reality of Dick and Jane's larger community and environment is expressed through other textual means as well, specifically, through information at the micro-propositional level of the word and sentence, and through the extensive use of pictorial information. The identification of what Eco calls 'content segments' which are 'articulated in larger sequences according to inferential links',[13] enables the detailing of the fictitious reality in question. By 'content segments', Eco refers to the elements which together constitute what Van Dijk identified as a 'frame'.[14] In what follows, I categorize words and meanings and note literary stylistics in order to indicate how this particular text represents an identifiable ideological fictitious reality: the idealized possible world of small-town America.

As noted, Gray and Arbuthnot wanted to control the input of new lexicon for pedagogical purposes, aiming to ease the developmental transition from oral to textual linguistic competence. Accordingly, the lexical structure of the text reflected a high repetition of key words. *Fun with Dick and Jane* was built upon a core 'pre-primer vocabulary' of 66 words established in *We Look and See*, *We Work and Play*, and *We Come and Go*. To this basic vocabulary, the grade one text added 99 new words. To illustrate: in episode one ('See it Go') 84 words are used. The words 'see', 'it', 'go' and 'up' are repeated 6–8 times each. As new words are introduced, they too are repeated to reinforce word attack skills and sight vocabulary. A scan of this 84-word structure also highlights how the text establishes narrative action: 66 words (.79) of the text consist of direct speech by characters. The remaining 18 words (.21) are devoted to attribution of dialogue, mainly reiterating the verb 'said' (e.g., 'Dick said . . .', 'Jane said . . .').

Herein is the key to the intentional developmental structuring of this early reader. The text as a whole consists of .60 direct speech and attribution; in the sequence of nine episodes examined in the previous section, this level is over .90. It is not until well into the textbook, in episode nine, that the narrator interjects descriptive statements: 'Up, up went the car' and 'Father went to the car.' This minimal narratorial intervention, when not functioning to mark direct speech, is almost exclusively devoted to the extremely literal provision of further descriptive data to augment pictorial cues (e.g., 'Away went the pony.')

Where the serial disclosure of information cannot be undertaken through pictures or dialogue, however, the narrator's role must expand. In three animal stories which follow the human-like adventures of Spot, Puff, 'Baby Quack' and other animals, the narrator provides a third-person recounting of events, augmented by the speech of intervening human characters. Unlike many characterizations in children's literature, these stories' animal characters are not afforded human voices, remaining restricted to 'mew, mew' and other onomatopoeic expressions.

In the larger text, only twice does the narrator describe what even vaguely resembles an inner mental state: 'Sally was happy' and 'Dick wanted to talk to Grandma.' In the latter instance, Dick's motivation or cognition is described, insofar as a 'want' could be said to reflect a cognitive state. For the most part however the narrative manages to operate without either mental state verbs or third-person observation: 'said' and 'laughed' are the predominant devices for attributing utterances to speakers. Hence readers are left to ascertain internal responses within the story grammar almost exclusively through characters' utterances and pictured actions.

What then provides contextual information about cognition, affect, setting, and spatial/temporal relations? How does the text manage to build a fictitious reality without a total reduction to a set of redundant exchanges between predictable speakers? The key lies in the pictures, which provide an identifiable environment for speakers to gesture and interact within. Following the conventional wisdom that picture books can serve to provide context clues for the making sense of text, the episodes are conveyed in a cohesive admixture of colour illustrations and text. The text semantics in the Dick and Jane series rely heavily on the temporal, spatial and inter-subjective context established in these pictures, without which it would be difficult, if not impossible, to comprehend the narratives. In this regard, the 1940s and '50s version of the Curriculum Foundation series differs fundamentally from the Elson–Gray or Elson Grammar School texts of earlier years. Text with pictures of thirteen colours appears on *every* page and, unlike earlier basals, there are neither sequences of illustrations without text nor is there text without pictures.

This system of text semantics, contingent on the total graphic and linguistic composition of the textbook *qua* sign system, was a significant aspect of the evolution of basal series. While the Elson–Gray textbooks often used cartoon-like colourful borders, the pictures in the Dick and Jane readers are without borders. Consequently, in the latter series the environment — the suburban community, the farm, the backyard, the school yard — is less claustrophobic, conveying a sense of limitless space. For instance, as depicted in figure 1, Dick's toy plane appears to be flying off the page altogether; trees and lakes extend off the page; cars and shops extend beyond the page; ceilings are implied but never drawn; and notably, paths, staircases and playgrounds lead off the page. The sum total effect of this textual semiosis, which is noticeable only by contrast to earlier readers, is a subliminally implied openness of the environment, and hence, of the children's movements and actions. Dick and Jane's universe thus is one of virtual but not actual movement and space.

The openness implied by the text's pictures, however, is connotative rather than denotative. Paradoxically, the outside, the pictorially implied world beyond the boundaries of the printed page, remains merely implied: neither real places, nor settings are textually (verbally) referred to. What one sees (and hears) is what one gets. Within this textually bracketed universe, all specific locales are generic; that is, service stations, schools, farms, streets, and zoos are not commercially identified or labelled. Whether this portrayal of an unbounded yet anonymous universe is fulfilled in the range of human actions and intersubjective relationships is, however, another matter.

These narratives thus rely on graphic cues similar to comic books: it is through pictures that this universe becomes fully inhabited and animated. Pictured but not named is an entire array of inanimate objects (e.g., telephone, books, newspaper, picture book, sandbox, various toys, furniture, gas pumps and garage in the service station, bus, various shop facades, barn, school) and human subjects (e.g., the uniformed bus driver, a middle-aged woman on the bus, the uniformed service station attendant, classmates at school). All are generic. Within this sign system, clothing acts as a primary cue for stereotypical character traits. Each character has an extremely limited and colour-coded wardrobe (e.g., Mother in pastel house dresses, Father in dark suits, Dick in dark shorts and striped knit and cotton shirts, girls in single-colour dresses, frocks and jumpers).

This reliance on pictorial cues, in conjunction with the emphasis on dialogue and direct speech, compensates for the limitations in volume and variety of nouns and adjectives. And if we combine these portrayed but not named objects with objects and individuals named in the text, a total picture of Dick and Jane's environment emerges. The *dramatis personae* reads as follows: Dick, Jane, Sally, Father, Mother, service station attendant,

Figure 1. Page Reproduction from *Fun with Dick and Jane.*
Source: William S. Gray and May H. Arbuthnot, *Fun with Dick and Jane* (Toronto: W.J. Gage, n.d.), pp. 6–7. Reprinted by permission.

Grandfather, Grandmother, Jack and Susan, three to ten unnamed (and in some cases, faceless) children without speaking parts, the bus driver, and the middle-aged woman on the bus. Animals include Spot (dog), Puff (kitten), Tim (stuffed bear), and unnamed horses, ponies, dogs, cats, kittens, 'Little Quack', 'Little Rabbit' and five zoo animals including a kangaroo. In addition to the inanimate objects portrayed, improper nouns used include: 'cookies', 'toys', 'dolls', 'tail', 'boy', 'girl', 'friend', 'school', 'eggs', 'house', 'barn'.

Within this universe the characters' actions are constituted by the use of simple and direct verbs. If indeed story grammars represent particular syntaxes of social action, verbs function at the micropropositional level to describe and constitute fictional actions, as lexical markers of intersubjectivity. In accordance with the aforementioned dissolution of real time, the present tense is predominant, with occasional variation of the simple past and future tenses. The high frequency verbs in *Fun with Dick and Jane* mainly express physical action (e.g., 'have', 'ride', 'go', 'sit', 'run', 'eat', 'jump', 'make', 'do', 'get') and observation (e.g., 'look', 'see'). Only two verbs could be seen to express cognitive or psychological action ('find', 'guess'), and this would seem to coincide with the text's omission of the cognate, the physically invisible.

To ascertain the particular inner states and perspectives on the world of the characters a similar survey of adjectives and adverbs can be undertaken. These include words which describe qualitative mental and emotional states ('good', 'happy', 'fun', 'well'), qualitative characteristics of physical objects (e.g., 'good', 'new'), and primary and secondary characteristics of objects relating to size, primary colour and speed (e.g., 'fast', 'baby', 'little', 'white', 'black', 'yellow', 'blue' and 'red').

The cognitive operations of the personae, then, are restricted in the main to basic pro-social emotions — fear, hatred, anger are omitted altogether — and the empirical observation of sense data. Notably, children never use mental state predicates which specify thought (e.g., think, imagine, understand) and dialogue is devoid of argument, metaphor, irony, idiom or other figurative and strategic uses of language which might indicate or encourage critical speculation or inference on internal responses, plans and cognition. The resultant preoccupation with the tangible and the immediate complements the thematic onus on immediate behaviour and social interaction. The aforementioned verbs and adjectives are matched by verbs which mark desire and possession ('want', 'like', 'have'), forms of social interaction ('help', 'work', 'play') and individual expression ('say', 'laugh'). These tend to underscore the theme of harmonious adaptation to existing social relations.

A range of other speech acts model rules of social decorum and authority: the social actions of giving and receiving ('please' and 'thank you'), greeting and departing ('hello' and 'goodbye'), and obligation/obedience (e.g., 'must') are enacted. These generally appear in conjunction with a particular set of social rituals pictorially or topically portrayed: e.g., shaking hands, getting service for the car, giving and receiving gifts, food preparation and table conduct, respect for the aged, riding the bus.

Given strict limitations to a lexicon of 159 words, the detail and complexity of the fictitious reality conveyed in *Fun with Dick and Jane* are remarkable, particularly in light of the noted omissions of verisimilitudinous settings, human subjects, actions, thoughts and emotions. Yet it is a possible world without overt cognition, one in which interaction supplants reflection. The fictitious reality, moreover, could be said to represent Gray and Arbuthnot's version of the possible world of the reader: a clapboard house, whitewashed fence, straight walkway, treed and turfed garden, all within driving distance of the Grandparents. All of this is located demographically within a clean, orderly community where citizens come and go like clockwork.

But the outstanding generic trait of this particular narrative world structure was its construction with minimal narration, through pictures and dialogue. Gray's aim was to create simple narrative reproductions of children's lived, experienced oral language and social interaction. Operating from core word lists, Gray and other American and Canadian textbook authors felt that by structuring text language around children's dialogue they could construct texts in which the themes, portrayals of social interaction and very words would not have to be acquired, but merely recognized. This reproduction of direct speech would bridge the gap between the oral language competence and the understanding of the social world the child brought to school, and the official textual language of early literacy training. Yet while Gray may have captured much of the vocabulary children commonly use, the regularity and simplicity of syntactical structure combine with the wooden attributions to preclude naturalism. *Fun with Dick and Jane* was not, and could not have been interpreted as real speech: it centres on fabricated dialogue with high repetition and unnatural, non-idiomatic expression.

On the basis of more recent sociolinguistic discussions of the spread and distribution of dialects,[15] we might speculate that this unique register of 'standard' American English probably was rationalized as common among particular classes and regional groups. Yet the stilted artificiality of the dialogue would have been unrecognizable even to these children. Gray and Arbuthnot's representation of direct speech lacks the patterns which characterize authentic conversation: never does a misfire, false start or local idiomatic usage occur. Carroll's comments on more recent basal series seem apt: he maintains that the language of most primers and basal readers is far short of what most children can handle in lexical and gramatical complexity.[16] What becomes clear is that while *Fun with Dick and Jane* reproduced the lexicon of many children, its fictions, aiming at mimesis, were inaccurate representations of children's natural speech and most children's sociocultural milieux.

In all, Gray and Arbuthnot did not provide any explicit authorial intervention. The author/narrator, the constructor and judge for the reader of this particular universe, was absent, speaking only through his/her characters. In lieu of providing information on motive, cause, possible outcome, psychological state, the narrator's presence only serves to denote motion in and through a physical universe pictured through text graphics (e.g., 'Away, away went the Cat' (where?), 'Father went to his car' (why?), 'Dick and Jane went to the barn' (to do what?)). And even then, describing human movement through space, the narrator in fact assumes the same repetitive voice, developmental limitations, and epistemological vantage point as Dick. Dick may indeed be the narrator. In this sense, the narrative never makes its generative status as authored artefact transparent to the reader.[17] The text has been stripped of the narrative conventions of children's literature, discourse options that commonly are used to situate the tale in time (e.g., 'Once upon a time') and space (e.g., 'In a universe far far away') relative to the teller and hearer.

In the Curriculum Foundation basal series, then, a curious and historically unprecedented genre of literature emerges: it was devoid of poetic tropes (metaphors, similes, story language); it was without an explicit or sustained narratorial/authorial presence; its serial disclosure of story schemata and contextual information was driven by dialogue and pictures. Ironically, by aiming to reproduce direct speech Gray effectively divorced the literacy textbook from the oral tradition. There is no epic poet, no story teller, no story language to make the audience aware of the artifice, no sense of historical lineage or tradition. The historical site is limited to a generic North American space and time. Gray and his contemporaries created composite artificial versions of natural language, and in so doing created a new kind of literature.

This literary form is characterized by micropropositional and macropropositional repetition. In the narrative designed for the maximum number of opportunities to practise word recognition, the same ideas and themes were repeated over and over again. Through the use of repetition at the multiple levels of lexicon, sentence syntax, and story grammar a total didacticism is achieved. Even given its 'secular humanist' values, this kind of text may have been a less overt but perhaps more effective transmitter of ideological values and rules for daily life than the previous generations of literary and moral textbooks. The sheer thematic repetition of play, fun, family, politeness, respect and the like coalesce at multiple levels of coding to represent a total ideological fictional reality.

What remains resembles a cartoon: a series of vignettes or scenes, of repeated actions and words, of speakers interacting in a visually/graphically displayed social environment. The words one reads are what Dick *et al.* say to each other, not the words of the storyteller which remind us that this is indeed a tale, or which might criticize and second guess characters' thoughts and actions. If the authors' goal was the portrayal of 'vicarious experience', in one sense they succeeded: in this universe of developing social speakers/actors, this pure unsullied dialogue could be construed as a kind of postwar modernist realism. But unlike cinematic realism, it does not follow the eye; unlike psychological realism, it does not reveal mental states, emotion or motive; unlike naturalist realism, it does not focus on eco-systemic relations. Rather it is a didactic sanction of certain social relations and attitudes, a portrayal and transmission of patterns of language, labour and interaction between child and child, child and parent, child and grand-parent.

It is perhaps too easy to surmise that the fictitious reality which resulted was chauvinistic, myopic and prescriptive. Indeed, a similar utopian vision of growing up in America was reappraised critically by sociologists like C. Wright Mills and novelists like Sinclair Lewis. But Dick and Jane were unsubstantial as children's literature. As Bettelheim and Zelan note, tra-ditionally valued fairy tales, poetry and biblical stories, overt ideological content notwithstanding, offered children a richness of language and imaginativeness of content which the modern 'controlled' basal, predictable and located in the perpetual present, could not.

One World: Possible Worlds of the Text

The linguistic properties of these children's textbooks, then, joined with pictorially presented information to portray a total fictional reality. In turn the particular ideological values, beliefs, social understandings and orienta-tions to action which constituted this reality were rendered official through their inclusion in a formally prescribed and taught textbook. Yet the portrayed version of culture, intersubjectivity and childhood is but one of the multiple possible worlds entailed in a text's authorship and readership. How these worlds are juxtaposed and valorized relative to each other can depend on the use of particular discourse options. For instance, an active and intervening narrator can encourage the reader to assume a divergent perspective on a particular portrayed world. The story within a story frame of the traditional fairy or folk tale, to take another example, can alter the reader's perceptions of the fictitious reality presented and of the framing environment within which the storyteller is telling the story. The ultimate interpretation, acceptance, rejection and mediation of the portrayed version of culture, therefore, is subject to the way that a given narrative situates that portrayed world in relation to the other worlds it implies and projects.

While the text's sentences indeed stand as formulae for the construction of possible worlds, they also mediate relationships between possible worlds. The portrayed fictitious reality necessarily stands to some degree in divergence with the authors' and readers' actual reality.[18] Defining a possible world as 'a possible state of affairs' and/or 'a possible course of events' expressed by a set of inferentially linked textual propositions,[19] Eco further argues that readers' ability to comprehend and interpret is constrained by the 'possible facts of our actual world',[20] as well as by how and to what degree the text 'invites' the reader to use that background knowledge and to speculate on the diversity of the characters' thoughts. So seen, interpretation is conditional, bound by the contingent conditions of possibility in the reader's actual milieu and by the relative degrees of 'semiotic freedom' the text invites and enables.[21]

Readers' experience and understanding of the text, then, involves a dialectical tension between their real worlds and their capacity to abstract beyond those worlds, for the construction of meanings proceeds from and may negate readers' actual senses of (psychological, social and physical) reality. While textual narratives may entail the unitary projection of a single fictitious reality, readership depends on the juxtaposition and layering of multiple possible realities:

> the text is not a possible world nor is the plot. It is a piece of furniture in the world in which the reader also lives, and it is a machine for producing possible worlds (of the fabula, of the characters within the fabula, and of the reader outside of the fabula).[22]

Eco here points out that even the most rudimentary of textual narratives calls a range of possible worlds into play, and it is through the interplay of explicitly portrayed and implicitly presupposed realities that messages emerge from a reading. For example, a densely layered literary text (e.g., Joyce's *Ulysses*, Tolkien's *Lord of the Rings*, or even a more popular work like *Watership Down*) attempts to create a field between portrayed realities and the fantasies projected by the characters. Correlatively, it presumes a prior knowledge of those realities on the part of readers, that they have access to schematic repertoires consisting in part of a range of previously portrayed

worlds and characters. Literary allusion thus operates as a kind of intertextual cataphoric and anaphoric device, referring to previous texts and
readings and laying the grounds for subsequent readings of other texts.[23]
These are played off against the primary backdrops of the authors' real *and*
ideal senses of reality, the characters' portrayed and imagined possible
worlds, and what the author presumes the reader has experienced and will
experience.

While all texts presume and interrelate diverse world structures, they
may or may not, depending on their literary and pedagogical intents, draw
interpretation into line with a confirmation of the portrayed fictitious
reality. This insight often has escaped those curricular critics who single out
portrayed (ideological) worlds for criticism, inasmuch as many condemna-
tions of the political content of particular narrative texts have been premised
on the assumption that the portrayed world is *the* didactically sanctioned or
approved world. It would be naive to assume, however, that Winston
Smith's experienced reality in *Nineteen Eighty-Four* was portrayed
favourably. As noted, many texts rely on the very divergence between
textually generated reality and readers' realities, or between portrayed
reality and characters' and narrators' hopes and aspirations, to metacomment
on or critique the moral or ideological worth of the portrayed world. Elementary distinctions enable readers to distinguish between possible, 'paper'
and real worlds, to situate themselves relative to narratively projected
worlds. The structure and literary style of narrative marks out boundaries
between these possible worlds such that readers come to recognize that
'narrators and characters ... are essentially "paper beings",' that 'the
(material) author of a narrative is in no way to be confused with the
narrator of that narrative'.[24]

The literal gloss of selected story grammars, stylistics and ideological
content of the text completed, a further examination of how the Dick and
Jane texts project and juxtapose possible worlds against the portrayed
fictional reality is in order. For this purpose, I want to look in detail at 'The
New Family' (see figure 2), a story from the reader which grade 1 and 2
students proceeded to after completing *Fun with Dick and Jane, Our New
Friends*. In the following discussion, the story grammar is outlined, the
implied and portrayed worlds charted, and implications for readership
noted.

> From their backyard (setting), Dick and Jane watch six workmen
> refurbishing the house next door (initiating event 1). Jane asks,
> 'Who will come to live in it?' (problem/goal). Dick deduces from
> the size of the house that it will be a large family (internal
> response/attempt 1). Jane hopes for girls for her to play with (inter-
> nal response/attempt 2/elaboration of 1); Dick hopes for boys

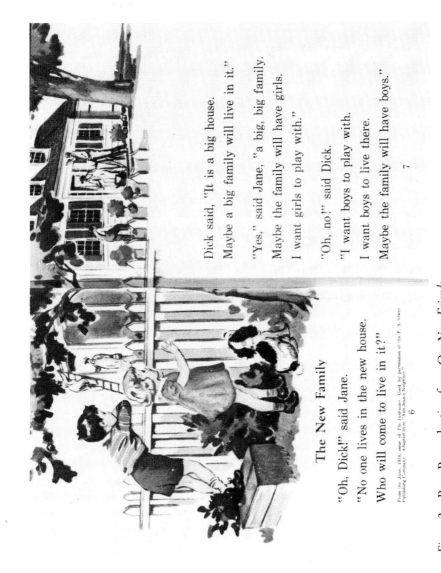

The New Family

"Oh, Dick!" said Jane.
"No one lives in the new house.
Who will come to live in it?"

6

Dick said, "It is a big house.
Maybe a big family will live in it."

"Yes," said Jane, "a big, big family.
Maybe the family will have girls.
I want girls to play with."

"Oh, no!" said Dick.
"I want boys to play with.
I want boys to live there.
Maybe the family will have boys."

7

From the June 1958, issue of *The Instructor*. Used by permission of The F. A. Owen Publishing Company. Adapted from "Ann Jane's Neighbor."

Figure 2. Page Reproduction from *Our New Friends.*
Source: William S. Gray and May H. Arbuthnot, *Our New Friends* (Toronto: W.J. Gage, n.d.), pp. 6–7. Reprinted by permission.

(hypothesis/attempt 3/elaboration of 1). 'One day', Jane observes a moving van with men unloading toys. Noting a doll house and dolls she views this as proof of her hypothesis (consequence 1). Dick sees toy horses and views this as proof of his hypothesis (consequence 2). A blue car pulls up and a young well dressed couple emerge. To Dick and Jane's despair, they are without children (consequence 3/refutation of all previous hypotheses). A black car pulls up and a Grandfather and Grandmother emerge (consequence 4/refutation as in 3); following are a boy and girl dressed similarly, and resembling Dick and Jane (consequence 5/confirmation of internal responses/attempts 1/2); Grandmother introduces the children, Peter and Ellen, to Dick and Jane (consequence 6). Jane introduces Spot to Peter and Ellen, declaring 'This is our dog Spot. He wants to say hello. He wants to say hello to our new friends' (reaction/didactic reiteration).

'The New Family' is a considerably more complex story than any presented in *Fun with Dick and Jane*: clearly, lexicon, concepts and complexity of story grammar increase incrementally throughout this, and other basal series. Here, for instance, the passage of time elapsed in the narrative extends beyond the actual reading time (e.g., 'One day'). The portrayed problem is cognate rather than behavioural, enabling readers to glimpse Dick and Jane's imaginations and aspirations. The story grammar resembles that of a mystery novel: Dick and Jane hypothesize, attempting to use clues to solve what is presented as an anomaly in their community/universe. As in *Fun with Dick and Jane*, the action of the characters stands as a parallel invitation to the child reader to forecast as well. The actual story grammar, then, bears potential for the juxtaposition of other possible worlds against Dick and Jane's lived sociocultural milieu.

   The pivotal choices presented by a textual narrative to the reader can be delineated in terms of similarity and difference. The modern novel, for example, typically uses the potential of text to layer, interrelate and refer to a range of possible worlds through the exercise of a range of discourse options. In Zola's novels, for instance, readers may distinguish the world of the author (W1), from the ideal world envisaged by Zola the social reformer (W2), from the 'paper world' of France during the Second Empire implied by the text (W3), from the portrayed worlds of the characters (W4). Most noticeably, Zola's narrator's world view in *Germinal*, for example, could not be equated with that of any of the characters. There is no necessary identity among W1, W2, W3, and W4. Add to this the possible worlds embodied by scenarios of future actions, fantasies and dreams of the characters (W5), and the world experience and knowledges which Zola assumed his readers would have (W6). In the case of later modernist narratives, like those of Joyce and Kafka, the very conflation and possible combination of (polysemous) possible worlds, enables an 'opening' of the text to diverse and potentially conflicting interpretations.[25]

To take a simpler example, a traditional fairy tale like Cinderella relies on the difference between Cinderella's portrayed existence from her projected ideal, invoking the imagination of the reader accordingly. Modern children's narratives by Dahl, Lobel and others juxtapose possible worlds through a range of literary techniques. For example, while pitched at a primer level audience, Lobel's Frog and Toad stories nonetheless employ such literary devices as stories within stories, dream and stream of consciousness sequences to portray and invite the further construction of imaginative possible worlds.[26] While readers, particularly child readers, may not be conscious of the positing and interrelation of world structures occurring in the text, how such structures are interrelated can encourage or discourage speculative interpretation, insofar as 'the pragmatic process of interpretation is not an empirical accident independent of the text *qua* text, but it is a structural element of its generative process'.[27]

In Gray and Arbuthnot's 'The New Family', a range of possible worlds are implied in the narrative structure:

W1 = The authors' real world
W2 = The authors' ideal world
W3 = The implied state of the real world referred to by the text
W4 = Dick and Jane's world portrayed by the text
W5 = The world projected/predicted by Dick and Jane on the arrival of the family
W6 = The readers' world as projected by the author/text
W7 = The readers' actual world
W8 = The readers' projected/predicted world of Dick and Jane on arrival of the family

In the narrative, the range of possible worlds is narrowed progressively: the text invites the reader to speculate, but then, as Eco's 'closed text', begins inexorably asserting 'its rights as a text' to 'say without ambiguity what is to be taken as "true" in this fictional world.'[28] That is, instead of leading towards 'pluriprobability', the text structure consists of a linear movement towards the closing down of interpretative possibilities. To begin with, W4 is equated with W5: Dick and Jane, verbally forecasting the arrival of a new family, are engaged in projective identification of their own ego identities onto the generalized other. That is, the possible world they imagine and predict reflects their deepest desires, for someone like themselves to play with. Competing versions of W5 are introduced: Jane hopes for a female counterpart and Dick for a male. In its movement and catharsis, the narrative synthesizes a unitary version of these ostensibly alternative possible worlds. Apparently, Dick and Jane are characteristically unable to disembed, with W5 standing as a narcissistic self-projection, later confirmed as valid, of W4. One can only assume that Spot as well is hoping for a new dog of identical pedigree.

In terms of its pedagogical function for an intended audience, Gray and Arbuthnot's 'high-interest' text can be taken on its word: that ideally W4 will bear some resemblance to W6, that the student readers will find in Dick and Jane versions of themselves represented and thereby recognize familiar patterns and language. To further the equation, by extension W5 = W8: if the sensibilities portrayed are similar to those of readers, those readers are in turn encouraged to share Dick and Jane's forecasts. The literary effect here is the cancelling of potentially divergent possible worlds into a single (highly ideological) fictitious reality. By plan, Dick and Jane's inferences are confirmed: the new neighbours are almost identical in appearance, bearing and social-class habitus to themselves: W4 = W5, and may = W8. The text thus directs the reader towards a singular version of culture: the formal prescriptive equation of the world portrayed in and by the text, with the world sought by the characters, with the knowledges and aspirations of the reader.

This is certainly common narrative practice, to generate a set of semantic equations in the hope that empathy and solidarity with the characters will result. Hemingway's use of long passages of dialogue, for instance, forces the reader to adopt the epistemic position of the main characters. Where the narrator steps in to provide further information, his voice is markedly similar to that of the protagonist. Accordingly, the author's world view is aligned intentionally with that of his male protagonists. But narratives, particularly those written for children, frequently invoke an autonomous, if obviously opinionated narrator who, if not an actual character in the story, through her/his omniscience implies or situates a third-person perspective and value position extrinsic to the portrayed characters' universe.

Such an explicit narratorial presence — which provides contextual information, a running commentary on actions, transitions, and also describes the inner workings of characters, motivations for actions, circumstantial information hidden from characters and so forth — enables readers to hypothesize W1 as different from W2, from W3, from W4, to differentiate the authors' real/actual world from their perspective on that world, from the portrayed world, and from the state of the 'real' world it implies. Texts can thus enable the reader to see, in Barthes' words, that *'who speaks* (in the narrative) is not *who writes* (in real life) and *who writes* is not *who is'*.[29] The established disjunctions between authors', narrators' and characters' epistemological perspectives have the potential to make more explicit the artifice of the text and hence render the text more criticizable.

In the case of Dick and Jane's tale, however, the relationships both within the text and between author and reader are effectively run together in a set of simple equations. It is assumed by the author that the reader's possible world is similar to the portrayed world and, not incidentally, the characters within that portrayed world are apparently unable to envision anything other than more of the same. In this manner the syntagmatic relationships in the text (and the paradigmatic cultural ones they imply) may act to cancel any divergent or conflicting cultural understandings and competing ideologies invoked by the reader. This literary effect is generated by the discursive options exercised in the narrative: the omission of an explicit third-person perspective and the resultant exclusion of an author's voice autonomous from that of the characters'. The sum result Eco would call 'ideological overcoding'.[30] All potentially different but related worlds, portrayed, real and implied, are joined in the text to become one, leading the reader (and Dick and Jane) back to the portrayed reality as 'correct' and constraining the possibility that the reader may second guess the text.

This portrayed world is highly invariable. Social conflict, ethnicity, cultural difference and divergent courses of action are absent. Here Dick and Jane (and apparently the authors) seem incapable of projecting difference and divergence. Instead of functioning as a fantasy, as a decon-textualized representation of another community and another epoch, the world of Dick and Jane is absolutely serious: the 'once upon a time' is now and the characters are the student readers. Readers are reminded of this in the closing story: Dick's class is portrayed sitting in a reading group study-ing basal reading storybooks with a teacher. The text not only prescribes the conditions for its own reception and its model readers but, through omission and the use of the variety of literary devices examined above, it offers up this particular social reality as the only possible childhood within the dominant culture.

The Mythology of the Modern Family

How ideology is coded at the level of the structure of the sign is explicated by Barthes and Eco in their complementary analyses of the nature of myth in modern popular culture.[31] It is Barthes' contention that certain signs and symbols of mass culture serve a complementary function to myth in primi-tive cultures. Like authentic myth, these portrayals serve to justify the ways of the sociocultural system to the populace, offering plausibility structures for the apprehension of everyday life. Modern 'mythologies', however, are forms of 'depoliticized speech' with the capacity to 'naturalize' and thereby render palatable the historical, the ideological and the artificial for a populace of 'myth consumers'.[32] He calls this a 'conjuring trick':

> What the world supplies to myth is a historical reality, defined, even if this goes back quite a while, by the way in which men have produced or used it; and what myth gives in return is a natural image of this reality. And just as bourgeois ideology is defined by the abandonment of the name 'bourgeois', myth is constituted by the loss of the historical quality of things: in it, things lose the memory that they once were made.[33]

Barthes construes myth as a structural metasignification, showing how, in various modern mythologies, the structure of coded information comments upon the literal or object level message. What it signifies can be broken down into a literal paraphrase, what Eco calls an ideological 'axiom'.[34] But its power rests on its interplay of structure and message. When a message is accordingly 'implicit in its metasignification', it becomes more subtle, subliminal and ultimately more effective at 'glossing over an intentional concept'.[35]

Ideology can be coded in modern mythology at two interrelated levels: at the literal level of the concept (axiom, theme, value, world view) and at the level of its deep structure, in the very principles which govern its organized expression. 'The very principle of myth' is its 'transformation of history into Nature' and to achieve this it must hide its very artifice. But, Barthes reminds us, 'myth encounters nothing but betrayal in language, for language can only obliterate the concept if it hides it, or unmask it if it formulates it'.[36] Close scrutiny of the linguistically coded myth can 'unveil or . . . liquidate the concept'. Eco argues further that 'the analysis of temporal structures' in textually inscribed myths can reveal 'the image of a way of telling stories which would seem to be fundamentally tied to pedagogical principles that govern . . . society'.[37]

In postwar society, a range of texts of popular culture — via television, mass education, print advertising, radio — increasingly superseded more traditional community, political and religious rituals as a source for the maintenance of ideological control and legitimacy.[38] Institutions which sustain a selective cultural tradition conceal the ideological character of that selectivity: presenting as 'natural' a 'particular way of seeing the world and human nature and relationships'.[39] The modern ideological mythologies forwarded gloss over difference, representing ideological consensus as somehow natural where such consensus may in fact not exist, or representing as 'timeless' fundamental expressions or certain properties of the human mind, and 'even . . . basic mental or psychological human organization'.[40]

Correlatively, such signs/symbols/texts may socialize their addressees into systems of social relations and social organization required by the dominant culture (e.g., the modern family as social institution).[41]

Within a closed textual schema, Dick and Jane are presented as mythological characters: that is, they are cultural archetypes, 'totalities of certain collective properties and aspirations'.[42] Dick, for instance, is mischievous, helpful, respectful of parental and community authority, disdainful of females, kind to animals and paternalistic towards his little sister, cooperative (and competitive) in play and enthusiastic at work. As such he is an 'emblematic' figure whose characteristics remain fixed and easily recognizable. Dick and Jane become phantom representations of a 1950s Everychild.

The mythological Dick and Jane, like Eco's Superman, are taken through a series of obstacles and time is literally suspended throughout. The passage of time, and hence character growth and development, is marked only by repetition rather than elaboration of rudimentary discursive structures, and hence, of intersubjective relations. Episodes string together causal chains, and time is marked only by an overcoming of or unknotting of successive problematic situations. We have no evidence, for instance, that Dick or Jane learn from these situations or change as a result of them, for both children are portrayed statically. The desired values are there at the onset and remain throughout.

Accordingly, characters' recognizability is heightened by virtue of the fact that they begin each set scheme with the same characteristics, traits and attributes.

> A series of events repeated according to a set scheme (iteratively, in such a way that each event takes up again from a sort of virtual beginning, ignoring where the preceeding event left off) is nothing new in popular narrative. . . . Nor are we dealing only with a schematism in the order of a 'plot', but with a fixed schematism involving the same set of sentiments and the same psychological attitudes.[43]

Herein lies a central paradox of the mythic characters in the closed text. Following Aristotle, Eco notes that the passage of events in narrative implies the passage of time: the passage of time implies change, growth, aging, development on the part of the human or human-like subjects within a given narrative. Accordingly, Eco argues that characters are 'consumable' *within* narratives. By contrast, the mythic character defies consumption, defies change, and conveniently can be resurrected in each succeeding episode intact, unchanged, and hence, recognizable. This in turn makes the character all the more consumable *by* readers.

Within this pattern of familiarity, each episode from these textbooks involves roughly the same set of sentiments and psychological attitudes. The pictographic and orthographic cues of the text are intended to connote familiarities, rather than to present new and varied situations. And the episodic structure becomes what Eco calls an 'iterative' series, each event is repeated according to a set scheme and each takes up in virtual beginning, ignoring contingencies of environmental and individual change which occur in real and open settings and texts. Moreover, the 'inferential walks' invited by the story grammar, encouraged by the serial disclosure of semantic information, are few, excessively guided by the authors, and limited to predictable or gratuitous outcomes. Hence, this iterative scheme, consisting of a recurrent repertoire of *topoi* — stock situations, stock reactions — both breeds and satisfies what Eco calls a 'hunger for redundance'.[44] Pointing to the success of other texts of popular culture, Eco argues that this kind of archetype working his/her way through thoroughly familiar terrain does not lead readers to a state of boredom but conversely creates in them a further dependency, a hunger for repetition. The text is 'consumed' by the reader, who is invited 'to repose' and accept a 'continuous load of information'.[45]

Eco would have it that all of the characters of popular literature, James Bond, Wonder Woman, Superman and so forth, are similar emblematic figures. Closed texts rely on a pattern of mere recognition of previously encountered characteristics. Thus, Eco concludes, the character is 'consumed' but not understood, the pattern of semantic disclosure of the text encourages readers to recognize rather than to interpret and criticize.

How did this particular official mythology — the whitewashed world of Dick and Jane, of untroubled progressive childhood, of the simplified nuclear family — fit into the postwar child's broader discursive universe of images and understandings? The postwar culture industry, armed with that new medium of television, forwarded a range of reciprocally confirming mythological images of the family and childhood which resembled both in content and form Gray and Arbuthnot's creations. Commenting on the television of the era, Gitlin[46] and Kellner[47] note that the family situation comedy/drama, like Dick and Jane texts, re/presented and justified for an international audience the emergent ideology of everyday life in industrial capitalism. Certainly there are striking schematic likenesses between Dick and Jane's universe and that of programmes like *Father Knows Best*, the prototype for the weekly family parable/drama. The lineage extended through *The Donna Reed Show, Leave it to Beaver, My Three Sons*, all broadcast in Canada as well as the US. The modern day exemplar, rerun after school hours for the consumption of the student audience, is *The Brady Bunch*.

Like Dick and Jane, each story does not begin where the last episode left off, but rather in virtual beginning. By contrast, while the modern soap opera relies on inter-episode continuity, each beginning *in media res* and reinitiating a process of serial disclosure, the characters in family dramas and situation comedies are the same week after week, episodes pick up in 'virtual beginning'. Rarely does the audience glimpse character evolution or growth: Beaver makes similar mistakes week after week, Eddie Haskell is nasty week after week, neither seems capable of growth and development. Largely, plots consisted of simple goal/problem-solving activities on the part of children. And, as in Dick and Jane, play, work, and other developmental activities are of focal importance, each concluding with some sort of parable or moral articulated by Mom, Dad or the character him/herself for the family and youth audience. Yet despite the moralizing tone of these narratives, it is as if the characters are never able to carry the learning which has occurred from one episode to the next.

Actions are set in a mid and late 1950s idealized suburb (Universal Studios) which is never named and without conflict or violence. These texts of popular culture graphically illustrate the same basic semantic structures (in a different communications medium) noted in Dick and Jane: a strict delimitation of possible worlds to be envisioned by readers/viewers and characters, and a flattening out of the characters such that their interaction with the environment becomes wholly schematized and predictable. In all, they close down the conceptualization of alternative courses of action, alternative possible worlds. Action/reaction/interaction: the sum total of syntaxes of human action in these postwar utopias is contingent on a reduction or elimination of real or authentic human characteristics.

Gitlin furthermore remarks that this particular genre of youth portrayal — within idealized family units, in suburban environments of inexact or mythical specification — was not superseded until the mid 1960s, when the first of the 'social issues' series was developed by Norman Lear and others in the United States.[48] Dick and Jane were by no means exclusively determining factors in the development of readers' attitudes and beliefs, for there is always overlap between the myths of popular culture in a given period. Texts of a variety of media and institutions complement, reiterate and perhaps contradict each other. All were manifestations of the possibility of the mass production of discourse. All were forms of standardized discourse themselves. The foregoing analysis has identified some points of convergence both at the level of overt ideological message, and at the level of discourse structure.

All as well prescribed the conditions of their own reception, actually working at remaking the human subjects which they took as their objects. Closed texts 'presuppose an average reader ... in the same way an advertisement chooses its possible audience'.[49] Mowitt locates the power of modern mythology in this, its ability to recast its viewers/readers in its own image.[50] In a critical analysis of *The Mickey Mouse Club*, another social text of the 1950s, Mowitt describes how a (video) message structure makes for the social organization of its own reception. The possible world of the Mouseketeers, Mouseland, is idealized perhaps to the point of portraying an 'alternative set of social relations'.[51] Therein dwells another set of mythological characters — Jimmy (head Mouseketeer), Big Roy, Annette (who later appeared in *Beach Blanket Bingo* with Frankie Avalon), Spin and Marty, and of course the Disney cartoon characters — with almost as extensive an audience as Dick and Jane. Mowitt describes the ritual of watching *The Mickey Mouse Club*: wearing their mouse ears and t-shirts, viewers crowded around the small black-and-white screens of the 1950s in martial array, watching the Mouseketeers watch them. He argues that the structure of this particular myth/message of popular culture made for the social organization of its reception. What Mowitt's analysis brings into focus is how message structure and content can prescribe the context and the character of its own reception. The final scene of *Fun with Dick and Jane*, with children arrayed in a reading group studying their basal texts, provides a similar sign.

What kind of readership might Gray's fictions have engendered among an audience? Indeed, the obvious criticism of the semantic structure of the Dick and Jane readers is that it presumes that the reader's lived experience, and encyclopedia of possible worlds is akin to the possible worlds portrayed in the text. Clearly, for those children whose backgrounds diverged, the text would have been less accessible and more 'irrelevant', to borrow the key word of 1970s curricular criticism. Indeed, the case that such basals discriminate against non-mainstream children's experience by failing to recognize and represent their background knowledge is at the crux of both liberal and neomarxist critiques.

But it is not a simple matter of convergence or nonconvergence of the readers' possible worlds with the possible worlds of the text. It is quite tenable that a steady diet of highly contextual, relevant texts may in fact inhibit readers from disembedding, from engaging fantasy and imagination,[52] and from assuming the epistemological, analytic point of view of significant others. The implication of this perspective on the developmental acquisition of schemata and possible worlds is that literate development requires an enhancement of one's semantic encyclopaedia, an elaboration of existing schemata. Accordingly, such texts may not only discriminate against non-mainstream learners, but may as well preclude the literate development of mainstream learners.

Eco points out that convergence/nonconvergence may be but one aspect of 'schematic accessibility' of the text.[53] In the closed 'high redundance' text the story grammar can be so dictatorial and delimiting in its representation of the familiar, in the extent to which it leans on and instantiates a mundane life context, that it may effectively constrain comprehension and criticism.[54] This is precisely what occurs in Gray and Arbuthnot's assemblage. The basal readers of the 1950s may have acted to close down interpretive possibilities for the reader. Lacking allusion, connotation, and nonliteral inference, missing temporal and spatial deixis, omitting a critical narratorial voice, they preclude the reader from expanding/testing his or her schematic repertoire, of constructing and overlaying multiple possible worlds. By portraying and modelling a universe of speakers (rather than thinkers), this effect is compounded. These textbooks express little about the possibilities of self-reflection or even the strategic use of oral language as mediating factors in social relations. According to Williams's explanation of the dilution of message for a mass media audience, by attempting 'to speak to everychild' such texts may have succeeded in addressing no one.

What does the closed text teach? The implication of the foregoing analysis is that texts teach a set of interpretive strategies, in Eco's words, a 'code' which will in turn be utilized in the processing of subsequent texts. Eco also argues that texts prescribe their 'model readers', creating a further dependency on certain ideological contents, discourse structures and literary conventions.[55] What might have been the characteristic ideological effects of the code of Dick and Jane? It would seem that the calculating reduction of semantic and lexical variability in the text, while it may have enhanced word recognition, also contributed to a reduction in semantic possibility. The causal, linear and episodic nature of the text does not encourage speculative transformations of the story grammar, the authentic interaction of children's background knowledge with the portrayed reality of the text. The text is not structured 'in such a way that each individual addressee can refashion the original composition devised by the author' to even the most minimal extent.[56] Hence, it would appear that the ideological function of the basal reader was not simply to convey a postwar mythology, but to do so in such a way that precluded criticism and enabled only a very literal, controlled readership. What children did acquire were special purpose schemata, a set stock of interpretive strategies for the correct consumption of this particular genre of text: the school reader.

Notes and References

1. Sara Zimet, 'Males and Females in American Primers from Colonial Days to the Present', in Sara Zimet (ed.), *What Children Read in School* (New York:

Grune and Stratton, 1972), p. 24; see also D.C. McClelland, *The Achieving Society* (Princeton: Van Nostrand, 1961).

2. O. Klineberg, 'Life is Fun in a Smiling, Fair-Skinned World', *Saturday Review* 87 (September, 1963), 75.

3. Sara Zimet, 'Values and Attitudes in American Primers from Colonial Days to the Present', in Zimet (ed.), *What Children Read in School*, pp. 80–5. For comment on the lexical and ideational content of current basal series, see Peter Freebody and Carolyn Baker, 'Children's First Schoolbooks: Introduction to the Culture of Literacy', *Harvard Educational Review* 55 (1985), 381–98.

4. Bruno Bettelheim and Karen Zelan, *On Learning to Read* (New York: Alfred Knopf, 1982), p. 266.

5. Ibid., p. 263; cf. Bruno Bettleheim, *The Uses of Enchantment* (New York: Vintage, 1976).

6. Bettleheim and Zelan, *On Learning to Read*, pp. 263–4. For further discussion of aspects of meaning in modern basal reading series, see Nancy L. Stein, 'Critical Issues in the Development of Literacy Education: Towards a Theory of Learning and Instruction', in Nancy L. Stein (ed.), *Literacy in American Schools* (Chicago: University of Chicago Press, 1986), pp. 175–8; Carolyn Baker and Peter Freebody, ' "Constituting the Child" in Beginning School Reading Books', *British Journal of the Sociology of Education* 8 (1987), 55–76.

7. See Roland Barthes, *Mythologies* (London: Paladin, 1973); Umberto Eco, *The Role of the Reader* (Bloomington: Indiana University Press, 1979).

8. William S. Gray and May H. Arbuthnot, *Fun with Dick and Jane* (Toronto: W.J. Gage, n.d.).

9. William S. Gray and May H. Arbuthnot, *Our New Friends* (Toronto: W.J. Gage, n.d.).

10. Gray and Arbuthnot, *Fun with Dick and Jane*, p. 133.

11. British Columbia Department of Education, *Programme of Studies for the Elementary Schools* (Victoria: King's Printer, 1947); *Programme for the Intermediate Grades* (Victoria: Department of Education, 1954); cf. Hilda Neatby, *So Little for the Mind* (Toronto: Clarke Irwin, 1953), pp. 132–54.

12. Eco, *Role of the Reader*, p. 116.

13. Umberto Eco, 'The Sign Revisited,' *Philosophy and Social Criticism* 3/4 (1980), 291.

14. Teun A. Van Dijk, *Text and Context* (London: Longman, 1977), p. 159.

15. For discussion of the issue of 'standard English', see, for example, Shirley B. Heath, 'Standard English: Biography of A Symbol,' in T. Shopin and M. Williams (eds), *Standards and Dialects in English* (Cambridge, Mass.: Winthrop Publishers, 1976), pp. 3–33; see also Peter Trudgill, *Accent, Dialect and the School* (London: Arnold, 1975).

16. John B. Carroll, 'Psycholinguistics and the Study and the Teaching of Reading', in Suzanne Pflaum-Connor (ed.), *Aspects of Reading Education* (Berkeley: McCutchan, 1978), p. 26.

17. For discussion of how traditional, closed texts can mask their own productive identity, see Julia Kiristeva, *Le Texte du Roman* (The Hague: Mouton, 1970).

18. See S.Y. Kuroda, 'Reflections on the Foundations of Narrative Theory — From a Linguistic Point of View', in Teun A. Van Dijk (ed.), *Pragmatics of*

Language and Literature (Amsterdam: North Holland Publishers, 1976), pp. 132–3.

19. Eco, *Role of the Reader*, p. 219.
20. Ibid., p. 12.
21. The notion of 'semiotic freedom' within the constraints of a code system is predicated on Peirce's concept of 'unlimited semiosis'; see Anthony Wilden, 'Semiotics as Praxis: Strategy and Tactics', *Semiotic Inquiry* 1 (1981), 1–34.
22. Eco, *Role of the Reader*, p. 246.
23. Ibid., p. 19.
24. Roland Barthes, 'Introduction to the Structural Analysis of Narrative', in Stephen Heath (ed.), *Image-Music-Text* (London: Fontana, 1977), p. 111.
25. Like cinematic montage, textual juxtaposition of possible worlds metacomments on the worlds situated relative to each other; see Anthony Wilden, 'Montage Analytic and Dialectic', *American Journal of Semiotics* 3 (1984), 25–47; *The Rules are No Game* (London: Routledge and Kegan Paul, 1987), esp. ch. 8.
26. Arnold Lobel, *Frog and Toad are Friends* (New York: Harper and Row, 1971).
27. Eco, *Role of the Reader*, p. 19.
28. Ibid., p. 34.
29. Barthes, 'Structural Analysis of Narrative', p. 112.
30. Eco, *Role of the Reader*, p. 22; Umberto Eco, *A Theory of Semiotics* (Bloomington: Indiana University Press, 1976), pp. 281–313.
31. Barthes, *Mythologies*; Eco, *Role of the Reader*, esp. ch. 4.
32. Roland Barthes, 'Myth Today', in Susan Sontag (ed.), *A Barthes Reader* (New York: Hill and Wang, 1982), p.116.
33. Ibid., p. 131.
34. Eco, *Role of the Reader*, pp. 11–27.
35. Barthes, 'Myth Today', p. 116.
36. Ibid.
37. Eco, *Role of the Reader*, p. 117.
38. Douglas Kellner, 'Television, Mythology and Ritual,' *Praxis* 6 (1982), 133–4.
39. Ibid., 146.
40. Raymond Williams, *Keywords* (London: Fontana, 1976), p. 212.
41. Cf. ibid., pp. 131–4.
42. Eco, *Role of the Reader*, p. 108.
43. Ibid., pp. 117–18.
44. Ibid., p. 120.
45. Ibid., pp. 120–1.
46. Todd Gitlin, 'Television's Screens: Hegemony in Transition', in Michael W. Apple (ed.), *Cultural and Economic Reproduction in Education* (London: Routledge and Kegan Paul, 1982), pp. 202–46.
47. Kellner, 'Television, Mythology and Ritual'.
48. Gitlin, 'Television's Screens', 217–18.
49. Eco, *Role of the Reader*, p. 18.
50. John Mowitt, 'Of Mice and Kids', *Social Text* 1 (1978), 53–61.
51. Ibid., 56; the domain of 'alternate social relations' later was reified through the establishment of Disneyland, with its replication of 'Main Street, USA', as a jumping off point for the possible worlds of the past, present, future and

fantasy. Within this discursive universe, social class was personified. The gifted, like Mickey Mouse, were set off from working-class characters like Donald Duck, an archetypal speaker of the restricted code.

52. Cf. Kieran Egan, *Educational Development* (Oxford: Oxford University Press, 1979).
53. Eco, *Role of the Reader*, pp. 224–5.
54. Ibid., p. 120.
55. Ibid., p. 53.
56. Ibid., p. 54.

Chapter 5

Revising the Text:
Nationalism and Canadian Content

The external imposition of an educational curriculum and the ideological system embodied therein upon a colonial people is a powerful form of cultural imperialism.[1] In the case of nineteenth-century Canadian education, British colonial authorities and Canadian school promoters developed a 3Rs, literature-based curriculum which was designed to engender Protestant morality and to maintain the cultural and political hegemony of Crown and Empire. Initially this entailed the use of versions of the Irish Reader series, which later evolved into textbook series like the British Columbia readers.[2] Subsequently, however, a new mode of external influence developed in the form of texts like the Dick and Jane series; in reading textbooks one form of external hegemony was superseded, however gradually and subtly, by another. By the mid-twentieth century, many Canadian school children learned to read and write using US developed textbooks, in some cases nominally adapted for Canadian schools, in cases like the Curriculum Foundation basals, simply reproduced by a Canadian-based publisher who had purchased the copyright.

As a legacy of Lord Durham's 1839 report condemning imported US textbooks in Canada, there remains continuing complaint against the use of American curricular materials in Canadian schools.[3] George Tomkins traces the growing 'Americanization' of Canadian curricula and an increasingly vocal nationalist response in the 1950s:

> The considerable Americanization of Canadian curricula since the mid-1950s, a process which underminded the old colonial curriculum in anglophone Canada, provoked a reaction in the form of demands for more Canadian content.[4]

The lack of explicit identification of settings, cultural activities and history in texts like *Fun with Dick and Jane* and *Our New Friends* certainly led to the omission of anything which could have been construed as distinctively Canadian. And the importation of foreign, albeit generic, cultural content is an exemplar of modern cultural imperialism. Carnoy describes this twentieth-century exportation of 'efficiency solutions to development', in this case of technocratic approaches to pedagogy, as a form of latter day 'neo-colonialism', a means whereby multinational capital markets are established and the mentality for the production and consumption of goods on that market is transmitted.[5]

By the 1950s several reading and language arts textbook series conscientiously attempted to represent for Canadian children distinctive aspects of Canadian sociocultural ideology and history. But did alterations in curricular *content* make a difference? As Tomkins further notes, the American technical/scientific approach to curriculum making crossed the border to Canada during the interwar years.[6] Alteration of overt ideological content notwithstanding, whether there was a substantial difference between Canadian and American learning materials in conception, development, linguistic and literary structure may be another matter altogether.

In what follows, the responses of Canadian educators, public figures and publishers to texts like Gray and Arbuthnot's are sampled. This description of changing conditions of textbook generation provides an historical backdrop for a critical analysis of the ideological content of selected texts from the other principal basal series used in British Columbia elementary schools in the 1950s, the Canadian Parade readers.[7] A review of selected narratives from the series indicates how these Canadian texts, despite the importation of US theories and approaches to curriculum development, attempted to address concerns about Canadian cultural content and in part succeeded in instilling in elementary literacy instruction a vision of Canadian culture distinct from the Dick and Jane mythology. In doing so, however, these textbooks may have embraced a version of postwar Canada as an economic colony devoted to primary, resource-based economic activity.

Changing Assumptions of Textbook Authorship: Nationalism and Curriculum

The war had signalled to the governments and peoples of Canada and the United States the extent to which the two countries' economic, military and cultural fates were intertwined by shared geography and political interests. Many postwar Canadian educators were reappraising remaining historical allegiances to the Commonwealth in light of an expanding economic and military alliance with the United States and a new-found cultural nationalism. The official British Columbia postwar syllabus noted 'the heroic resistance of the people of the British Isles in the struggle of other countries for freedom' and encouraged 'the teachers of British Columbia . . . to foster those loyalties to the throne, to our fellow countrymen, and to democratic institutions'.[8] At the same time, ranking Departmental officials never tired of directing teachers' attention to modern, 'child-centred' and democratic pedagogies favoured in American schools and universities. It was this enthusiasm for the distinctively American approach to the application of scientific research and to the development of humane, non-traditional pedagogies, particularly strong among King, Weir and Conway, which weighed in favour of selecting American texts and related pedagogical schemes like Gray and Arbuthnot's basal series.

Nevertheless a burgeoning nationalist sentiment remained among artists, intellectuals and educators, reflecting a profound scepticism towards cultural and economic dependence on the United States. In 1949, the federal government named Vincent Massey, heir to the Massey industrial empire and longtime supporter of the arts, to lead a Royal Commission inquiry into the state of the arts and culture, including broadcasting, book publishing, performing arts and related areas. While a study of formal education as such was not included in the Commission's official mandate, its critiques of American influence on the culture industry extended to encompass a discussion of public educational systems. This orientation reflected the participation of Norman MacKenzie, president of the University of British Columbia, and Hilda Neatby, head of the History Department of the University of Saskatchewan, whose criticism of Deweyianism we examined in Chapter 2. What emerged was a nationalist document which put forward policies designed to defend the autonomy of Canadian publishing, media, art and culture.

The Commission's specific comments on education were in line with this general orientation. Canadian educators' reliance on American training and expertise was singled out for criticism.

> How many Canadians realize that over a larger part of Canada the schools are accepting tacit directions from New York that they would not think of taking from Ottawa.[9]

The Commissioners disdainfully noted that it was the common practice of Canadian teachers seeking to upgrade their professional status 'almost automatically [to] make their pilgrimage to Teachers' College at Columbia or to one of half a dozen similar institutions'.[10] Returning with upgraded US credentials, these teachers would rise through the ranks, noted one British Columbia teacher, 'to occupy senior positions in elementary or high schools and to staff our normal schools and colleges of education'.[11]

The Massey Commission's critique of the English–Canadian

educational establishment extended further to the fiscal dependency of writers, artists, publishers, libraries and educators on such US donors as the Carnegie Corporation and the Rockefeller Foundation.

> Granted that most of these American donations are good in themselves, it does not follow that they have always been good for Canadians. We have been content with an unnecessary dependence on the contributions of our rich neighbor. We have been tempted by her too easy benevolence. This has left us in an undignified position, unworthy of our true power. We have been content to focus on the bounty of our neighbor.[12]

As for the cultural effects of economic dependence, the Canadian Writers' Committee testified before the Commission that 'a mass of outside values are being dumped into our cities, towns and homes. . . . We would like to see the development of a little Canadian independence, some say in who we are, and what we think, and how we feel and what we do'.[13] Further considering the manifestations of this kind of cultural imperialism in schools, the Commission criticized the overreliance on US curricular materials, stating that 'the dependence of English-speaking Canada on the United States for such teaching aids is excessive'.[14]

Massey's personal perspective on Canadian education and the use of imported curricular materials was stated in his own best seller, *On Being Canadian*:

> It is no doubt simpler to accept a ready-made book from the United States than to encourage the production of one at home on the same subject . . . but it is of obvious importance that Canadian scholars should be employed in such tasks . . . and that the Canadian character of Canadian education should be preserved.[15]

In the early 1950s this general critique of the 'passive acceptance' of US textbooks was sustained in provincial and national teachers' journals. One British Columbia teacher writing under the pseudonym of 'A Canadian' put the case for Canadian content before provincial teachers:

> Great numbers of Canadian teachers . . . will agree that far too many of the texts authorized for our elementary and secondary schools, and far too much of the supplementary reading material, are American, with an emphasis and a direction appropriate for American students but unsuitable for Canadian boys and girls. What is the situation with regard to textbooks in British Columbia? . . . The official list of texts issued by the Textbook Branch shows . . . large numbers of American books.[16]

To avoid accusations of xenophobia, the author claimed not to be aiming 'to sponsor bitterness against the United States, its people or schools', but simply, to be agreeing with the Massey Commission that

> Canada is a nation in her own right, that she is not part of the United States, and that textbooks prepared for the use of American schools are not necessarily suitable for use in Canadian schools if our children are to be educated as Canadians.[17]

'A Canadian' closed with a call for 'our educational authorities in British Columbia . . . [to] accept the challenge with which the Massey Report confronts them in this matter of building up a stronger and truer Canadianism in our schools through the greater use of Canadian textbooks'.[18]

Dick and Jane's days in Canada, it appeared, were numbered. Massey's comments were a reassertion of Durham's initial bar of US texts a century earlier, although in this instance support for Canadian curricula was seen not as a defence of British colonialism but rather as the means for nurturing a distinctive Canadian culture. Empire still was at issue here, but the expansion in question was that of American corporations and related academic and cultural institutions. Historical objections to the overuse of American curricular materials pivoted on two crucial arguments: first, that importation of (educational) culture was hindering the autonomy and financial independence of the Canadian culture industries in print and electronic media, the arts, literature, and related research; and second, that the use of such materials was preventing the further development of an independent Canadian national identity.

Regarding the claim of economic dependence, the large-scale adoption of US textbooks led to a movement of public funds, taxpayer capital, to firms like Scott Foresman via their Canadian subsidiaries and licensees, in this case Gage. Following existing economies of scale, Gage and other companies paid a percentage of their profits on locally licensed US series back to US publishers, and by extension, to US curriculum authors like Gray, Arbuthnot, Russell, Witty and others. So in terms of definite fiscal effects, the use of imported learning materials led to a movement of capital from Canada and discouraged the development of texts by smaller Canadian houses. Regarding the argument that such licensing agreements enabled independent Canadian publishers like Gage to retain their financial viability, it is notable that, by the mid-1960s, both Gage and Ryerson Press — two of the remaining independent Canadian producers of educational materials — had sold out to US companies, effectively becoming official and no longer *de facto* 'branch plants'.[19]

The foregoing inspection of the Dick and Jane texts confirms the second concern of reports like the Massey Commission, that such texts portrayed something less than an indigenous cultural heritage. Granted, there was little in the ideological content of the Curriculum Foundation textbooks which could be seen to contradict some Canadians' sense of national destiny. The industrial and military power of the US was held in awe by many and no doubt some Canadians would have aspired to the idealized suburban life-style portrayed. Indeed, 1950s English-Canadian curriculum documents spoke glowingly of the parallel interests of America and Canada, Canada and Britain: all were seen to aspire to 'democratic' principles and 'industrial progress'. Long before Sputnik and the perceived Soviet military threat to North America led to even closer military, economic and cultural ties, the two countries had become each other's largest trading partners and closest defence cohorts. In the field of education, this internalization of a distinctively American ethos, of a progressivist/technocratic sense of the normative goals and scientific means of modern education, remained largely unchallenged until the Massey Commission and the contemporaneous criticism by Commission member Neatby.

But textbooks like *Fun with Dick and Jane* obviously failed to generate and enhance children's understandings of local, provincial or even national culture. This is not to suggest that this ideological content and structure in early reading and language arts curricula was not as limiting on American children, inasmuch as the postwar United States also featured an increasingly diverse populace, divided by social class, ethnic and geographical boundaries. For American urban Black children, rural Midwest farm children, west-coast Asian or Hispanic children of the 1950s saw little more of their lived experience portrayed in these readers than their Canadian or Fillipino counterparts. By omission, then, Dick and Jane-style US textbooks served up an assimilationist ethic: they were based on a supposition that schools should recast culturally different children into Americans and transmit a middle-class 'American dream' to children of all different class, cultural and geographic backgrounds.

Accepting at face value the analytic distinction between 'melting pot' and 'mosaic' cultures, emergent in the late 1950s and early 1960s[20] — that bicultural Canadian society reflected a different set of assumptions and attitudes towards ethnic and social-class variation — it would appear that the Dick and Jane/*Leave It to Beaver* mythology served the former. Accordingly, nationalist critiques hold with some justification that such texts represented another nation's ideology and culture, in spirit if not in name, and thereby precluded in Canadian children an understanding of how their culture was distinct from a generic North American culture.[21] Furthermore, if we consider the export of educational products as a sign of economic expansionism by the US corporate sector, it becomes apparent that this development potentially, at least, endangered the indigenous Canadian textbook industry, which to this day struggles for economic viability.

The Dick and Jane series was not the only US basal used in early primary literacy instruction. Taught in British Columbia schools as second issue, early primary readers were other texts like the Chicago-based Beckley Cardy Company's basal series Functional Phonetics, by Anna Cordts of Rutgers University.[22] Series like Cordts', which emphasized a systematic teaching of phonics, became increasingly common in the midst of the Flesch's popularization of phonics as an instructional panacea. Cordts' reader, which taught colour-coded 'phonetic cues', was used in some schools as an auxilliary text for 'slow readers'. To understate the case, *I Can Read*,[23] the first text in the series, has a paucity of semantic structure and content which made Dick and Jane seem like rich literary works. As in many modern phonics series, each lesson was designed to teach a specific phonetic word attack skill. Words were colour-coded and on each page stick figures pointed to the specific digraph or dipthong to be taught. Sustained narrative was lost altogether in this systematic, hierarchical decoding training. On a page-by-page basis the text shifted arbitrarily from topic to topic, setting to setting, never attempting to establish a viable story grammar. The culture imported in these series could not really be construed as highly ideological, inasmuch as the messages and discourse structures conveyed no coherent values. Rather the neo-colonial imposition here entailed the importation of a technical approach to literacy: reading conceived of as a set of decontextualized, meaningless skills. The use of such texts was yet another marker of the departure from Canada's long history of value-laden, didactic colonial readers and the replacement of this residual tradition by the application of US-developed technocratic approaches to curriculum.

Also used in British Columbia as an augmenting text was John C. Winston Company's Easy Growth in Reading basal series.[24] Unlike Cordts' texts, the Winston series was designed as a competitor to the Curriculum Foundation texts: simple narratives based primarily on dialogue introduced children to a controlled sight word vocabulary which increased incrementally with each story. Principal author Gertrude Hildreth was a leading American reading expert, having written several professional books on reading.[25] Her series resembled Gray's: adjunct materials, tests, and guides were provided; the semantic content reflected strict vocabulary controls; the licensing agreement covered the UK, the Phillipines and Canada. In this series, early primary grade children followed Dick and Jane clones Nancy and Bob, with cat Muff and dog Mac, neighbour twins Tom and Don through regimens of play, going to school, learning through experience, all detailed in multi-coloured illustrations. As with Gray's series, the lack of temporal and spatial referents made it such that local contexts were impossible, if unnecessary, to identify.

But the Easy Growth in Reading basals also model an emergent response by American publishers to charges of lack of local involvement in development and hence lack of verifiable Canadian content. The strategy used by John C. Winston Company was to list on the 'Canadian Edition' as co-authors local consultants. In this case Elsie Roy, primary supervisor of the Vancouver School District, and F.C. Biehl, of London were listed as authors with Hildreth and others. At the time Roy was an active force in professional development in the Vancouver area; she held curriculum workshops every fortnight for beginning teachers to discuss the range of approaches and methods for the teaching of early reading.[26] The documentation to establish the extent of her actual involvement in the authorship of Hildreth's series is lacking. But, significantly, it should be noted that there is nothing distinctively Canadian, or more precisely British Columbian about these texts.

This historical footnote is crucial in following the distinctive techniques of textbook exportation, for the prototypical marketing strategy of 'Canadianization' had been initiated by publishers like Winston. The use of local consultants and collaborators stamped the text with the veneer of local relevance. Of course local teachers, district consultants, and practitioners have taken part in the curriculum development process for the last century; Charters and Bobbitts's and later Tyler's curriculum development schemes employed local teachers and consultants in pilot testing and implementation phases. But this system of local consultantship, emblazoned on subcontracted editions of US series, was an increasingly popular development and marketing strategy of publishers and one which potentially could deflect spreading popular, professional and academic hostility towards the importation of US curricula. The strategy remains to this day.

Yet there was a significantly more educationally legitimate response of publishers and Canadian academics to complaints of the lack of Canadian content: in the 1950s British Columbia and other provinces adopted several series of early literacy texts which were distinctively Canadian in origin, authored by Canadian researchers and curriculum developers. Specifically, an Interprovincial Committee on Readers,[27] appointed jointly by provincial departments of education, influenced the development, adoption and revision of texts like the Canadian Parade readers and the Canadian Spellers.[28] The intent of the former series was, in the words of its authors, 'to offer books with a truly Canadian atmosphere which present ideals of the Canadian way of life'.[29]

A Technocratic Approach to Canadian Content

The Canadian Spellers, developed and published by Gage, featured stories by Canadian educators and were based on a detailed University of Saskatchewan study of the writing of Canadian children. The primary author, Frank Quance, shared with contemporary commentators a concern with the cultural content presented by US textbooks. His was a unique approach to the inclusion of Canadian content, and the conception and development of the Canadian Spellers embodies the tension between US developed and researched technical approaches to curriculum development and the provision for Canadian content.

While principals and teachers could choose, depending on availability, to augment and supplement the prescribed Gage/Scott Foresman readers in the early primary grades and the Canadian Parade readers in the intermediate and upper primary grades, Quance's spellers were prescribed exclusively by provincial officials for *all* elementary school children from grades 2–6 on a *daily* basis.[30] Hence, between their licensing agreement with Scott Foresman for the Dick and Jane series and their indigenous development of the Canadian Spellers, Gage had assumed a dominant role in the production and marketing of textbooks for the teaching of reading, spelling and related language arts.

Quance's textbooks provided a systematic instructional program based on extensive psychological research and development. The texts were sequenced developmentally, progressing through all elementary grades. For approximately thirty minutes each day, schoolchildren throughout English Canada studied Quance's series and the Monday through Friday word study/pre-test/review/post-test instructional sequence became a staple of early literacy training.

Quance believed that 'the essence of a good textbook is the guidance of learning' and that 'this, too, is the essence of good teaching'. Consequently, he instructed teachers that 'to obtain the best results,' they should 'study the text, learn its goals, its underlying principles, its general plan, and its program of specific activities for both the pupils and the teacher'.[31] Spelling was conceived 'not . . . as an isolated subject, but as one of the related language arts'. Quance, then, shared with his contemporaries a concern that various aspects of early instruction in literacy and oracy be as fully 'integrated' as possible via highly systematized and interconnected curricula and pedagogy.

Spelling itself was considered part of a child's total literate development:

> Before school age, he sees signs and advertisements on the streets, and large headings in newspapers, and thereby discovers that the symbols that we call letters convey meaning. . . . Soon, occasions arise when he . . . meets the need to express his own ideas by means of written symbols. He finds, however, that he does not know how to write the words he needs to use to express these ideas. He knows neither the letters, nor their order; in other words, their spelling. By this time, he has learned that not only what he reads but also what he is to write is filled with meaning . . . Therefore, spelling is associated in the pupil's mind with meaningful experience.[32]

Like many of his contemporaries, Quance thus saw the key to the teaching of literacy in the representation of meaningful, recognizable experiences. In accordance with his general concern for the meaningful integration of spelling instruction with the teaching of reading and writing, Quance commissioned a team of authors to develop prose passages and stories to accompany each weekly list. Their task was to lodge the teaching of 'basal words' to the point of 'automatic response' within portrayals of 'living experiences'.[33]

Like the modern basal reading series, then, the Canadian Spellers was a complete, comprehensive curricular package, featuring adjunct exercises, tests and reviews, and, of course, the teachers' manual. The pedagogical structure which Quance's program imposed on the daily classroom routine of literacy learning will be examined in Chapter 6. For now I want to focus on Quance's scientific/technical approach to the Canadianization of the curriculum.

Although he drew dictionary passages from the *Thorndike-Century Beginning Dictionary* and *Thorndike-Century Junior Dictionary*[34] and correlated selections with American word lists by Gates and Dolch,[35] Quance saw the need for textbooks which would reflect 'Canada's social, political and economic life'.[36] Hence, he argued that a course in spelling should reflect Canadian content as faithfully as 'a course in Canadian history'. American courses, he noted, tended to have 'a much lower validity' for Canadian school children.[37]

> Courses built, for instance, on counts made in the United States would omit hundreds of words like rugby, tractor, bazaar, poppy, toboggan, municipal, British, and dandelion which Canadian children use with considerable frequency in their free writing.[38]

To develop a more appropriate textbook for Canadian students and teachers, Quance undertook a major research project. He and his graduate students examined 'nearly 600,000 running words of children's writing' drawn from a 'representative' group of Canadian school children in an attempt to develop 'the most valid word count extant on which to base a series of spellers for Canadian schools'. His study 'rigidly controlled factors' like 'national origin of parents, occupation of parents, rural and urban residence, regional areas of Canada, and sex of pupils' to assure the 'validity' of his selection.

Quance, then, viewed the task of generating a truly Canadian curriculum in technical terms. He was confident that the matter of Canadian curricular *content* could be addressed through a simple and direct application of existing empirical research methodology. The solution was highly conventional: the development of readers and spellers on the basis of empirical studies of the lexicon of children's oral and written language had been pioneered by Gates, Gray, Dolch and Thorndike in the United States. But unlike Dickie and other Canadian textbook authors who continued to rely primarily on American word lists, Quance undertook the development of a Canadian data base from which he would cull the words for spelling instruction. This done, he developed prose selections 'closely integrated with the spirit and aims of the curricula of Canadian schools, particularly in the social studies, health, language, and science phases'.[39] These selections would provide a 'meaningful' prose context for each weekly spelling list. The result was a series of spellers which were truly 'Canadian', inasmuch as they were developed exclusively on the basis of Canadian research and published indigenously. Nonetheless they mirrored basic approaches to curriculum development and the technical form of modern curricula pioneered by American educational researchers: like the Dick and Jane readers, their content reflected an empirical approach and pedagogical theory which entailed the breaking down of the literate competence in question into subskill components.

The postwar atmosphere of scepticism towards the importation of US educational materials thus led to a change in the assumptions guiding Canadian textbook generation and adoption, spawning various publishing, marketing and curriculum development strategies. These ranged from the alteration of provincial textbook adoption policies under the aegis of consultant bodies like the Interprovincial Committee on Readers, to the use of local consultants by publishers to augment multinational textbook series, to schemes like those of Quance which drew heavily from technicist approaches to curriculum development. The ideological content presented in curricula like Gray and Arbuthnot's had become the target for an emergent nationalism among Canadian educators and by the early 1950s a response from policy-makers, educators, curriculum developers and researchers was forthcoming. However, in Quance's case at least, the approaches to 'Canadianization' may have mirrored a research and development orientation to curriculum development, the same model upon which the imported US texts were based.

Locating the Reader in Time and Space: The Canadian Parade Readers

Apart from Quance's spellers, the Canadian Parade readers were the most widely used Canadian textbooks in the British Columbia primary reading and language arts curriculum. Many student readers in British Columbia and other Western provinces began their literacy training in early primary school with the Dick and Jane series, moving on to Canadian Parade texts in the intermediate grades. Like Quance's texts, they too embodied emergent historical contradictions and tensions within the curriculum development process. While they were founded on assumptions drawn from educational research, the kind of curriculum development via empirical study undertaken by the likes of Gray, they were also self-conscious attempts to vest educational material, and early literacy instruction, with culturally significant content and knowledges.

Dickie, of the University of Alberta, was a leader in the progressive education movement in Canada. Her book *The Enterprise in Theory and Practice*,[40] was later said to have 'considerably influenced teaching methods' throughout Canada.[41] Dickie advocated the progressive notion that the purpose of education was social adaptation, rather than the acquisition of rote knowledge. Writing in the *British Columbia Teacher*, she paraphrased the Deweyian ideal of social learning through 'problem solving':

> Pupils who are to learn to adjust themselves satisfactorily to any social situation in which they find themselves need daily experience in adjusting themselves to the stream of situations that group living continuously provides . . . any and every social situation presents the participant with a problem to solve. The afternoon is sunny, you go out or remain at home to work; you need a new suit, it must be chosen; you are to teach a lesson or make a speech and must prepare it; there is a community bowling game, a church supper, an election and you do your part.[42]

But this emergent model of training through community activities, leisure and family life, and the idyllic possible world of civic life implied, was tempered by a recognition of the role of schools in training industrial workers. Dickie saw the school by necessity taking on the role traditionally performed by business:

> Modern commercial life has no place for apprentices, the competition is too keen; industry now demands workers ready trained. As the home and industry have ceased to train for social and industrial adjustment, the school has been forced to add these fields. . . . Preparation for industrial life is now almost completely in the hands of the school and education for social adjustment is rapidly being taken over.[43]

Dickie viewed education essentially as a 'preparation for industrial life'. Problem-solving, creativity, independent thought and action were not ends in themselves, but rather means for maximal participation in the production of capital and the preservation of democratic civil institutions. This dual sense of the sociocultural purposes of education was reiterated in the British Columbia Department of Education's official syllabus, which stated that 'a democratic state such as Canada' required 'integrated personalities', 'socially efficient and capable of further growth'.[44] In a paraphrase of the American progressive philosophy, the Canadian curriculum was conceptualized as follows:

> The materials of a curriculum should be a selection of subject matter and experiences chosen and arranged to stimulate the growth of the child and to assist him in fitting into his environment.[45]

For Dickie, this kind of social and industrial adaptation required not 'drill for the inculcation of skills and facts' but rather that 'teacher and pupil together take up a social situation, identify the problem it presents and, as a group . . . undertake the solution of that problem'.[46] Learning, then, was considered to occur optimally through an approximation of modern life itself: goal-seeking cognition and intersubjectivity towards the solution of 'problems' arising in social, cultural and economic reality. Humane pedagogy, the cornerstone of child-centred education, was seen as a means towards the production of sensibilities suited to postwar industrial capitalism. In the midst of this, somewhat ironically, Canadian identity was to be fostered by the adoption of this distinctively American approach to education.

Dickie's work, then, marked the reiteration and extension of Deweyian approaches into the postwar era. The 'enterprise' was the 'unit work' or 'project approach' advocated in western Canadian and American curricular syllabuses.[47] It entailed a unified, thematic approach to teaching, whereby teachers would teach projects across the primary school curriculum. Dickie defined the enterprise as 'the co-operative achievement of a social purpose that a teacher presents to her class with a view to having them use it as intelligent social behaviour'.[48] In the interwar years, the British Columbia curriculum had heralded the 'socialized recitation' and 'project method' as universal pedagogies, while during the war the Summer School of Education at Victoria had offered teachers a course on 'integrative teaching'.[49]

Yet the enterprise method was seen not only to require an integrated, project-centred approach to pedagogy, but also to depend on adequate curricular materials. In the political and educational climate which had spawned the Massey Report and the Interprovincial Committee on Readers, Dickie, with coauthors including an interwar president of the British Columbia Teachers Federation and early local advocate of the teaching of silent reading,[50] set out

> to offer Canadian boys and girls, in whom an interest in community
> life is dawning, books with a Canadian atmosphere; to build into
> the consciousness of their readers a general picture of Canada and a
> definite impression of the ideals of the Canadian way of life.[51]

Their efforts were supported by J.M. Dent and Sons, a British publishing house which, like Macmillan, Oxford University Press and Thomas Nelson and Sons, had established a Canadian branch in Toronto after World War I.[52] It is somewhat ironic that Gage, an independent Canadian publisher, chose to purchase reprint rights to the Scott Foresman series while Dent's Canadian branch plant supported the development of a series expressly designed to respond to the call for nationalism in educational materials. Although the quest for profit was clearly Dent's intent, it should be noted that the Canadian Parade series, by virtue of its national content, had limited sales potential on the multinational English-speaking market. Eventually the series was authorized as a required textbook in Alberta and British Columbia and for 'permissive use' in Ontario.

Dickie and colleagues' stated goal was not 'to foster a narrow Canadian nationalism', indeed they claimed that Canada is 'perhaps the least nationalistic' of Western nations. But, they argued, 'she has a personality of her own, the expression of the way of life created by the Canadian acting upon the inherited tendencies of her people'.[53] Hence, they reasoned, it was only through the development of 'her national personality' that 'Canada can make her contribution to the development of the world'.[54] Clearly, in spite of its financial link with a British publishing house, this basal series was a Canadian enterprise. The authors further recognized that in initial literacy training broader political socialization was indeed taking place: 'boyhood and girlhood', when 'the beginning reader must grasp ... that printed symbols present ideas,' was the time 'to make conscious' that national sensibility. This, they argued, was 'too often forgotten' in the belief 'that reading ... is just a mechanical process'. To rectify an emphasis on skills at the expense of national cultural and moral content, they proposed that early elementary school literacy training needed to 'present ideals of the Canadian way of life', of 'Canada's achievements and of her place among nations'.[55]

It would appear that the 'project' approach to the teaching of literacy and a stress on Canadian ideological content were the two guiding principles behind the development of the Canadian Parade series. Not surprisingly the design of the curriculum also derived theoretical presuppositions from modern reading research, this despite critique of the 'mechanization' of reading instruction. It too provided a total curricular package: teachers' guides, lists of adjunct standardized reading tests, a 'wordbook' for student exercises, and so forth. It would appear that by the mid-1950s, successful development of a basal reading programme depended on the provision of this standard range of adjunct materials. Avoiding a narrow phonics emphasis, the series stressed a whole word approach to the teaching of 'reading for pleasure' (cf. Gray's 'recreational reading' noted in the provincial syllabus) and 'reading for information' (or 'work-type reading').[56] The former was used to rationalize the selection of literature, myth, and cultural tales while the latter was used to justify content-area reading.

Like Gray and Arbuthnot, the authors of the Canadian Parade readers were committed to the systematic and gradual introduction of new vocabulary and syntactic structures, recognizing that 'word burden is the most common difficulty confronting the average or new reader'. Accordingly, they generated a 'general scheme of progression in word burden, sentence structure and punctuation',[57] under the assumption that the 'good reader' in grades 3 to 5, for instance, could handle 'one new word in 25', the 'average reader . . . one in thirty five' and the 'poor reader . . . one in fifty five'.[58] Consequently, the grade 3 text *Young Explorers* offered an 'average word burden' ranging from 4.3 to 5.4 per page; the grade 4 reader *Gay Adventures* ranged from 5.3 to 7.3.[59] Some allowance was made for passage to passage variability, and the teachers' guide commented on the relative 'difficulty and use of each selection'.

As in Gray's textbooks, 'the sentence structure and punctuation' were 'adapted to that being taught the grade in the language class'.[60] But the authors additionally noted the kinds of pedagogical ramifications of too systematic control, arguing that 'if the word burden is too light, the material ceases to be a challenge to the good and average readers'. There was, then, a clear recognition of the pitfalls of contemporaneous series, an understanding that excessive limitation of the lexical variation of the text would hinder reader motivation and might not challenge 'good and average' readers. In a 'general purpose reader', the solution lay in the 'varying of word burden'.

This variation was to be achieved through a range of editorial strategies. First, Dickie and colleagues refused to 'interfere' with the 'sentence structure and punctuation' of poetry, plays and short stories. Though only segments or abridgements of existing literary works were presented, their lexical, syntactic, and (partial) semantic structures were left intact such that 'the pupil meets constantly, as he should do, with new and advanced forms'.[61] Their second solution was aligned with their stated ideological mission to represent Canadian culture. In controlled 'informational passages and stories of current quality', the series attempted to provide for the reader 'a context which will enable him to make out its [the new word's] meaning'. This entailed the discussion of identifiable Canadian locales, myths and legends which would offer the reader a semantic context with which to attack new vocabulary. Third, in a like departure from convention, teachers were encouraged to teach the text in a non-linear manner. Teachers could, using the charts of 'average word burden per page', move children through chapters 'in ascending order of difficulty' as advocated in the US series,[62] or they readily could jump from story to story according to student reading competence, grouping, or interest in particular themes.

With these approaches the Canadian Parade series attempted to surmount the semantic and literary problems which the strict control of basal reader lexical content and syntactic structure gave rise to. Certainly, given their broad understanding of the significance of ideological content in early reading instruction, the authors of this series had in mind a range of considerations regarding semantic structure and content not shared by their US counterparts. Moreover, their work evinced an awareness of the central problems of the scientific oversystematization of learning materials, namely the loss of literary quality and related matter of ideological trivialization.

The grade 4 reader, *Young Explorers*, consisted of 123 stories, poems and articles, with a Dictionary, 'word list', and a listing of prose selections 'in order of vocabulary and concept difficulty'.[63] The pieces are arrayed in nine thematic sections: 'Canada is Our Country', 'Good Citizens', 'Round the Fairy Ring', 'Animal Friends', 'Good Neighbours', 'The Workers', 'Workers' Helpers', 'Skyways', and 'Out of Doors'. Canadian authors are broadly represented throughout, including Myles, Benson, Connor, Moorhouse, and Woodhead. These are interspersed with more traditional works by Longfellow, Milne, Carmen, the Brothers Grimm, Andersen, Stevenson, Roberts, Lowell and Grahame. As noted, 'literary works', like Longfellow's *Hiawatha*, and Andersen's 'Princess and the Swineherd' are presented excerpted but unedited.

Young Explorers thus offers a variegated set of possible worlds and meanings for nine- to ten-year-old readers. Recall that the Curriculum Foundation texts used in British Columbia were intended for grades 1 and 2 (six- and seven-year-old readers) and that Gray's texts incrementally developed more complex lexicon, syntax and semantics. Nonetheless, all of the multinational texts lacked that crucial ingredient noted by Quance, Dickie and the aforementioned critics of US curricula: regional and local context and content meaningful to Canadian children. While it could be argued that the difference between the Dick and Jane texts and Dickie's series represented differing developmental orientations, the fact remains that the two prior generations of reading textbooks in British Columbia schools, the British Columbia Readers and the Highroads to Reading series, introduced children to traditional folk tales, English literature and English-Canadian content at the earliest primer and pre-primer levels.

The Canadian Parade textbooks, like their nineteenth-century Irish, Ontario and British Columbia predecessors, began by foregrounding national identity and ideology. In the initial passage of *Young Explorers*, the authors point out that 'Canada is a good country for boys and girls. The sunshine is bright. The air is fresh and clear.'[64] Here children encountered a form of direct address to the reader not found in any of the imported series. In addition to locating the readers in a particular national context, the text states explicitly to its readers a normative agenda of industrial and social adaptation:

> There is also a great deal of work to do here. Canada needs her boys and girls. Everywhere in Canada there are boys and girls about your age. They go to school and work and play just as you do. Let us go to see what they are doing.[65]

As with Dick and Jane, the child reader was to see her/himself in the text. Yet the ensuing portraiture would not present an imaginary Everychild from Anytown, North America. Instead, the overt purpose of this text was to portray however prescriptively a range of children's experiences, English-Canadian, French-Canadian and foreign. Readers were introduced to Jill and Angus Maclean, English-Canadian children who go fishing with French-Canadian Gaston and his father Henri; Rural Quebecois Juli, Henri and Petit Jean; Jim and Joe Sandford, eastern Canadian children holidaying in Niagara; Barbara and Ted visiting Manitoba; Albertan 'Speed' Cannon in a roping contest; and a host of others engaged in suitably civic and industrial learning and 'doing'.

Notable here is the manner in which the text utilizes both characterization and direct reference to situate geographically and culturally the narratives. Though the text was constructed using the *Thorndike Twenty Thousand Word Book*, direct references to Canadian locales are integrated throughout. Cities mentioned include Vancouver, Montreal, Niagara, Calgary, Shady Creek, Winnipeg, Banff, Lytton, Yale and Lilloet; provinces noted include Manitoba, Ontario, Alberta and Quebec. As texts adopted in Alberta and British Columbia and written by educators working in those provinces, the Canadian Parade series not only expresses Canadian content, but reflects a distinctively western provincial orientation. Specific localities familiar to western Canadian children like Hell's Gate, Lake Kamloops, the Fraser Canyon, and the McLeod River provide story settings. In later chapters these locales are interleaved with stories set in Brazil, El Salvador, 'Cathay', Holland, France, the Middle East, Babylon, and 'Buckingham Palace'. The effect of this geographical location is to make the reader aware that s/he is moving from one locale to another, from one time period to another.

Three major sets of themes emerge in *Young Explorers*: stories about Canadian children at work and play; stories about contemporary children from other cultures; folk tales, myths and legends; and content-area texts linked to social studies and science curricula (e.g., a series of poems and stories about modes of transportation, a poem about shipping and trade, stories about primary resource-based economic activities). The folk tales include European fairy tales, Biblical tales, Canadian Indian legends and an American tale of 'Young Tad Lincoln'. The collection set out, then, to put children in touch with aspects of a modern Anglo-Canadian/Protestant selective tradition. The identification for children of key texts within their cultural tradition is augmented by the construction and themes of the stories about contemporary Canadian children.

Cultural Assimilation through Individual Enterprise

In what follows I want to examine in detail two stories: 'Dutchy Becomes a Canadian' and 'Boots are Very Grown Up in Quebec'. They are nominally about Canadian children, yet they discuss two identifiable groups which comprised a significant segment of the Canadian school-age populace definitely excluded from the aforementioned US series: postwar migrant children and French-Canadian children. Both were written expressly for the textbook and neither was among the aforementioned literary texts left lexically and syntactically intact. As in previous analyses, the reading moves from a story grammar outline to a discussion of the interrelationship of discursive form and ideological content, and of the possible worlds implied by the narrative. First, 'Dutchy Becomes a Canadian', from the 'Good Citizens' section of *Young Explorers*, is considered.

> At Garry school, Heinrich, a grade six Dutch immigrant student known as 'Dutchy', stands dressed in Dutch clothing 'at the edge of the crowd'; he is quiet, detached and generally alienated from the

other Canadian school children (setting). Try outs for the school speedskating races are announced (initiating event); Roger, 'captain of the elementary hockey team' and Dutchy volunteer (internal response). Dutchy beats Roger in the preliminaries and wins the praise and recognition of his classmates (attempt/consequence). Roger, Dutchy and two other students are chosen to represent the school at the city relay races (consequence), to be held in the City Arena (setting); Roger is to race third and Dutchy the final leg. Dutchy exchanges his ethnic garb for a school sweater which, metaphorically, doesn't quite fit right (internal response/metaphor). The race begins (initiating event). Roger trips and falls (sub-attempt); Roger crawls on the ice to reach Dutchy (sub-consequence), who begins the final leg of the race far behind the competition (attempt). Dutchy imagines himself racing past windmills and canals (internal response) but then, realizing that he is in Canada and that 'he must win his place as a Canadian away from his Canadian school mates', wins the race (major consequence). Dutchy is accepted, 'thumped on the back by his teammates' (reaction). 'Now he was one of them; now he was a Canadian' (didactic reiteration by narrator).

Commentary: 'Dutchy Becomes a Canadian' is a densely layered parable. Like many other stories in the reader, 'real life' conflicts are presented and the protagonist is forced to overcome successive problems: speaking out to volunteer, beating Roger, recovering from and compensating for Roger's fall, and finally, and significantly, contending with his own fantasy. Each internal response ➔ attempt ➔ consequence sequence forms a metaphoric hurdle for the establishment of his assimilated identity: Dutchy defeats the archetypal Canadian child ('captain of the hockey team') at a Canadian national sport; he receives and wears the ill-fitting school sweater 'proudly', 'like a King's robe'. This use of simile underlines the message of cultural assimilation. Subsequently, the protagonist achieves hero status before Canadian cheerleaders in a civic event after having compensated publicly for a Canadian child's mistake. Throughout, an explicitly judgmental narrator signals the reader that this is more parable than simple schoolyard tale.

The narrative thus portrays in microcosm the very assimilation process of postwar European migrant children into mainstream Canadian culture. And despite 'old world' trappings — Dutchy wears 'heavy Dutch skates with their long curling ends' — the migrant child emerges victorious, having won the spoils of acceptance by peers, teachers, community and by self as an authentic Canadian child. This is indeed a tale of adaptation to set and subtly non-negotiable social situations and cultural circumstances, of exemplary progressive 'problem solving behaviour'.

It is Dutchy's self-acceptance which is most curious: the narratorial voice explicitly describes Dutchy's inner mental state, and what emerges is an internal psychological conflict over cultural identity. Dutchy's final attempt/consequence focuses on a psychological problem generated within the self, rather than a mere physical or social obstacle. The race itself is epiphanic: Dutchy's realization that he is not in Holland but in Canada enables him to win the contest and thereby to reconcile his cultural identity crisis. This signals that the problem of culture shock and assimilation largely rests in the psychic state of the immigrant child, for while the Canadian school children's response to Dutchy is modelled, no negative or blatantly discriminatory behaviour emerges.

To illustrate: Roger, the archetypal Canadian boy, is but a character foil. The reader hears of his actions but never hears or, though the narrator, gains any insights into what the Canadian children are thinking. Pictorially, the text portrays Canadian girls in cheerleader outfits egging Dutchy on. They gossip about his victory over Roger, but they too are cardboard portrayals. The focus of the story, then, is not on the Canadian children's reaction to the migrant child but on his psychological battle to win acceptance. This message is reiterated figuratively by the ritual 'thumping on the back' and literally by the narrator's didactic reiteration.

This particular ideological message notwithstanding, 'Dutchy Becomes a Canadian' models the multilayered semantic structure of the Canadian Parade series. The macropropositional structure consists of successive goal-formations and sub-attempts, and partial outcomes which lead to further psychological and social problems. The narratorial presence enables insight into the protagonist's mental states. Hence, not only does the student reader encounter a series of sub-resolutions leading to a major, pro-social catharsis, but as well s/he confronts a much more complex interrelationship of explicitly projected possible worlds than in the early primary texts:

W1   The authors' world
W2   The narrator's world
W3   The narrator's projected ideal society
W4   Dutchy's world view
W5   The portrayed Canadian children's and teacher's world view
W6   The reader's actual world as assumed by the author
W7   The reader's actual world

First, there is an unmistakable synthesis of the authors' point of view with that of the narrator. It is clear that the nationalist but egalitarian (viz., assimilationist) perspective of the narrator is also held by the authors and hence, $W1 = W2$. Notably the author/narrator does not assume any immediate identity between the world view of the protagonist and the world view of the reader (W4 ≠ W6). This story is about the social other the reader encounters in an actual school setting. More importantly, it is confirmed that Dutchy *does* see the world differently, that W4 ≠ W5 or W6. While their stated intents indicate that Dickie *et al.* hoped that W5 = W6 = W7, that the readers would see themselves in the Canadian schoolchildren portrayed, there remains a fundamental recognition that non-mainstream children, in this case migrant children, actually do conceive of the world with different categories and referents. Upon conclusion of the narrative, however, this observation is overridden by the conflation of W4 with W5 and W6 within the ideal possible world, racially integrated and harmonious (English) Canada (W3). Through the appropriate 'enterprise', the skating race as school-based, problem-solving activity, Dutchy has learned to adapt and adjust.

The reader thus is led to the conclusion that, having psychologically and symbolically 'become a Canadian', Dutchy will now share experiences, aspirations, competences and knowledges with the other children. Even Dutchy, who has altered his mental projections to fit Canadian social reality, shares this egalitarian ideal. In other words, to win the race and thereby acceptance, Dutchy has sacrificed W4 for W5: he has relinquished cultural difference in order to be fully accepted and to 'succeed' in this new culture. An attendant, yet extremely subtle, conflation also occurs with the story's resolution: the initial conflict-laden situation is transformed into the author/narrator's ideal Canadian society realized for all. Through the omniscient and interpreting narrator (W2), the text establishes that indeed W1 = W4 = W5 = W6. The greater didactic presumption is that W7 might/will change accordingly, that in future Canadian school-children/student readers will be more prone to accept migrant children and that migrant children will make the psychological adjustment to become Canadians.

In this way, the ideological message that cultural assimilation is primarily the responsibility of the immigrant is encoded in the story grammar and literary stylistics. The multiple physical and social goal → attempt → consequence pattern of the narrative parallels an interior psycho-logical sequence which occurs within, and as a result of, the physical and social situation. In a correlative manner, the catharsis, the 'happy ending' and moral of the narrative are contingent on a psychological act, the sacrifice of Dutchy's ethnic identity. The symbolic shedding of ethnic clothing, of fantasies, and of illusions is confirmed by the ritual 'thumping' and chanting.

What is notable about the story is that it does tackle explicitly the weighty postwar social problem of increasing numbers of migrant children in Canadian schools, implying the problem of discrimination and ostracization. Beyond its willingness to address a contentious postwar social issue, 'Dutchy Becomes a Canadian' differs from the aforementioned Dick and Jane type narratives in that it represents for readers a world view and psychological sensibility which is explicitly 'other' than those of its primary intended audience of student readers.

The literary structure of the text furthermore underlines the text's didactic function: a ritualized vicarious participation in a familiar activity is invited. Granted, the layering of conflicts and subconflicts, and the presentation of an identifiably foreign protagonist might enable conflicting interpretations better than the literal and repetitive texts of the Dick and Jane series. The chance of a 'pragmatic accident' on the basis of the reader's racial and cultural intolerance (or in the case of the migrant child reader, actual cultural difference) indeed might cause him/her to take issue with the narrator, who at least is present and thereby criticizable. But, as in Gray and Arbuthnot's texts, the didactic reiteration is univocal and unambiguous. The English–Canadian child reader is steered towards a ritual participation in a familiar form of social bonding with the protagonist, and thereby towards an appropriate interpretation. In this way the closed text attempts to pull the reader's world view into alignment with the portrayed worlds and with the authors' normative ideological position.

This particular story structure is characteristic of *Young Explorers*: semantic choices are available to the reader as a consequence of a wider selection of portrayed characters, easily marked and identifiable settings, a more complex story grammar, and the disclosure of information about characters' mental states by the narrator. All of this demands the participation of the reader not just in inferring the outcome (happy endings abound) but as well in inferring the mental states of the characters. In this regard, the text's more complex semantic structure invites interpretation of portrayed motivation and action more explicitly than texts like *Fun with Dick and Jane*. Yet the invitation to forecast is overridden by the univocal didactic reiteration, through which the text reasserts its claims on what will count as a valid outcome and interpretation.

As noted, the text was adopted for use primarily in English Canada. The story 'Boots Are Very Grown-Up in Quebec' offers another portrayal of characters who for British Columbia and Alberta schoolchildren would have constituted a social other. It too takes an explicitly didactic, parable-like form.

> On a rural Quebec farm (setting), children Henri and Juli wish for their new boots and hats (goal). Papa Jean has slipped by the barn door, twisting his leg and cutting his foot (initiating event); Mama

Jean has taken him to the hospital on their two wheel cart. Now Henri and Juli will have to take on daily adult labour (sub-goal), transporting their farm milk to town to exchange for goods and supplies (plan). They realize that their hopes for new boots, and a new hat are now dashed, as money will be lacking (internal response). Henri, Juli and dog Bobo hitch up the cart to go to the village (attempt 1); Bobo cannot pull the heavy cart (consequence 1/sub-problem 1); Henri and Juli push the cart to get it moving again (consequence 2/resolution of sub-problem 1). Reaching the village (consequence 3 to attempt 1), they are unable to unload the cart (consequence 4/sub-problem 2); 'Old Louis, the woodcarver' helps them unload (consequence 5/resolution to sub-problem 2). The children order the goods, returning home (consequence 5/resolution to major attempt 1). Mother returns from the hospital, informing them that Papa will be in the hospital for a week (consequence 6). Papa Jean returns with new boots for Henri, a new hat for Juli, a pink dress for petite Marie, and a bone for Bobo (consequence 7/resolution to major goal).

Commentary: The assumption of real adult responsibilities as a constituent part of development is foregrounded here. The children are forced out into the community by a conflict situation which has generated a disequilibrium in their family. Following Dickie's notion of the enterprise, the characters are portrayed in a multiple long- and short-term goal → attempt sequence which requires learning *qua* 'problem-solving' and perseverance. In this sense, the macropropositional structure of the story grammar models the particular version of goal-seeking human intersubjectivity and social adaptation favoured by progressives. Hence, as with Dutchy's portrayal and others throughout the series, the ideological lessons (e.g., how children live in Quebec, loyalty to family, the work ethic) are accompanied with a deeper message about ingenuity and problem-solving. At another level, readers learn that even within a culturally different context, certain universals about child development and learning, human intersubjectivity and needs are asserted.

In this case however the children are not simply rehearsing adult roles by choice, or modelling for the reader constructive patterns of play: fictional versions of real problems and conflicts are at work. Physical injury to the male head of family is the catalyst for the enterprise, and the austerity of rural life, while romanticized to some extent, is not avoided. If anything, poverty is implied throughout: the family is depicted eating 'cold breakfast'; the children must assume adult responsibilities or there will be disastrous economic ramifications. Stereotyping of culturally specific needs and wants is, of course, involved here. Students are told that 'all Quebec boys and girls' desire new boots and hats, that 'in Quebec boots show that a man's work is to be done', and that 'Hats with trimmings add to the grown upness of girls'. But, as in Dutchy's story, a real conflict is portrayed, begetting a pattern of multiple attempts/resolutions, each of which in turn is overcome by the children.

Summary Comments: It could be argued, as no doubt many 1950s designers of basal series would, that the semantic complexity in these and other Canadian Parade narratives is appropriate for children in the eight- to ten-year-old age group, and that the simple story grammars in the Dick and Jane series are incomparable with the multiple attempt/resolution sequences of these texts for older students. The point is indeed valid, inasmuch as children developmentally are able to comprehend progressively more complex syntaxes of human motivation and action. There is nonetheless a very different approach to the portrayal of the contexts, structures and relationships of human intersubjectivity in the Canadian Parade readers than in the US-based series.

As in its late-nineteenth-century and early-twentieth-century predecessors, this Canadian reading series foregrounds themes of national ideology and regional identity. However sanitized, the portrayals of Canadian experience in this textbook reflect a principal thematic preoccupation of Canadian literature: conflict with a hostile social and geographical climate. The more complex story grammars signal to readers that life is not conflict-free, but rather fraught with both environmental and social dangers, pitfalls and potential problems: the alienation of the migrant child, rural poverty and family illness, physical injury to loved ones and peers. This Canadian possible world is not one of simple adherence to authority and law. Nor is it limited to the childhood construction of play situations for the rehearsal of adult-like roles and behaviours. The inferences invited by the text require participation in the cognitive and social problem-solving processes of the characters, which often occur against archetypal aspects of the Canadian environment.

The likes of Dutchy, Henri and Juli, and their English–Canadian counterparts do not while away their time watching firemen in action, waiting for Father to return from the office, or even meeting new friends next door. Their ontological status is not one of imminence, one in which they await and somewhat gratuitously practice adulthood, but rather one of immediate experience brought about through direct conflict with the social and physical environment. Clearly, Dickie *et al.*'s interpretation of the progressive cliché of 'learning through experience' had a distinctive Canadian dimension. Despite the inclusion of the mundane summer vacation and animal stories which pass as 'high interest' children's fiction, many stories in the Canadian Parade readers feature versions of real conflict with the physical and social environment, however sanitized.

The didactic message of many of these stories then is not simply an ideological statement of the value of Canadian identity and nationality. As indicated by the kind of semantic messages embedded in the story grammars, it is obvious that children, both fictional characters and model readers are instructed in the value of social and cognitive autonomy: they are learning to analyse situations, to develop action plans and to modify or adapt those plans to subsequent change. They are being taught that rewards, gratification and the realization of goals are contingent on a strategic admixture of short and long-term goal-seeking action. Conflicts which are seen to require autonomous and moral behaviour are not limited to childhood's egocentric preoccupations (e.g., a lost toy, a silly domestic pet, or meeting new kids on the block) but rather are concerned with adult problems, often requiring direct confrontation with both natural and social forces beyond immediate control. At the conclusion of Henri and Juli's tale, the characters had foregone the expectation arising from egocentric desires for material, but culturally significant objects. It is as if their 'forgetting', their suspension of immediate childlike wants and their subsequent assumption of adult responsibilities, had led to the gratification of those wants.

In these texts — characterized as they are by a narratorial presence which enables detailed portrayals, story grammars which beget multiple prospects for 'forecasting' and interpretation, and spatial and temporal denotation which enables the reader to situate portrayed patterns of inter-subjectivity — a complex, subtle and effective didacticism occurs. For they remain tales of adaptation, of children 'fitting in', albeit cleverly, to an extant social order and a harsh physical environment. The 1954 British Columbia *Programme for the Intermediate Grades* frames this kind of socialization:

> The school assists the child in his adjustment to society. As society is constantly changing, the adjustment must be flexible and progressive. The child not only must make a temporary adjustment, but he must acquire capacity for readjustment.[66]

In accordance with Dickie's notion of industrial socialization, the child was to be assisted in 'making adjustments to his environment, and, it may be, in modifying this environment'. However, this dialectic within educational progressivism between education for social stability and social progress, between individual adjustment and the need to alter the economic and social environment was not fully reconciled in the text semantics of the Canadian Parade basals. From Dutchy to Henri, social adaptation entails an acceptance of and working within pre-established social and economic relations. Goal-seeking action requires wit, ingenuity and adult-like labour on the part of both fictional children and real student readers, but in these texts goals and outcomes remain non-negotiable.

The Semantics of Being Canadian

The possible educational and cultural effects of the overt ideological content of US textbooks did not escape the gaze of increasingly vociferous postwar Canadian nationalists. Accordingly, both Quance's Canadian Spellers and the Canadian Parade series were designed with an eye towards the preservation of explicit ideological content. The dissemination of a Canadian way of life was a paramount consideration. Following the earlier analysis of the effects of scientific/technical approaches to textbook authorship and curriculum development, it would seem that the pitfalls of modern curriculum, national content notwithstanding, lay in the very technical form of the modern textbook, and the possible ideological effects of closed semantic structures on readership. Certainly, Quance, Dickie and others operated within a tradition which drew suppositions about the nature of literacy and the forms and purposes of the pedagogical text from mainstream American educational research and from progressive educational philosophy. However, even though constructed within the conventional confines of 'word burden', the Canadian Parade textbooks were identifiably more traditional in literary orientation and national ideology. Representing a range of cultural experiences, locales, values, myths, legends, and genres of short poetry and prose, these textbooks remained anthologies of literature representative of a distinct, if somewhat fabricated, cultural tradition.

Dickie and colleagues expressed an identifiable Canadian ideological content in the series. Considerations of lexical and syntactic control did not prevent the building of fairly complex story grammars in those texts written expressly for the textbook. Moreover, these were augmented with 'uncontrolled' poems and literary passages. This Canadian content is achieved not only through the aforementioned lexical reference to Canadian scenes, but also through both characterization and the thematic addressing of contemporary social and economic concerns (e.g., European migration, expanding trade and transportation links, rural poverty).

In contrast with Dick and Jane's idealized suburbia, the fictitious realities of the Canadian Parade basals are inhabited by identifiable historical and contemporary characters. In the series as a whole, English-Canadian characters (modern workers and children, eighteenth-century United Empire Loyalists, major past political figures, etc.) are intermixed with token French-Canadians, Manitoba Cree, European migrants. These stories alternate between Canadian portrayals, characters from traditional societies (e.g., Babylonians, Biblical figures, fairy-tale characters) and more modern international 'neighbours' (e.g., peasant Latin Americans, quaint Eastern Europeans, anachronistic Chinese of undesignated historical origin and, of course, patriotic Americans).

Indeed, all characters are portrayed in (albeit positive) stereotypes, garbed in culturally typical clothing, engaging in culturally typical activities, expressing local concerns. Canadian Indians are characterized as pure, unsullied and close to the environment. French-Canadians are hard-working and stoic, while English-Canadians are portrayed as the norm: adventurous, hard-working, clever and fair. This kind of stereotyping is typical of modern basal series. But, unlike in the multinational basals, it occurs here in identifiable geographic and historical contexts. Coupled with a present, if explicitly directive and didactic narrator, this location in space and time of the characterizations at least makes for the possibility of criticism, for the rejection or acceptance of the text's veracity.

But what of the prescriptive version of postwar social and 'industrial' order which readers were to learn about, adapt and aspire to? As in American texts of the period, overtly didadtic sanctions of 'citizenship' and 'work' were included. In the basal reader possible world of Canada, children and adults are portrayed working in primary resource-based occupations which constituted the very heart of the postwar Canadian economy. Trapping in the North, farming wheat, logging, fishing, constructing houses and highways are among the portrayed kinds of labour. Elsewhere, readers catch glimpses of the transportation and communication infrastructure which was a constituent element for this resource-based colonial economy and culture.[67] Children are introduced to several stories on the Trans-Canada airline, on life in logging camps, on bush piloting, ferries, the construction of the highway system in northern British Columbia, and so forth.

Notably, the anonymous suburban style community of Dick and Jane is absent altogether. In *Young Explorers*, no adults in urban white collar occupations appear; never is a character portrayed, as Dick and Jane's father, in dark three-piece business suit and matching hat. The rural scenes of *Fun with Dick and Jane*, set in their grandparents' hobby farm, stand in sharp contrast with the distinctively Canadian settings. In the Canadian textbooks, grain silos, rugged mountainous terrain, rushing and dangerous rivers, and stands of timber all present clear environmental obstacles for the characters. In the aforementioned story of rural Quebec, there is little of the pastoral allure of life on a farm: the children, even the youngest, have no time for playing with chickens or chasing pets. In all this is a textbook representation for children of archetypal themes of Canadian life and literature. The setting, characterization and story structure do indeed teach a prescriptive kind of social realism: surviving in, and domesticating, a potentially harsh and predictably wild environment, moreover, requires particular kinds of understandings and patterns of action.

Readers of Dick and Jane learned a curious admixture of Amy Vanderbilt and John Dewey: polite manners, respect for elders, cooperative play, participation in domestic life. These messages were coded by way of repeated, redundant semantic structures and lexis; this kind of text in turn precluded divergent or varied interpretations. By contrast, readers of the Canadian Parade texts encountered a universe in which children had to learn to contend with adversity from social and economic sources extrinsic to the family unit. This is conveyed at the semantic level as well. The story structures convey a series of clearly identified alternative possible worlds which, even if reconciled and explained by the narrator, are nonetheless presented. Although the message finally is one of cultural assimilation, that even Quebecois and Cree children share rudimentary universal concerns, various lifestyles and contexts, however stereotyped, are portrayed. Moreover, the ideological message of testing and adaptation to problems in the biosocial environment is coded at the level of story structure. To be Canadian is to be adaptable, tough and ready for environmental and social challenge.

And yet there remains a curious historical irony here. The likes of Massey, 'A Canadian', Quance, and Dickie believed that the representation of distinctive aspects of Canadian culture would generate an authentic sense of nationhood and selfhood, one unfettered by Americanisms. These basals, moreover, came a long way towards that goal in spite of the importation of dominant scientific/technical approaches to curriculum making. Yet, as Carnoy suggests, cultural imperialism in modern industrial states can entail far more than the imposition of an identifiable version of culture: as well it can involve the preparation of students for participation in neo-colonial, multinational capitalist relations.[68]

The kind of 'social adjustment' espoused in Canadian textbooks of the era was archetypally Canadian in a number of contradictory ways. Indeed, Dickie's version of progressivism was a self-styled effort to prepare children for 'industrial life'. Children were to adjust to a broad vision of social progress which entailed perpetuation of western Canada's role as a provider of primary resources for eastern Canadian and American manufacturers. Taking into consideration the contemporaneous and current literature on Canada's cultural *and* economic dependency[69] — much of which is based on a reexamination of concerns voiced by Massey, Innis and others — we might conclude that the maintenance of *this* sense of national, regional and individual destiny may have historically perpetuated the very dependency it set out to reverse.

Notes and References

1. Martin Carnoy, *Education as Cultural Imperialism* (New York: David Mackay, 1972).
2. See Suzanne de Castell and Allan Luke, 'Models of Literacy in North American Schools: Social and Historical Conditions and Consequences', in Suzanne de Castell, Allan Luke and Kieran Egan (eds), *Literacy, Society and Schooling* (Cambridge: Cambridge University Press, 1986), pp. 95–100.
3. See, for example, Rowland Lorimer, *The Nation in the Schools* (Toronto: Ontario Institute for Studies in Education, 1984); Paul Robinson, *Where Our Survival Lies: Students and Textbooks in Atlantic Canada* (Halifax: Atlantic Institute of Education, 1979).
4. George S. Tomkins, 'Foreign Influences on Curriculum and Curriculum Policy Making in Canada: Some Impressions in Historical and Contemporary Perspective', *Curriculum Inquiry* 11 (1981), 165.
5. Carnoy, *Education as Cultural Imperialism*, p. 235.
6. See Tomkins, 'Foreign Influences on Curriculum and Curriculum Policy Making in Canada', 157–66; 'Tradition and Change in Canadian Education: Historical and Contemporary Perspectives', in Hugh A. Stevenson and J. Donald Wilson (eds), *Precepts, Policy and Process: Perspectives on Contemporary Canadian Education* (London, Ont.: Alexander Blake, 1977), pp. 1–20; 'The Moral, Cultural and Intellectual Foundations of the Canadian Curriculum', in Douglas A. Roberts and John O. Fritz (eds), *Curriculum Canada V: School Subjects Research and Curriculum/Instruction Theory* (Vancouver: Centre for the Study of Curriculum and Instruction, 1984), pp. 1–24.
7. The Canadian Parade reading series, by Donalda Dickie, Belle Rickner, Clara Tyner and T.W. Woodhead, was published between 1947 and 1962 by J.M. Dent in Toronto and Vancouver. Sheila Shopland of the University of British Columbia acted as series consulting editor.
8. British Columbia Department of Education, *Programme of Study for the Elementary Schools* (Victoria: King's Printer, 1947), p. 7.
9. Royal Commission on National Development in the Arts, Letters and Sciences, *Report* (Ottawa: King's Printer, 1951), p. 15.
10. Ibid.
11. 'A Canadian', 'Must We have American Texts?', *British Columbia Teacher* 32 (1952), 257.
12. Royal Commission on National Development in the Arts, Letters and Sciences, *Report*, p. 14.
13. Ibid., p. 225.
14. Ibid.
15. Vincent Massey, *On Being Canadian* (Toronto: J.M. Dent, 1948), p. 103.
16. 'A Canadian', 'Must We have American Texts?', 257.
17. Ibid.
18. Ibid., 259.

19. Pat Hindley, Gail M. Martin and Jean McNulty, *The Tangled Net* (Vancouver: Douglas and McIntyre, 1977), p. 17.
20. See, for example, John Porter, *The Vertical Mosaic* (Toronto: University of Toronto Press, 1965).
21. See, for example, Satu Repo, 'From Pilgrim's Progress to Sesame Street: 125 Years of Colonial Readers', in George Martell (ed.), *The Politics of the Canadian Public School* (Toronto: James Lewis and Samuels, 1974), pp. 118–33; Lorimer, *The Nation in the Schools*.
22. The Functional Phonetics series, by Anna Cordts, was published in Chicago by the Beckley Cardy Company in 1953.
23. Anna Cordts, *I Can Read* (Chicago: Beckley Cardy, 1953).
24. The Easy Growth in Reading series, by Gertrude Hildredth, Elsie Roy, A.L. Felton, F.C. Biehl and M.J. Henderson, was published in Toronto by John C. Winston in 1950.
25. See Nila B. Smith, *American Reading Instruction* (Newark, Del.: International Reading Association, 1965), pp. 273, 322.
26. Margarite Cronkite-Weir, personal communication, 12 June 1981.
27. See Donalda Dickie, Belle Rickner, Clara Tyner and T.W. Woodhead, *Teaching Reading in the Intermediate Grades* (Toronto: J.M. Dent, 1957), p. 8.
28. The Canadian Spellers series, by Frank M. Quance, was published in Toronto by W.J. Gage from 1930 to 1950. The third edition series, spanning grades 2 through 6, was adopted for use in British Columbia schools in 1951; see British Columbia Department of Education, *Programme for the Intermediate Grades* (Victoria: Department of Education, 1954), p. 65.
29. Dickie *et al.*, *Teaching Reading in the Intermediate Grades*, p. 3.
30. British Columbia Department of Education, *Programme for the Intermediate Grades*, pp. 65–77.
31. Frank M. Quance, *Teacher's Manual to the Canadian Speller* (Toronto: W.J. Gage, 1951), p. 1.
32. Ibid.
33. Ibid.
34. See Ibid., p. 14.
35. Ibid., p. 17.
36. Ibid., p. 5.
37. Ibid., p. 6.
38. Ibid., p. 4.
39. Ibid., p. 9.
40. Donalda Dickie, *The Enterprise in Theory and Practice* (Toronto: W.J. Gage, 1941).
41. For comment, from a 1960s 'progressive' perspective, on the influence of Dickie's work, see F. Henry Johnson, *A History of Public Education in British Columbia* (Vancouver: University of British Columbia Publications Centre, 1964), p. 164.
42. Donalda Dickie, 'Enterprise Education', *British Columbia Teacher* 20 (1940), 19.
43. Ibid., 18.
44. British Columbia Department of Education, *Programme for the Intermediate Grades*, p. 7.
45. Ibid.
46. Dickie, 'Enterprise Education', 19.

47. See, for example, British Columbia Department of Education, *Programme for the Intermediate Grades*, p. 16.
48. Dickie, *The Enterprise in Theory and Practice*, p. 125.
49. Johnson, *A History of Public Education in British Columbia*, p. 164.
50. See T.W. Woodhead, 'What Kind of Silent Reading?', *British Columbia Teacher* 10 (1930), 33–6.
51. Dickie *et al.*, *Teaching Reading in the Intermediate Grades*, p. 2.
52. Hindley *et al.*, *The Tangled Net*, p. 16.
53. Dickie *et al.*, *Teaching Reading in the Intermediate Grades*, p. 2.
54. Ibid.
55. Ibid.
56. British Columbia Department of Education, *Programme for the Intermediate Grades*, pp. 51–62.
57. Dickie *et al., Teaching Reading in the Intermediate Grades*, p. 2.
58. Ibid., p. 3.
59. Ibid., pp. 4–5.
60. Ibid., p. 3.
61. Ibid., pp. 2–3.
62. Ibid., p. 5.
63. Donalda Dickie, Belle Rickner, Clara Tyner and T.W. Woodhead, *Young Explorers* (Toronto: J.M. Dent, 1947), p. ix.
64. Ibid., p. 1.
65. Ibid.
66. British Columbia Department of Education, *Programme for the Intermediate Grades*, p. 72.
67. Harold A. Innis, *The Fur Trade in Canada: An Introduction to Canadian Economic History* (Toronto: University of Toronto Press, 1970).
68. Carnoy, *Education as Cultural Imperialism*, pp. 343–4.
69. See Anthony Wilden, *The Imaginary Canadian* (Vancouver: Pulp Press, 1981); Dallas W. Smythe, *Dependency Road: Communications, Capitalism, Consciousness and Canada* (Norwood, N.J.: Ablex, 1981).

Chapter 6

Teaching the Text:
Enforcing the Norms of Literacy

Text content and structure make for specific levels and kinds of readership, projecting, Eco reminds us, a 'model reader'.[1] Nonetheless, readership always occurs within a specific historical and, in the case of the reading of the school textbook, institutional context. Books like *Fun with Dick and Jane, Young Explorers*, and the Canadian Spellers were not read autonomously, but were experienced under the institutional restrictions and guidance of teachers in classrooms. In what follows the postwar institutional rules governing what children were entitled and encouraged to do with text are examined.

In schools children's apprehension of the text is *mediated* by variables of institutional context. Through discourse, teachers in classroom shape and constrain what children learn to do with text, deliberately setting out to engender particular attitudes towards and behaviours with text.[2] In this regard, the teaching of text in the classroom is governed by the intentional application of an ensemble of pedagogical practices. Through instruction, assessment and related daily classroom interaction, a hidden curriculum is established which may augment, enhance, complement and, in instances, contradict the ideological messages expressed within and through the text.[3] As Apple has argued, the imposition of a prepackaged instructional regime can lead to the reduction of curricular knowledge to bodies of prespecified skills and behaviours, and to a correlative reduction of teaching and learning in the classroom to standardized social interaction.[4]

This chapter examines the texts about the teaching of textbooks, outlining the official rules for and theoretical assumptions about teaching literacy to children. The focus here is on another level of historical textual artifacts, teachers' guides and government-issued pedagogical guidelines. This level of educational discourse on literacy stands as a metatext to the children's text: a text with instructions and conventions for the teaching of early reading and language arts texts. Following a brief discussion of the central role of classroom codes in the mediation of the acquisition of literate competence and textual knowledge, I examine the postwar texts of rules for the organization of the teaching of literacy in the classroom, viewing them as a centralized administrative technology for the structuring of that teaching. The expansion of standardized testing as a means for the classification and grouping of students in British Columbia schools is described. My intention is to show how this emergent meritocracy placed teachers in a contradictory situation, at once enjoined to follow the ethical and moral imperatives of progressive education while at the same time bound to an increasingly comprehensive body of technicist practices.

Historical Classroom Literary Events

Reading and criticism presuppose interpretative norms, codes of interpretation learned and shared by and within an interpretative community.[5] These codes are historically specific and themselves subject to interpretation and reinterpretation; this differentiates them from what Wilden calls 'ciphers'.[6] Ciphers, like Morse Code, are simple sets of 'rules about how to make one-to-one transformations from one kind of message to another'. A code, Wilden argues, is different from a cipher in that it constrains the information exchanged and the behaviour permitted in a given system, but does not simply dictate or determine it. Following this definition, the codes of readership taught in a given model of literacy training can be seen as 'sets of constraints' on the relative interpretative freedom of student readers and writers.[7]

Codes and norms of readership are taught/learned within codes and norms of pedagogic action.[8] The code at issue here is the institutional rule system for reading and learning to read: the set of school rules which mediates curriculum *qua* text into school knowledge *qua* messages drawn and derived from the text by student readers under the direction of the teacher. That teacher in turn is guided by his/her learned and administratively enforced assumptions about teaching and learning in general, and about teaching literacy in particular. The resultant structures of intersubjectivity entailed in teaching/learning situations constitute instructional events. Those events which involve text we can classify as specialized classroom 'literacy events', occasions in which a piece of writing is integral to the nature of participants' interactions and their interpretative processes.[9] What differentiates classroom literacy events from daily uses of literacy is that while the latter may indeed influence the development of particular literate practices,[10] the former are designed especially for teaching and learning particular literate behaviours. That is, they are intentionally didactic and deliberately structured to accommodate this didactic function.

All text has the potential to be 'autodidactic', as Goody maintains, because reading does not necessarily require mediation by any human subject other than the reader.[11] Student readership of textbooks, however, is a uniquely rule-bound and mediated form of readership. It is didactic not only in its intent to teach particular ideological content, but it also entails the equally ideological superimposition of codes of readership, of officially sanctioned and culturally acceptable behaviours with the technology of literacy. This is achieved through the intentional intervention of the teacher, who may follow to varying degrees a standard script which specifies appropriate relationships between texts and student readers. In this way, the teacher acts much as the medieval cleric did, mediating the 'word' by omitting, emphasizing, and reinforcing particular readings and interpretations, and by calling for specialized kinds of speaking and writing in response to the text.[12] As Baker and Freebody indicate, teachers lead children to particular kinds and levels of reading practice, discursively structuring what will count as a legitimate classroom reading.[13] Through this structured and constrained form of intersubjectivity — at the behest of the teacher who acts as a custodian and principal interpreter, with privileged access to the text — the student learns what counts as writing and reading, what counts as response and interpretation, and what counts as a legitimate function and use of literacy.

The discourse on the teaching of text, a textual record of official rules, norms and prescriptions for student/teacher interaction with and around the text, is recoverable. While we cannot presuppose that it or any other official code was strictly adhered to, this record stands as a trace of the generalized pedagogical norms for the acquisition of literate norms. In its original historical context of use, this discourse signalled to teachers of the era the official school rules for the incorporation of students into literate culture. It was thus the expression of a selective tradition of institutional practices which opted for and against specific textual knowledges and literate competences.

Such regimes of school practice are putatively descriptive, drawing from an allegedly 'true discourse' of empirical observations, coded into 'rules imposed and reasons given, the planned and the taken for granted'[14] for the teaching of literacy and the optimal conditions for its acquisition. Moreover,

> These types of practice are not just governed by institutions, prescribed by ideologies, guided by pragmatic circumstances — whatever role these elements may actually play — [they] possess up

to a point their own specific regularities, logic, strategy, self-evidence and 'reason'.[15]

In this way, the official discourse on the teaching of literacy, while ostensibly standing on the basis of the description of extant and prior onto-logical, psychological or social conditions, also potentially makes and standardizes those conditions according to its own intrinsic 'logic'. Perhaps more importantly, it is a discourse of institutional power that stands as a yardstick against which daily classroom practice and human subjects can be measured.

A Grid of Specification: Centralized Control of Literacy Training

How were basal textbooks to be read? By which children? And under what pragmatic conditions and constraints? What kind of interpretative responses were to count as signs of successful reading and writing? While centralized administration of schools had been an earlier innovation throughout North America,[16] 'prepackaged' curricular material came to the fore in the 1950s.[17] Postwar British Columbia teachers encountered two principal sources of formal bureaucratic documents which prescribed rule systems for the teaching of literacy: regionally developed curriculum documents, and teachers' guidebooks and monographs produced by textbook publishers. Many of these have been alluded to in previous chapters: the Department's professional magazine, *British Columbia Schools*, the British Columbia Teachers' Federation's official organ, *The British Columbia Teacher*, and of course the Departmental syllabus. In the postwar period among the most influential and ubiquitous were those articles, memos to principals and teachers, and sections from the provincial curriculum written by C.B. Conway. A sample of Conway's guidelines for the teaching of reading enables the specification of one level of the official code governing early literacy training, and of the scientific rationale upon which it was based.

Conway, postwar Director of the newly created Division of Tests, Standards and Research in the British Columbia Department of Education,[18] was versed in the work of Thorndike, Gray, Gates and others. A psycho-metrician by training, former Victoria Normal School principal, and regional leader in the Canadian Educational Research Association, Conway saw his task as that of interpreting the findings of psychological research in education for teachers. In a Department which consisted of Conway, a secretary and graduate students hired during the summer to assist in tabu-lating test scores, he was personally responsible for standards and testing in the province, and was therefore ideally placed to select and implement policies and practices based on the findings of educational research. Throughout the 1940s and '50s Conway's articles appeared in scholarly journals, teachers journals, and, of course, in the memos and guidelines sent to principals and teachers.[19] Additionally, he had significant influence on the writing and formulation of curriculum guides. The Division was charged with the preparation of the sections on reading, assessment and grouping.

In all, Conway generated a comprehensive statement on the teaching of reading and writing; his texts offered direct guidelines for the construction and organization of instruction and assessment. They were compatible with the academic research, articles and books on reading by reading researchers like Gray and Gates, the teachers' guides authored by reading and language arts researchers and curriculum specialists like Dickie and Quance, articles in teachers' journals, and of course the Departmental guidelines issued by the curriculum branch. For example, his Division's circulars, like 'Suggestions for the Improvement of Reading',[20] referred teachers to works by Betts, Gates, Dolch, Hildreth, and Russell. These texts together form a complex discursive field, putatively descriptive though ultimately prescriptive, selectively theoretical though primarily practical.

Though Conway went to lengths to assure teachers that his official word was non-binding, certainly his was an administrative discourse of power, intentionally constructed to standardize instruction.[21] His official tasks included the development of local and provincial norms on US and Canadian IQ and achievement tests. Having orchestrated the administration of standardized testing in the province since the early 1940s for King and Weir, Conway was interested in longitudinal changes in achievement. For example, he readministered Stanford, Metropolitan, and Iowa reading achievement tests at ten-year intervals to establish BC norms. Additionally, he administered tests in selected districts throughout the province, wary of the kind of bureaucratic and financial problems, with hand scoring and scaling, that might have resulted from too frequent province-wide testing. Conway also tried his hand at test construction but with limited success. In the late 1940s and early 1950s he undertook to develop standardized tests of composition and of reading in the content areas.[22]

Adding to his administrative influence, Conway used achievement test and IQ data to scale yearly provincial examinations administered to secondary-school students. This system in turn functioned to regulate matriculation and subsequent university entrance.[23] These curriculum examinations, Conway noted, worked to 'enforce minimum standards', while the use of achievement tests provided 'a stimulus for good teaching'.[24] Through 'cross referencing' IQ with curricular exam results and test achievement, Conway enabled the local teacher 'by using the norms . . .

[to] discover how the achievement of other classes of equal ability compares with his own'.[25]

To convince teachers of the need to heed modern reading research, Conway noted that by 1955 provincial students had fallen below the US norms on reading achievement, and discussed an array of causes of 'reading failure'.[26] He speculated that 'perhaps the comic books are having an effect', but this, like his attribution of declining handwriting standards to the advent of the ball point pen,[27] was as far as Conway went towards a speculative blame of falling achievement on general cultural changes extrinsic to the school. Declining achievement in literacy, he argued, could be located in the child's background, previous education, and innate ability. Among the scientifically verified sources of reading failure he included: 'language difficulties' encountered by 'recent immigrants' and others; 'poor home environments' without sufficient 'books, newspapers and magazines'; 'consistently poor teaching' which may deny children of 'educational opportunities' (e.g., 'teachers who had not used standardized tests'); and 'insufficient maturity and low mental age'.[28]

Conway thus saw home and community background as a primary cause of literacy problems. 'Meagre backgrounds', he argued, had a 'retarding effect' on reading comprehension. While children had to be physiologically capable and emotionally motivated, they were seen to require ample opportunities for reading at school and home. These and like guidelines foreshadowed a cultural deficit model, setting out to alert teachers to the danger of 'underemphasizing' the effects of specific cultural 'experience' and background knowledge on the development of literacy.

Teachers were also warned that children's personal immaturity or 'brightness' might create problems with the attainment of 'satisfactory reading ability'. This assumption of the relationship between IQ and reading achievement was widely accepted by American and Canadian educational psychologists. But perhaps more focal for provincial teachers was Conway's insistence that teaching, particularly when not guided by standardized diagnostic procedures, could create deficit.

To contend with this myriad of possible 'causes', teachers were to focus attention on the scientific 'location of poor readers', the absence of which was itself seen as a sign of 'poor teaching'. Conway noted that 'individual difficulties in reading' may be caused by diagnosable and remediable psycho-physiological causes, including:

1) Poor visual perception and visual defects.
2) Lack of auditory acuity . . . .
3) Lack of interest . . . .
4) Emotional factors . . . .

5) Lack of practice . . . .

6) Poor sight vocabulary and limited word meaning vocabulary.

7) Lack of general information and lack of experience or background knowledge in the fields on which reading materials are
based.[29]

Reprinted in the Departmental syllabus,[30] this hierarchy of causes was
extremely conventional, drawn as it was from the work of Gates, Gray and
others.

Failure to acquire competent reading 'skills' thus was seen to result from
physical, motivational, or cognitive deficiencies. These could be compensated for by adjustment of regular instruction or by the introduction of
'remedial treatment'. In cases where lack of interest was a problem, Conway
argued that 'reading materials [should be] adapted to the basic curiosities
and desires of the individual pupils'.[31] This approach would better enable
children to develop a 'positive reaction . . . toward reading'.

Yet for the daily conduct of the reading programme, knowledge of
root factors in reading failure in itself was not enough. In the 1947 curriculum, the Department referred teachers to Gray's five 'stages in the
development of reading abilities':

1. *The stage at which readiness is attained* . . . pre-school years, the
kindergarten, and often the early part of first grade . . . .
2. *The initial stage of learning to read* . . . usually during the first grade
. . . .
3. *The stage of rapid progress in fundamental reading attitudes and habits*
. . . usually during the second and third grades . . . .
4. *The stage at which experience is extended rapidly and increased power,
efficiency, and excellence in reading is acquired* . . . normally during
Grades IV, V, and VI . . . .
5. *The stage at which reading interests, habits and tastes are refined* . . .
occurs as a rule during the junior high school, senior high school,
and junior college periods.[32]

Gray's hypothesis of developmental stages became part of the conventional
wisdom about reading acquisition for over four decades subsequent to its
formulation.[33] This developmental hierarchy could enable teachers to
diagnose and group students, offering appropriate curricular materials and
instructional approaches.

Indeed the Departmental curriculum noted that those 'reading
disabilities' not caused by external factors might 'arise from using methods
and reading material suitable for a higher stage when the pupil has not yet
reached this stage'.[34] Teachers were to watch for particular symptoms

associated with each stage and act accordingly: in stage 1, for instance, 'steps should be taken to overcome physical and emotional deficiencies that might interfere with progress'. To pass from stage 3, students 'should read silently more rapidly than orally'.[35] Hence, these stages set out a theoretical template which could be translated into practical criteria for achievement and place-ment. The scientization of literacy training clearly was leading to a quasi-medical, clinical approach to instruction and assessment.

The processes of diagnosis and treatment could be assisted by the use of standardized tests issued by Victoria and local school boards. To confirm a standing in stage 3, for example, 'a grade score of 4.0 in silent reading should be attained'; for stage 5, 'a grade score of 7.0 in silent reading is desir-able by the end of this stage of development'. In spite of the caveat to teachers that 'the stages, while recognizable, naturally merge one into another',[36] the stages were linked administratively with quantitative achievement on standardized reading achievement tests. Hence, the stages, and the attendant psychometric means for evaluating literate development, acted as a grid of specification used by administrators and teachers to categorize students for differential curricular and instructional treatment.

The set of classroom procedures which Departmental administrators and university-based curricular experts advocated proceeded from the use of a 'diagnostic test' for the sorting of children into instructional groups: 'The purpose of grouping is to adapt the curriculum and the learning environ-ment to the individual abilities and needs of the pupils and to provide appropriate means for their continuous development.'[37] Again teachers were reminded that within each grade and classroom children would differ widely in 'maturity, health, social and cultural background, intelligence, interests, attitudes and habits'. But in literacy training the standardized reading achievement test, used in conjunction with various IQ tests, was to be their key apparatus in the implementation of a thoroughly modern approach to literacy instruction. The centralized monitoring of students and teachers was at issue here. For the learner, the test was crucial: the kind of instructional treatment and text the child received was contingent on initial diagnosis. For the teacher, the test was equally crucial: the efficiency of his/her teaching and of specific curricula could be gleaned by local and regional administrators on the basis of test score results. While British Columbia schools were not on a system of 'payment by results', such matters as promotion, tenure, district and school accountability could be adjudicated by reference to achievement test results.[38]

The 'location' and 'classification' of students for reading groups was provided for in two basic formats sanctioned by the Department: tests of 'oral reading ability' and 'standardized tests of silent reading'. The former, such as Gray's *Oral Reading Paragraph Test*, required that children read paragraphs aloud. Teachers were also encouraged to use paragraphs of their own choice. Problems in 'word reading, incorrect method of attack on new and unfamiliar words, mispronunciation and reversals, or defects of vocalization' could be noted. The teacher was to 'jot down' these errors so that 'corrective work' could be laid out for the student.[39]

The second technical apparatus for pre-instructional classification was the standardized test of silent reading. These tests could assess students' knowledge of vocabulary, paragraph meaning, recall of significant details, word recognition and knowledge, and prediction of given events: 'most . . . test the pupil's ability to understand stated facts, comprehend implied facts, uncover the central idea of a paragraph, read and understand directions, and understand word meanings'. Notably, *Gates Basic Reading Tests*, for grades 4–8, tested higher semantic level competences such as the 'appreciation of general significance', 'prediction of outcome of given events', as well as more conventional skills of 'noting details', and 'understanding directions'.[40] The resultant test scores in reading and related linguistic competences and knowledges could be charted on a graph provided by Victoria against IQ test results.[41] This would enable the teacher to determine whether the child was working below her/his innate 'ability' or whether 'low ability' was being compensated for through effective instruction and student effort. The same system would allow principals to assess the relative progress of classes and efficiency of teachers.

Armed with this quantitative data, and taking into account afore-mentioned factors of innate ability, level of development, individual character and sociocultural background,[42] teachers were advised to group the children for separate texts and instruction in all of the 'tool subjects of Reading, Arithmetic, Spelling, etc.'.[43] Far from being arbitrary, this kind of scientific grouping was seen to reflect closely the children's sense of their own achievement:

> Teachers will find that the children tend to divide themselves into three groups: first, those who are unquestionably mature; second, those who are capable of making average progress; and, third, the slow group who have much immaturity to overcome.[44]

These groups apparently would enable the teacher to 'plan her time [so] that she may move from group to group, giving her attention where it is most needed'.[45] This would encourage 'faster-learning and more mature pupils' to be 'challenged to work to capacity'.

For 'slow learning pupils' from 'poor home environments', 'special adaptations' were necessary: 'possibly the assignments will be simpler and shorter'. In the case of slow readers, perhaps 'remedial' instruction was in order, and the aforementioned 'disabilities' might be remedied with special-ized textbooks, decoding drills, and 'certainly . . . more first-hand experi-ences, more illustrative material, and more repetitions to fix any learning'.[46] In other areas of the language arts such as oral and written expression, these same deficit students might need 'corrective teaching'. The following list of common grade five usages offers an official inventory of illustrative kinds of oral and written expression which were seen to require 'corrective teaching' (viz. remedial drill).

> Correct forms to be learned.
> (a) Those books — *not* them books.
> (b) Haven't any paper or have no paper — *not* haven't no paper.
> (c) Haven't any or have none — *not* haven't none
> (d) I have two hands — *not* I have got two hands.
> (e) I have gone — *not* I had went.
> (f) Jack and I (as subject) — *not* Jack and me, or me and Jack.
> (g) Correct use of *may* and *can*.
> (h) Correct use of *an* and *a*.
> (i) The one who (that) — *not* the one what.
> (j) Correct use of *two, too, to; hear, here*, and similar homonyms.[47]

Consequently, those students grouped for remediation were to receive a greater degree of direct instruction, drill and continual diagnosis. By con-trast, 'fast learning' students were seen to require from the teacher 'not more instruction, but inspiration to enable them to make extended use of their abilities to become creative learners'.[48]

Through this diagnosis, grouping, and treatment process, and through the conceptualization of literate development in terms of hierarchical stages, then, the Department offered a scheme for the differential transmission of literate 'habits' and 'skills'. Within this system, standardized testing provided the basis for pre-instructional classification of students. Moreover, it enabled the verification of the efficacy of particular curricula, peda-gogies, schools and teachers. For province-wide yearly surveys of reading achievement, ranking administrators relied primarily on conventional measures of reading, stressing vocabulary, levels and speed of comprehen-sion, paragraph meaning, etc. These tests were available for local teachers' use, but generally they were administered throughout the province by Con-way's division, which also provided materials for systematic record keeping of each child's test results. Additionally, individual districts like Vancouver and Victoria regularly administered such tests. Norm-referenced achieve-ment testing was augmented by the maintenance in secondary English education subjects of the traditional British-style year-end examinations. In

Division reports to teachers, principals and the legislature, provincial examination results were cross-correlated with data from yearly standardized tests of IQ, achievement in reading, math, content-area reading, and even handwriting.

The lynchpin of the assessment and instruction system in reading and language arts was the modern silent-reading test. Descended from Thorndike's first use of short paragraphs, these tests entailed textual stimuli and objective questioning to measure student response. It is not my purpose here to enter into the ongoing controversy over whether these test actual reading, comprehension, and so forth. This question has been taken up both by critics of educational measurement and measurement experts themselves, who continue to debate the very nature of comprehension in particular and literacy in general.[49] There is of course the actual measurement issue of construct validity, whether such tests actually measure what they purport to measure. However, my primary concern remains with how such tests provided a set of taken for granted truth claims and epistemological assumptions for the categorization of students and for the deployment of classroom practices.

It was not as if Conway was unaware of the 'disadvantages and many dangers in centralized testing'.[50] In the mid-1950s, following two decades of experience at province-wide testing, he noted that teachers 'may be led to depend entirely' on one particular type of test and hence, that 'desirable flexibility and high instructional validity of the teacher-made test may be lost'.[51]

> The programme may become inflexible, particularly if 'package' tests are used. If separate answer sheets and machine scoring are used, the great advantage of teacher marking, and the correction of mistakes by the pupils of their own test papers may be neglected.[52]

Conway clearly saw the principal dangers of standardized testing in terms of instructional abuse. He further highlighted for teachers the dangers of inexact, hackneyed use of scientific instruments, pointing out the potential effects on the learner:

> There is also a danger of too great a dependance on the results of standardized testing programmes. Promotion may be based entirely on such tests instead of the results of local tests and local evaluation.[53]

Again, Conway did not take issue with the educational legitimacy of centralized testing but with its potential abuses. But in this passage he seems more concerned with the possibility that standardized test results might be used by the teacher at the expense of local tests, again taking for granted the very efficacy of testing *per se*.

Conway did address the potential political ramifications in terms of both pedagogical and administrative abuse: 'by resisting tendencies toward the use of too many tests and toward testing teachers rather than pupils, we hope to maintain that attitude'. Yet nowhere in his memos, journal articles, teachers' articles and contributions to Departmental programmes of study are there signs that he or his colleagues in the Department of Education questioned the total social and educational effects of mass testing in an extended educational jurisdiction. One possible effect was that children from lower socioeconomic and non-mainstream cultural backgrounds might have fallen into the classification of 'slow learners', receiving drill-centred remediation which bore remarkable similarities to the nineteenth-century rote instruction Conway and other self-styled progressives purported to abhor. By contrast, the treatment of 'fast learners' of innate ability and literate backgrounds was to consist of 'high motivation' activities and 'enrichment' materials. What Departmental officials of the era did not appear to anticipate was that the centralized prescription of a script for the assessment and teaching of literacy, in its provision of differential placements and treatments, may have selected for and against specific groups of children.

As for the rationale underlying this officially sanctioned ensemble of practices, Conway and his colleagues in the Department conceived of the teaching of literacy as a thoroughly scientific enterprise, which could be engineered systematically on the basis of empirically derived under-standings and decontextualized measurements of literate competence. This view of literacy afforded a theoretical grid of specification, thereby enabling the placement, treatment and certification of children and the gearing of classroom practices towards maximal instructional efficiency. Using the systematic interpretation of standardized and non-standardized test data, teachers could group for differential treatment and thereby cater for 'individual difference'.

With inspectorial and school administrative vigilance, and the compilation of exam and standardized test data throughout the postwar period, Conway had the means for enforcing this code throughout the province. While he and many of his fellow civil servants saw their role as the imparting of empirical data, pedagogical concepts, social facts, and practical guidance, their bureaucratic machinery in fact constituted a discursive technology of power reigning over the teaching and learning of literacy in provincial classrooms.

The Teachers' Guides: Standardizing the Instructional Event

Under the aegis of psychometrics, then, there was a strong Departmental bias towards standardization, towards the norming of literacy instruction in line with the NSSE state of the art, towards the drawing in of both traditional and new practitioners into centrally controllable, meritocratic models of teaching and assessment. But the Deweyian orientation towards thematic, integrated approaches continued to coexist with this technicist orientation. The duality of modern literacy instruction — the child-centred and humanistic with scientific and systematic — was reflected as well in the teachers' guidebooks issued by publishers.

All postwar reading series came with guidebooks, usually in a smaller and less durable format than the textbook. Although they came into common usage in the interwar period, in the 1950s these guidebooks had become a central component in sophisticated 'packaged curricula' due to both aggressive marketing by publishers and the conviction common among educators that the quality of teacher training and the potential for Cold War ideological deviation in the classroom necessitated stricter and more precise guidelines for teaching.[54]

In their guidebook to the Dick and Jane basals, sections of which were reprinted in both the Departmental curriculum and *British Columbia Schools*, Gray and Arbuthnot explain their intents:

> We have not merely given a general philosophy of teaching, but we have implemented this philosophy by carefully worked out suggestions to the teachers at each step, whether it be preparing the child to read, guiding his reading from the book, or interpreting and applying the ideas gained. We subscribe to the idea that at each grade level guidance is needed.[55]

As noted, the introduction of these guidebooks was one marker in the historical transition from traditional readers to more modern, complete, and scientifically designed packages. It should suffice to note that by mid-century any series lacking this kind of reference guide would have encountered major problems in the search for regional adoption and sales.

Likely the first of such guides had been offered by Ryerson/Macmillan with the interwar Highroads to Reading series. *The Highroads Manual*[56] offered a short course in theory, model lessons, and a range of strategies for structuring classroom environments, assessment and related skills teaching. The guide provided for teachers the latest explanations of 'the reading process', describing the relative roles of oral and silent reading instruction, 'phonetics instruction', and so forth. In a section entitled 'Applying Our Theories', it presented systematic approaches to testing and grouping, advocating the use of Gray's standardized reading tests. Suggestions for Deweyian 'project work', 'supplementary work to improve reading habits', and the building of a 'classroom library' were included. The interwar model for teachers' guides, then, included explanations of the theoretical basis of the series, model lessons and activities. The stress on assessment and classification was directed to both beginning and traditional teachers with minimal training in reading, language arts or pedagogical method.

It is significant that, unlike postwar manuals, *The Highroads Manual* did not offer step-by-step, lesson-by-lesson procedures, only noting 'model lessons' for the teaching of prose and poetry, phonics and comprehension, silent and oral reading. Additionally, it refers the teacher to a host of other texts on reading pedagogy by Gates, Gray and others, and a bibliography of children's literature. It reads, then, more like an introductory course in the practice *and* theory of teaching reading and language arts, not as a denotative script for regimenting interaction around the textbook. By the postwar period, however, this format had changed.

The Canadian Parade basals also featured a manual: *Teaching Reading in the Intermediate Grades*,[57] which differed from its historical predecessor in its minor emphasis on theory and its specificity in the direction of daily instructional practice. Although shorter in length, of eighty-seven pages, this guidebook offered much more detailed instructions for the teaching of the intermediate basals in the series. Additionally, this handbook reiterated the Department's stress on scientific grouping and assessment while retaining an emphasis on the child-centred 'enterprise'.

The manual provided teachers with an overview of the particular approach to reading instruction embodied in the basal series. Two types of reading were to be taught: 'interpretive type' and 'work type'. The latter was akin to Gray's notion of 'recreational reading': 'children learn to read by reading and only by establishing that attitude that reading is a joy-giving activity will they be persuaded to give themselves the constant practice necessary'.[58] By contrast, children were to be taught 'the mechanics of work-type reading'. Reading was thus conceived as 'work-type and literary skills' and, Dickie *et al.* reasoned, 'to acquire facility in any skill, two types of practice are necessary: "Whole process practice" ... and "element drill"'.[59] In other words, children were seen to learn best through practising the total reading act but they also were seen to need to practise particular subskills in isolation. These included 'moving the eyes from left to right in long eye spans, rhythmically; word recognition; phrasing, or word grouping; fusion, fusing word meanings together into thoughts; getting the meaning of a word from the context; using phonics to make out the pronunciation of the word'.[60] These were all conventionally recognized subskills of reading, cited in Departmental circulars and memos. But the unmistakable emphasis here was on a whole word approach which did not afford phonics a focal position in instruction.

Moving from the Curriculum Foundation basals to the intermediate grades, students were expected to 'use a reading vocabulary of from 2000 to 3000 words, including those listed in the Gates Primary Reading Vocabulary' and to 'read silently at the rate of about 95 words a minute'.[61] What the authors of this reading series aimed for, then, was an admixture of 'whole process' practice and skills training. Dickie *et al.* noted, moreover, that 'good readers' would focus on the former, while 'poor readers' would require the latter.

The Canadian Parade manual restated the maxim that the instructional program should 'begin with tests':

> The modern teacher knows that it is a waste of time to try to teach pupils who are good and poor in a subject together. Both suffer. For efficiency, working groups must be formed on the basis of ability. It matters little how long a child has been in school. Good readers are good readers whether they are in Grade Two or Grade Six. They need one kind of treatment. Poor readers are poor readers in whatever grade they are found. They need a different treatment.[62]

Teachers, then, were to begin from a set of pretests and groupings 'according to ability'. Several standardized tests are recommended in a separate appendix (e.g., *Gates' Basic Reading Test, Gray's Oral Reading Tests, Gray's Oral Reading Check Tests, Metropolitan Reading Tests*).[63] In lieu of these, teachers are encouraged to use short passages and questions (e.g., 'find the main thought'; 'locate definite pieces of information'; 'recognize word meanings') and to develop their own 'informal' tests of oral and silent reading. Eight sample tests on basal narratives are provided and guidelines on how to diagnose oral reading problems are noted.[64]

Again, there is nothing particularly unique or innovative about this description of diagnostic assessment. But this section on assessment, in sharp contrast with the Highroads to Reading manual, comprises virtually a fifth of the total manual. Testing and grouping are seen as essential preconditions for teaching the text:

> Following the tests, the teacher should divide her class into reading groups: the senior class, the good readers, those who are up to standard in the mechanics of reading and ready to be trained in the special skills of reading for information; and the junior class, those who are below standard in the primary skills and need additional element drill in them as well as training in the new skills.[65]

Within this systematic approach, teacher and student record keeping were crucial: model individual 'progress charts' for tracking the rate of silent reading and percentage scores on comprehension quizzes were provided.[66] The notion of 'senior' and 'junior' groups as well indicates the kind of stratification by test results which was advocated. While the former would 'be expected to proceed rapidly through each chapter' and progress to 'the available supply of supplementary material', the latter would alternate between 'group discussions' of stories with the senior group and remedial 'element drill' drawn from Dolch's, Thorndike's and Munroe's 'Word Lists from Remedial Reading'.[67]

Testing and grouping thus acted as a psychometric prelude for the larger instructional programme. There was to be joint 'discussion with a short interpretative activity' before the breaking off into groups for 'comprehensive or technical activities'.[68] 'Reading and literary skills' (listed as 'comprehension skills', 'technical skills', and 'techniques for the appreciation of literature') were to be taught in order, following the format of 'progressive development' through 'game-type element drills' and other specific lessons.

Many of the skills, however, were covered in (disposable) 'Reading Activity Books' provided for each student. Intended to 'supplement, but . . . not supplant, the blackboard lessons',[69] these books were alleged to

> give invaluable training in word perception, in read-and-do, in thinking-while-you-read. They introduce new words in context, review old words in new contexts, give word and phrase recognition practice. They train also in selecting, associating, comparing and evaluating both facts and ideas.[70]

Teachers then could treat different reading groups with a range of experiences. They could provide a 'formal, full-dress teaching lesson' which entailed introduction to topics, motivating the children to read, vocabulary, 'setting' or 'word study'. This would lead to 'silent reading' and a post-reading discussion to check and 'correct' 'the pupil's grasp of new ideas and new words'. Or they could alternate these typical silent reading lessons with 'element lessons' or 'practice lessons':

> a ten to fifteen minute lesson in which the pupils practice one or another of the different skills of reading as: eye movement, word or phrase recognition, fusing, getting the meaning of a new word from the context, the different types of phonic exercise, reading at different speeds, practice in different types of comprehension exercise.[71]

These, according to the manual, were 'generally blackboard lessons . . . preparing for and supplementing the Workbook Exercises'. Additionally, the teachers' handbook cited examples of specialized drill exercises to contend with 'poor readers' ' habits (e.g., 'faulty eye movement', 'vocalization', 'single word reading', 'inadequate phonics', 'inadequate reading vocabulary').[72]

These basic formats — silent reading lessons, drill lessons and workbook exercises — could be alternated with sustained supervised silent reading and oral reading. In sum, these were the major instructional treatments specified for the Canadian Parade series at the intermediate elementary level. With Quance's weekly spelling lists, these skill-based activities formed the core of early literacy training.

Yet Dickie's approach did not exclude totally a range of other activities and the resultant pedagogy is a curious and ostensibly contradictory synthesis of old and new, traditional and progressive. To teach literature, such traditional, classicist activities as choral reading, practice at 'reading aloud' literary passages, poems, and plays, and 'speech training' are noted. In the latter, students of the 1950s, like their nineteenth century predecessors, were to learn to 'stand in correct posture' and practise 'breathing, voice production, and resonance, and articulation'.[73] 'Breathy voice', 'harsh voice', and 'shrill' and 'nasal' voices were to be overcome through the 'proper reinforcement of tone'.[74]

In the rush to systematize instruction Dickie and colleagues had not neglected either the contemporary preoccupation with Canadian content or the Deweyian concern with the 'enterprise'. Throughout the guidebook teachers were encouraged to 'integrate' the particular contents of stories with social studies, and follow up their lessons with 'projects and activities'.

The following sample lesson, on the story 'Kidnapped' from the grade 5 textbook, *Gay Adventures*,[75] exemplifies the directive quality of the teachers' guide and the particular ideological focus on Canadian content to be taught.

Explain to pupils that in those days the United States as well as Canada belonged to Britain. Then the people of the United States quarrelled with Britain over the taxes. . . . The quarrel went on until many Americans decided that the only thing to do was to separate from Britain and form a country of their own. The two countries went to war and the Americans won their freedom. Most of them were anxious to form a separate country, but a number of people did not approve of this. They wished to . . . remain as part of the British Empire. These people were called United Empire Loyalists. The Separatists treated the Loyalists very harshly, taking their property . . . ill-treating many and even killing some. Many of the Loyalists moved to Canada where they could be free and yet remain British.[76]

This complex rendering of background knowledge and story content obviously is as much for the teachers' benefit as for the students'. It epitomizes the way in which modern teachers' guides provided teachers with a script to follow not only for the prescription of activities and lessons but for the highly ideological explication of text content. This passage was followed in the guidebook by a specification of teaching strategies:

> Before the pupils commence reading the selection, show them a map of Canada and the United States and point out the Richelieu running through the State of New York and the Province of Quebec.[77]

Teachers were encouraged to use the basal reading series as a departure point for the integrated teaching of history, geography, sciences, as well as a means for the systematic inculcation of reading skills. This 'pre-reading' motivation, and provision of background knowledge (which mediated how the child interpreted the text) was followed by 'post-reading' activities: 'arranging events in story order'; 'dictionary work'; 'listing of main points'; 'making an outline', 'tests of achievement in map reading', and so forth. Subsequently, teachers were instructed to 'assign workbook exercises on pages 28 and 29 of *Workbook for Gay Adventures*' for most students, and to turn to 'element drills' in 'word perception' and 'dictionary practice' for 'poor readers'.

As regards the 'project method', teachers were told that 'this story might be useful in a unit or enterprise on Pioneer Life' which might involve the construction of 'The Durham boat, the bateau, the locks, the camp of the Indians, the bear's nest in the hay' or the painting of 'a frieze . . . depict-ing . . . the trip, making a cabin, finding Ann'.[78] However, the compre-hensiveness which this exemplary instructional script provided for structur-ing the teaching of text may have discouraged the development of fuller, more extended enterprises.

On the one hand, teachers of the Canadian Parade basals were encouraged to mix instructional activities and to vary their teaching to meet the needs of specific groups of children. On the other, a rigid pedagogical agenda was laid out. On the basis of their reading of standardized reading achievement test results, they were to select from prescribed pedagogical treatments and prepared workbook exercise sheets. No doubt in many class-rooms the aforementioned format, comprising pre-reading discussion/silent reading/post-reading discussion/exercise and worksheet, became the staple of literacy instruction, repeated daily for months at a time as children moved lock-step through the text in sequence. The cumulative effect of this exhaustive set of textual directives was the establishment of a machinery of literacy instruction which entailed the teaching of standardized texts in standardized classroom literacy events. This is exemplified most graphically in the guidelines for teachers laid out in the *Teacher's Manual for the Canadian Spellers*.[79]

As described, Quance developed for teachers a systematic and comprehensive approach to spelling that could be undertaken for roughly fifteen to thirty minutes on a daily basis for the full Canadian school year:

> The plan followed . . . is that of dividing the work of each grade into thirty-six lessons, and each lesson into five parts — one part for each of five days. . . . Thirty of the lessons are used for the development of new work.[80]

This Monday-through-Friday pre-test/post-test system was adopted by various Canadian Departments of Education and in the US and Australia. To implement this scheme, the textbook series provided two running scripts: the textbooks provided daily instructions to the pupil ('What to Do Each Day') which were matched by the manual's instructions for the teacher ('The Weekly Program'). There was exacting complementarity between the rules for students expressed in the textbook and the guidebook specifications of teacher behaviour. Consider for instance, the day-by-day injunctions laid out for grade 3 teachers and students.

On Monday ('Look at Your Words'), the student turned to his/her textbook and was told to 'Read the story. Your teacher will say each of Your New Words. Look at each and say it after her. Find each word in the story. Write each on the paper.'[81] The teacher was told to undertake a 'conversation about the picture' as a 'stimulating approach to the reading . . . and the study of the words of the lesson'. Following this, the manual instructed the teacher:

> The next step is for the teacher to pronounce each word in the list . . . and to have the pupils say it after her. The teacher's pronunciation should be natural (not exaggerated), distinct, and accurate. Check the children's pronunciation for such mistakes as 'goin'' and 'jist'. . . . When the words are being pronounced by the teacher and the pupils, the pupils should look at them in the word list. They should then find them in the story, and write them on a piece of paper.[82]

This Monday procedure, like the total programme, was to be followed by both teacher and student with little or no deviation. Throughout, the teacher's text reinforces this with enjoinders to 'follow the regular steps', 'follow carefully each step in the procedure', and so forth. The only variation arises in the specification of possible discussion topics (e.g., 'Talk about going to the store and shopping for Christmas') and in the notation of particular mispronunciations to guard against. The resultant regimentation of classroom interaction is particularly interesting in light of the observation that 'on Monday the pupils [have] looked at *their* words and saw them in *meaningful context — their* story' [emphasis added].

On Tuesday ('Learn about Your Words'), students were asked to 'Do what it asks you to do under Learn about Your Words. Look at each word before you write it. Write each word carefully.'[83] In individual lessons, students were told to 'be sure to write the number of each part on paper', while undertaking exercises in the placement of apostrophes, syllabification, filling in missing letters, recognizing compound words, and other subskills of spelling. The guide explained to the teacher that these exercises were 'inductive procedures' optimally suited to teach the 'essential generalizations in word meaning and in word building'.[84] It instructed the teacher 'to supervise all their work closely at first, and continue to do so until they show that they have gained the power to do it independently'.[85]

On Wednesday ('Test on Your Words'), students were told to 'write each of Your Words on a piece of paper as your teacher says it. Keep this paper. Draw a line through each word that you missed. Beside each of these, write it as it is in your book'.[86] The teacher was instructed:

> The correct procedure in giving the test is, first, to say the word distinctly; second, to read the sentence in which the word is used, stressing the word very slightly; then to say the word again, when the pupils write it.[87]

Recall that Quance believed that sentences should provide the words in 'contextual material'. Consequently, his series not only provided the words but also specified sentences for the test. For the words 'has', 'three', 'coming', 'where' and 'hot' in lesson twenty-one of the grade 2 speller, he offered the following:

1. The postman has a parcel.
2. Grandpa has three pigs.
3. Is Jim coming to the ball game?
4. Where is my coat?
5. The sun is hot.[88]

Regardless of whatever authentic contextual meanings may have been generated either in ('their') discussion or reading of the story, the teacher was told to adhere to these pre-stipulated sentences and follow exact procedures for stress, intonation and repetition.

After this pre-test, the teacher was expected to monitor students, ensuring that 'words that have been misspelled should be rewritten correctly beside the wrong form'.[89] The list was to be retained by the students 'until after the study period on Thursday'. On Thursday ('Make Sure of Your Words'), students were told to 'study the words that you missed last Friday and yesterday'.[90] If they had few errors, they were told to expect that 'your teacher may ask you to learn the More Words to Study'. A five-point system for further memorization was laid out:

1. Look at the word. Say it softly. If it has more than one part or syllable, say the word again, part by part, as rab bit, while looking at the letters in each syllable.
2. Look at the word and say the letters to yourself two times. If the word has more than one syllable, say the letters in each syllable by themselves.
3. Without looking at the word, write it.
4. Find the word in your list. See if it is right. Write it two more times.
5. If you spelled it wrong, study the word again as in steps 1, 2, 3, and 4, looking carefully at the letters that you missed.[91]

During this study period, as the student followed this script, the teacher was to play an 'active and helpful role': 'she should take extreme care to see that the pupils . . . study their words in accordance with the method of studying a word outlined at the beginning of the pupils's book'.[92] As in Tuesday's preliminary study, then, the teacher was required to do little direct (much less creative) instruction. In all, the teacher's role was to monitor and enforce student adherance to procedures laid out in the textbook.

On Friday ('Test on Your Words Again'), students were made to 'Write Your New Words and Your Review Sentence as your teacher says each'.[93] The final test was similar in format to the pre-test but pupils were also to be tested on words they had missed in previous weeks ('Words You Missed Last Friday') and on 'enrichment' words ('More Words to Study'). Teachers were also provided with a marking procedure: 'Pupils may mark their own test papers with benefit but only if this is done under careful supervision.' Following the test, each pupil was to mark her/his score on a chart entitled 'Your Spelling Record', adding errors to her/his 'spelling notebook' for next week's retesting.

This system of charting student results in figure 3, matched by those provided in various basal reading series, was designed to generate student pride in achievement and incentive for improvement. Each student was provided with a progress chart on the back of her/his speller. A more subtle management effect was achieved insofar as such charting provided teachers with a systematic record-keeping system for tracking student progress.

To complete the curricular package, Quance provided teachers with 'a modified plan' designed for occasions when 'the five-day week is broken by

YOUR SPELLING RECORD

WEEKLY FRIDAY TESTS

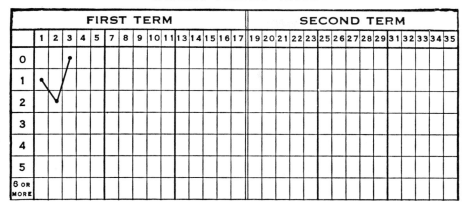

How to Mark Your Record.—Draw in Your Spelling Notebook a Record like the one above. The numbers along the top tell the weeks. Those along the side tell the number of words that you miss. Mark Your Record in this way. If you miss 1 word the first week, 2 words the second, and 0 words the third, put dots in the centre of the spaces and join the dots as above. If you have no words wrong each week Your Record will show a straight line along the top. Try to keep it there.

YOUR REVIEW TEST RECORD

	FIRST REVIEW		SECOND REVIEW		THIRD REVIEW		FOURTH REVIEW		FIFTH REVIEW		SIXTH REVIEW		1ST TERM REVIEW		2ND TERM REVIEW	
0																
2																
4																
6																
8																
10 OR MORE																

How to Mark Your Record.—Draw in Your Spelling Notebook a Record like the one above. During the year you will have six Review Tests and two Term Review Tests. You will write these tests in two parts, one on Tuesday and one on Thursday. Mark Your Record in this way. If you miss 4 words on the Tuesday test put a dot in the space opposite 4. If you miss 3 words on the Thursday test, put the dot on the line between 2 and 4. Join the dots as above.

Figure 3. Student Progress Chart from *The Canadian Speller.*
Source: Frank Quance, *The Canadian Speller* (3rd. Ed.) (Toronto: W.J. Gage, 1950), back cover. Reprinted by permission.

a holiday'. A full 'six weeks review' was similarly structured, giving students a week to study again words they previously had found difficult. Quance also experimented with the development of an adjunct 'text-workbook' for the series, a disposable exercise book to be used during review weeks.[94]

This mode of spelling instruction, then, epitomized the kind of technocratic approach to curriculum, instruction and assessment advocated by many postwar administrators, researchers and educators. Teachers and students were provided with correlating instructional scripts, which relied on redundancy of interaction, exercise and procedure for effectiveness. The *technical form* of the curriculum thus circumscribed instruction and assessment and this scheme for the management of daily instructional events was virtually 'teacherproof'. Teachers were provided with step-by-step instructions, many of which, as noted, concerned keeping the students (and the teachers themselves) in line with the total scheme provided. Assessment was systematized. Variables such as teacher-generated sentences and student response to the prose passages were eliminated from the pre- and post-test procedures and a gridlike recording system for monitoring student progress was included in the curricular package. Little was left to chance.

In all, this kind of standardized literacy pedagogy, recognizable to most Canadian or American postwar students, allocated distinct activities for each day of the week, and was repeated weekly. This routine was broken only by a review lesson every six weeks. Parallel curricular technologies were developed for the teaching of grammar, handwriting and mathematics. In this case, each week, each day and each moment in the classroom literacy event would follow an 'orderly procedure'. It is not that this is necessarily bad pedagogy, and no doubt many researchers and teachers would make the case that the effectiveness of each procedure (e.g., the steps for 'word study') is empirically verifiable. In this manner, the total standardized textbook/instructional event/assessment sequence operated tautologically. It was a closed system capable of providing its own justification and confirmation. For there can be little doubt that such test-driven instruction and test-based curricula would yield higher test scores, verifying their own validity in terms of the application of the technical criteria and apparatuses upon which they had been developed and implemented.

Yet the sum educational effect of this kind of instruction entails far more than the simple learning of spelling. For the textbook here provided a strict and inflexible sequence of behaviours for literacy learning: the teacher's manual provided a like sequence of behaviours for literacy teaching. Accordingly, a strict code of teacher and student conduct reigned over the teaching of the interpretative code for the actual reading and writing of and speaking about text.

A defensible historical justification for this kind of explicit control over teachers could be mounted. With a postwar teacher shortage, burgeoning enrolments, and the wholesale induction of war veterans into teaching ranks throughout English-Canada, many classroom teachers were grossly under-trained.[95] It is certain that many teachers would have been unable to provide, for example, the kind of detailed (or biased) information about the United Empire Loyalists offered by the Canadian Parade teachers' guide-book. Without Quance's handbook, others might have reverted, for better or worse, to a nineteenth-century rote, drill approach to the teaching of spelling, teaching as they were taught. But these total curricular packages could hardly be expected to engender the humane, 'socialized recitation' of the 'enterprise' advocated by progressives like King and Dickie.

As discursive practices they were, apart from all else, forms of control, management systems whereby both teachers and students could be deskilled and reskilled for the full thirty-six weeks of the school year. As forms of ideological incorporation, they were means for the imposition of attitudes and behaviours. Students learned to function on the basis of impersonal oral and written instructions *and* to accept classification and grouping on the basis of scientific survey information. As a theoretical basis for the understanding of literacy and the literate, they corroborated the provincial Department's dominant categories of description and justifications for particular forms of literate and oral intersubjectivity.

Teaching Literacy by Numbers and the Pedagogical Double Bind

While the likes of Conway advocated more standardized testing, grouping and record-keeping — hallmarks, according to Bowles and Gintis, of twentieth-century meritocracy[96] — many teachers' guides and curricular documents tended to advocate both this technocratic approach and more overtly progressive methods. Some analyses maintain that industrial-style education of the progressive era yielded an inexorable machinery of social reproduction: that schools, in the disbursement of literate competences and social understandings, were flawless imitations of factories, producing masses of acquiescent workers under quality controlled conditions, selecting against children of the poor and ethnic and in favour of those of a white collar elite.[97] There is, however, a set of discursive and ideological contradictions within the postwar discourse on practice. The dual strands of progressive pedagogy, the scientific and humanistic, continued to coexist side by side.[98] Accordingly, literacy was conceived of both as a set of 'mechanical skills' and as a cultural process capable of enriching individual social experience.

We could speculate that in consequence the teacher was caught in what psychologists and communications theorists have termed a 'double-bind' situation. In his classic contribution to the study of schizophrenia, Gregory Bateson draws attention to the role of context in the generation of conflicting messages: when 'unresolvable sequences of experience' occur, the human subject is confronted with the 'double-bind situation'.[99]

Bateson explicates what he considers necessary conditions for the double bind. Two or more persons must be involved and the injunctions 'inflicted' upon the subject must occur from 'repeated experiences'. Bateson does not locate the source of schizophrenia in a 'single traumatic experience' but rather in 'habitual expectation'. The actual double bind emerges from the contradiction between 'primary' and 'secondary negative injunctions'. First the human subject is confronted with an injunction to do something to avoid punishment. The next 'necessary ingredient' entails a 'secondary injunction'. Bateson draws on Russell's theory of logical types to explain that this secondary injunction stands 'conflicting with the first at a more abstract level' though, like the primary injunction it too is enforced with possible negative consequences. The double bound individual, then, is confronted with conflicting injunctions to action, each with potentially negative consequences. Finally, a 'tertiary negative injunction' prohibits the subject 'from escaping from the field'; that is, the choice between primary and secondary injunctions is enforced. Bateson concludes that this sequence 'may then be sufficient to precipitate panic or rage'.[100]

Following Bateson, others have outlined instances and ramifications of double-bind situations in everyday life. Watzlawick, Beavin and Jackson designate how one form of the double bind, the paradoxical injunction, can place people 'occupying the one-down position' in 'untenable positions'.[101] Their examination of paradoxical injunctions — single utterances, imperative statements, commands and orders which in themselves embody paradox — indicates how all of Bateson's conditions can be met simultaneously. First, an institutionally bound interactional context may itself serve as a tertiary injunction. To use Watzlawick *et al.*'s example, a captain's order to a subordinate is binding; the subordinate has no choice but to comply by the nature of the codes and rules governing that relationship. Furthermore, they note that

> the most frequent form in which paradox enters into the pragmatics of human communication is through an injunction demanding specific behaviour. ... The prototype of this message is, therefore, 'Be spontaneous!' Anybody confronted with this injunction is in an untenable position, for to comply he would have to be spontaneous within a frame of compliance, of nonspontaneity.[102]

This example, of the person enjoined to 'be free', or 'be spontaneous' or of the child told 'Don't be so obedient',[103] may be an apt description of the plight of the postwar teacher. Bound by the ethical injunctions of progressive education, s/he was encouraged by the likes of Dickie and provincial inspectors trained under the auspices of King's 'socialized recitation' to exercise spontaneity, to tailor the curriculum and instruction to local and individual needs, to be flexible in the teaching of text according to her/his reading of the situation and human subjects in question. Following the requirement that teachers 'begin with testing' and 'grouping', the authors of the Canadian Parade teachers' manual left actual procedures up to the teacher. Echoing Conway, they assured teachers that 'suggestions made are suggestions only. The teacher will use them only when and as she thinks best.'[104] Apart from the aforementioned drilling of 'poor readers' in subskill areas, a variety of patently child-centred interventions were recommended: the enterprise method, a programme of curricular integration, the informed modification of textbook passage selection, and so forth.

Yet the converse side of this paradoxical injunction was the scientific standardization of literacy training within the very discourse that demanded innovation. While invited to extrapolate and to a certain extent experiment in order to address individual and local needs, teachers were confronted with an exhaustive, comprehensive and binding set of instructional procedures *and* an increasingly vigilant system of centralized administrative surveillance and control. There is some evidence in the Public Schools reports of the 1940s and 1950s that teachers who did not appear to be embracing the 'new pedagogy' were subjected to criticism by local administrators and inspectors. However, no correlative institutional apparatus for enforcing the humanistic strand of progressivism was developed. This would seem to be in part the result of the very character of Deweyian child-centred education, for while the 'scientific' element was being fully implemented via a body of technicist practices, the humanist injunction was formulated as an ethical/moral responsibility. As such it was less easily enforced through such devices as testing and standardized curriculum. King and Weir's 1940s frustration with overt 'formalism' in secondary English teaching attests to this. But this is not to say that such ethical imperatives, though more abstract, were any less binding once instilled through teacher training and repetition at all levels of institutional discourse.

More concretely, though, teachers did have to contend with yearly provincial standardized achievement testing, traditional year-end curricular examinations, and inspectors and principals armed with curriculum documents. With additional complementary guidelines issued by publishers, these conditions imply an educational scenario which encouraged pedagogical (and hence, literate) conformity. The teaching of reading and language arts was undergoing an historical reformation towards increased standardization. Teachers were encouraged to view the process of teaching as a technical enterprise, entailing the systematic and exact deployment of a curricular technology. In tandem with this recasting of the teacher as curricular manager, literate competence was normed into a series of discrete, technically imparted skills. The related *universal* assessment programme, moreover, functioned as a tertiary injunction, making adherence to the humanist injunction unlikely, if not contradictory.

A correlative pressure resulted from the premium which all of these instructional materials placed on 'integration'. As we have seen, teachers were encouraged in publishers' guidebooks and Departmental curriculum guides to teach language arts in an interrelated, cohesive manner: Quance's texts, for example, were supposed to complement 'related language arts'. Dickie's enterprise method was premised on the melding together of lessons in various modes of oracy and literacy around particular themes and pieces of literature, many of which covered social studies and science topics. Indeed both the Canadian Spellers and the Canadian Parade readers actively challenged teachers to join reading and language arts instruction with other curricular subjects. Yet, as in many present-day classrooms, the rhetoric of curricular integration may have been, in practice, hollow. The very format of these modern curricular packages — adjunct materials, comprehensive exercises, scripts for managing instructional events, workbooks and tests — may have operated as a pedagogical straitjacket, its very comprehensiveness forming a disincentive to deviate from prescribed guidelines. At the very least, it led to a compartmentalization, a set of discursive and behavioural boundaries for the classroom organization of knowledge and intersubjectivity.

Consider, for instance, the contradiction in Quance's spelling programme. Clearly he conceived of spelling as something which occurred in the context of writing, with correlative effects in students' reading. His lists were derived from children's school writing, and he argued that spelling was optimally taught in relevant texts which expressed a clear and direct relationship to children's experiential and cultural background. If this was the spirit of his venture, its effect was the opposite. The strict daily spelling routine — fully spanning the thirty-six weeks of the school year, linked by periodic 'review tests' every sixth week and recorded on comprehensive progress charts — heralded a mechanization of spelling instruction matched in its comprehensiveness perhaps only by the 'muscular movement' approach to the teaching of handwriting used in the 1930s and '40s. Quance's system of dictionary work, skill exercises, pre- and post-tests, effectively wrenched the teaching of spelling from the context of the teaching of writing. This disjunction, advocates of 'process' approaches to writing instruction note, remains today.

The identifiably progressive spirit and intent of many of these curricular packages, then, stood in contradiction with their technical and dramaturgical form: the result of ever more sophisticated curriculum development and marketing, and of the perceived need to systematize, to simplify and to standardize instructional procedures for the classroom teacher. In its totality, the code left little to chance.

In sum, the 'innovative' and creative teacher would not have been encouraged by the growing use of standardized curricula and assessments. Quite the contrary, s/he might well have felt stultified by the ever more comprehensive code of rules, injunctions, and guidelines governing how s/he should mediate children's reading and writing of text: meet local and individual needs; teach in a way which will yield results verifiable by centralized authorities; be creative and innovative, allow the children to explore language and literacy through experience; administer standardized tests, drills, spelling tests, and remediation; meet the needs of every child in a non-discriminatory manner; use IQ and reading achievement tests to assess, classify, group and treat children; integrate language and literacy across the curriculum; and teach spelling and reading for two hours each day following a repeated, set scheme.

The code of literacy instruction, made explicit in a voluminous discursive script on 'how to' teach literacy, constrained teachers' freedom to design classroom instructional events. It simply needed to be enacted by numbers. The primary injunction for teacher behaviour was to implement practices which systematized and standardized the teaching of literacy; the secondary injunction was the more abstract ethos of progressive education, to 'teach the child, not the subject'. This is not to suggest that postwar teachers were aware of this contradiction or of possible related educational ramifications. Indeed, many retrospectively appraise the situation by noting that 'we just didn't know that IQ tests were working against certain children'.[105] But they were double-bound, caught between what must have appeared to curriculum developers, departmental officials and many of their colleagues to be complementary prescriptions, but what seem in historical retrospect a significant theoretical and practical rupture within postwar literacy instruction.

Inasmuch as those progressive, child-centred practices could yield *measurable* improvement in students' literacy as assessed by standardized tests, there was no overt contradiction between these dual strands. For, as noted, the standardized texts of literacy instruction — themselves generated according to empirical research by Thorndike, Gray and others — offered systematic pedagogy which if adhered to would no doubt yield systematically assessible progress. The technocrat approach was predicated on the match between curriculum development (and hence control over the selection and design of the textual stimulus), systematic grouping and treatment (and hence control over access to different texts), and assessment of the acquisition of competence (and hence control over reader response). For teachers, traditionalists and progressives alike, to assert their individual proclivities in developing truly divergent instructional settings and events would have potentially thrown a major hitch into this seamless system which Departments of Education, university-based researchers and curriculum developers, and publishers together were endeavouring to establish.

By the mid-1950s the bureaucratic and discursive machinery for a standardized approach to literacy instruction was in place, vestiges of which remain with us today. The categories of the textual code for the teaching of literacy, moreover, though putatively descriptive, had the power to select for and against certain kinds of teaching and certain kinds of reading, in effect *making* a distinct kind of literacy in the aspiring child.

Notes and References

1. Umberto Eco, *The Role of the Reader* (Bloomington: Indiana University Press, 1979).
2. See Carolyn Baker and Peter Freebody, 'Talk Around Text: Construction of Textual and Teacher Authority in Classroom Discourse', in Suzanne de Castell, Allan Luke and Carmen Luke (eds), *Language, Authority and Criticism: Readings on the School Textbook* (London: Falmer Press, forthcoming/1988). Cf. Courtney B. Cazden, 'Texts and Contexts: A Response', in de Castell, *et al.* (eds), *Language, Authority and Criticism.*
3. See Jean Anyon, 'Social Class and School Knowledge', *Curriculum Inquiry*, 11 (1981), 3–32.
4. Michael W. Apple, *Education and Power* (London: Routledge and Kegan Paul, 1982), p. 114.
5. For discussion of the concept of 'interpretive norms', see Jonathan Culler, *The Pursuit of Signs: Semiotics, Literature, Deconstruction* (Ithaca: Cornell University Press, 1981), esp. ch. 1. Interpretive communities are examined in the context of reader response theory by Stanley Fish, *Is There a Text in This Class? The Authority of Interpretive Communities* (Cambridge, Mass.: Harvard University Press, 1981).
6. Anthony Wilden, 'Semiotics as Praxis: Strategy and Tactics', *Semiotic Inquiry* 1 (1981), 25–6.
7. Ibid.; see also Anthony Wilden, *System and Structure: Essays in Communication and Exchange* (London: Tavistock, 1980), ch. 7.
8. See Pierre Bourdieu and Jean Claude Passeron, *Reproduction in Education, Society and Culture* (London: Sage, 1977).
9. Shirley B. Heath, 'Protean Shapes in Literacy Events: Ever-Shifting Oral and Literate Traditions', in Deborah Tannen (ed.), *Spoken and Written Language: Exploring Orality and Literacy* (Norwood, N.J.: Ablex, 1982), p. 93.
10. See, for instance, Shirley B. Heath, *Ways with Words: Language, Life and Work in Classrooms and Communities* (Cambridge: Cambridge University Press,

1983); Deborah Keller-Cohen, 'Literate Practices in a Modern Credit Union', *Language in Society* 16 (1987), 20.

11. See Jack Goody, *The Logic of Writing and the Organization of Society* (Cambridge: Cambridge University Press, 1986).

12. Ibid., pp. 16–17; Carmen Luke, Suzanne de Castell and Allan Luke, 'Beyond Criticism: The Authority of the School Text', *Curriculum Inquiry* 13 (1983), 111–27.

13. Baker and Freebody, 'Talk Around Text'.

14. Michel Foucault, 'Questions of Method', *Ideology and Consciousness* 8 (1981), 5–6.

15. Ibid., 6.

16. See David Tyack and Elizabeth Hansott, *The Managers of Virtue: Public School Leadership in America, 1820–1980* (New York: Basic Books, 1982); Raymond B. Callahan, *Education and the Cult of Efficiency* (Chicago: University of Chicago Press, 1962).

17. Apple, *Education and Power*, p. 150.

18. For a description of the division's postwar foundation and activities, see Clifford B. Conway, 'Research and Testing in British Columbia', *Canadian Education* (June, 1949), 59–79.

19. See, for example, ibid.; Clifford B. Conway, 'Fundamentals of Testing', *British Columbia Schools* 2 (No. 2, 1947), 38–9; 'Further Fundamentals of Testing', *British Columbia Schools* 2 (No. 4, 1947), 29–33; 'The Holding Power of British Columbia Schools', *British Columbia Schools* 2 (No. 4, 1947), 33–4; 'Centralized Test Programs in Education', *Education* 1 (No. 13, 1956), 49–52.

20. Clifford B. Conway, 'Suggestions for the Improvement of Reading', (Victoria: Division of Tests, Standards and Research, 1955).

21. See, for example, Conway, 'Centralized Test Programs in Education'.

22. See Clifford B. Conway, 'Survey of English Composition' (Victoria: Division of Tests, Standards and Research, 1952); 'Ability to Read in the Field of Mathematics: Results of an Experimental Test Survey' (Victoria: Division of Tests, Standards and Research, 1956); 'Report on the Ability to Read in the Field of Social Studies' (Victoria: Division of Tests, Standards and Research, 1956).

23. Clifford B. Conway and Ellen L. Brown, 'The Establishment of University Entrance Standards in Required and Optional Subjects', *Canadian Education* 11 (No. 2, 1956), 17–30.

24. Conway, 'Centralized Test Programs in Education', 51.

25. Ibid.

26. Conway, 'Suggestions for the Improvement of Reading', p. 2.

27. Clifford B. Conway, 'Handwriting in Grades V and VII' (Victoria: Division of Tests, Standards and Research, 1949).

28. Conway, 'Suggestions for the Improvement of Reading', p. 2.

29. Ibid.

30. British Columbia Department of Education, *Programme for the Intermediate Grades* (Victoria: Department of Education, 1954), p. 53.

31. Conway, 'Suggestions for the Improvement of Reading', p. 2.

32. British Columbia Department of Education, *Programme for the Intermediate Grades*, pp. 52–3; see also, William S. Gray (ed.), *Thirty-sixth Yearbook of the National Society for the Study of Education: The Teaching of Reading* (Chicago: University of Chicago Press, 1937).

was not, for instance, following the researched practice of phonics instruction.

How did this reigning model of literacy-related curriculum, instruction and assessment weather historical change? A brief return to the context of Canadian and British Columbian educational politics highlights subsequent criticism of this dominant postwar approach to teaching language and literacy.

Historical Aftermath: Back to the Basics Again

Certainly if any historical event marked the reevaluation of the educational status quo it was the launching of Sputnik in 1957. The apparent success of countries like Canada and the United States in managing the unprecedented growth of public education in the aftermath of World War II was called abruptly into question and public opinion was galvanized into a thorough reappraisal of schooling. In a Cold War atmosphere marked by fear that the Russians were capable of technologically superseding the West, public and academic assaults on what Johnson eulogized as 'the democratizing tide' of Progressivism were renewed.[10] The Principal of Toronto's University College, for example, held that

> So-called progressivism has been universally accompanied by an immediate and drastic decline in the subjects that have hitherto furnished the formal disciplines.[11]

Many educators renewed Neatby's criticism of progressivism as thwarting the achievement of literacy. Noting that 'the movement towards universal education . . . [is] ideally a movement towards universal literacy', George Whalley, head of the English department at Queen's University, revisited the 'inadequacies' of reigning pedagogical approaches, namely 'the assumption that language can be fully explained as instrumental, as "a medium of communication"', and 'as a "technique of communication"'.[12] He, like many classicists, found fault with the actual materials for the teaching of literacy, arguing that 'the prescribing of inappropriate reading — of books too trivial to nourish imagination or respect' generated in students 'weariness of response'.

Teacher educators and educational researchers attempted to allay public anxiety over the state of education, sensing that the greatest danger lay in reform and innovation for its own sake. Some, like Phillip Penner, critiqued the emergent human capital arguments:

> For as long as 'Sputniks' and 'Luniks' circle the earth and sun and seem merely to maintain the age-old balance of terror, there is no

new frontier in space, nor is it in an education conceived only in the narrow terms of defense. ... One of our tasks as teachers and educators is to disabuse ourselves and the public of false hopes.[13]

In British Columbia, led since the early 1950s by the populist, conservative Social Credit government of W.A.C. Bennett, the response was a fresh criticism of the school system. On 11 January 1958 the *Province* ran an editorial which called for BC schools to go 'Back to basic education', reporting on the move of Ontario Education Minister Dunlop 'to reintroduce new regulations to reintroduce competition to Ontario schools and return to the fundamentals in elementary and secondary schools'.[14] Dunlop credited the 'Sputnik publicity on Russia's approach to education' with the reform movement sweeping North America. Once again the target was progressivism: it was assumed in the editorial that elementary schools did not emphasize the '3R's sufficiently, and that the current curriculum was not competitive'.

This mood was exacerbated by periodic hysterical articles by a press sceptical of educational standards. In 1959 a front-page *Vancouver Province* headline exclaimed 'Illiterate Entered Grade Seven'.[15] The case of an eighteen-year-old Burnaby student who completed grade 7 without being able to read and write was documented and the boy's subsequent prison record — he was charged with fifty-three cases of breaking and entering — was used to indict the school system.

A climate of public uncertainty and fear thus led to the Chant Royal Commission. Then Minister of Education, Leslie R. Peterson, recently described his sense of the situation:

> They were unsettled times. When you add to that the very large increases in numbers of students each year to cope with and the lack of funds ... we had a great shortage of teachers in those early years. In the late fifties and early sixties I had to establish personnel whose responsibility was to recruit teachers from England and I'd raid other countries.[16]

In addition to the growing political pressure for educational change, and an acrimonious public debate fuelled by Cold War rhetoric, the British Columbia system had continued to grow in accordance with high birth rates and migration. Between 1957 and 1959 the total enrolment rose from 301,523 to 327,987 students, with a rise in elementary school enrolment of over 12 per cent.[17] Nor had the province overcome the postwar shortage of qualified teachers: despite the move towards more university-level training, the number of teachers with two years or less of post-secondary training continued to hover around the 55 per cent mark throughout the 1950s.[18]

In January 1958, at the height of the furore over schooling, the W.A.C.

Bennett government appointed a Royal Commission to enquire into 'various phases of the provincial educational system with particular attention to programmes of study and pupil achievement'.[19] Between 1950 and 1958 Royal Commissions on education had been undertaken in Ontario, Nova Scotia, Manitoba and Alberta.[20] By the early 1960s they had proliferated to such an extent that one editorial writer was prompted to refer to the 'Royal Commission Industry' as a means for 'cooling off' any 'hot political potato'.[21] But from its inception in the 1920s the progressive/scientific model implemented in British Columbia by Weir, King and colleagues had escaped official governmental scrutiny. The Social Credit government deliberately chose Commissioners without ties to the educational research or teacher-training communities in the province: S.N.F. Chant, Dean of Arts and Science at the University of British Columbia, along with the Vice-President of the Powell River Paper Company, and the general manager of British Columbia Tree Fruits Ltd. The business and resource-based industrial orientation of two of the Commissioners certainly reflected the post-Sputnik concern with economic competitiveness and productivity, the primary industry base of the provincial economy, and the strong rural constituency of Social Credit.

After hearing over 360 formal briefs and visiting 116 schools, the Commission submitted its report in late 1960. The report noted that 'the survival of mankind will very largely depend upon learning more intelligent ways for dealing with problems that threaten the human race' and called for a reorganization of the existing system to accommodate better a two-stream academic/vocational system beginning in grade 8. Although its criticism of school standards and practices was not as negative as anticipated in many quarters, the Commission called for a re-emphasis of 'basic skills and knowledge' and a reorientation of the curriculum away from subjects like art, music and drama towards specialized scientific and vocational studies.[22] This was hailed publicly as a 'depressing, disappointing and reactionary' document by N.V. Scarfe, Dean of Education at the University of British Columbia, who noted that 'it was aimed at destroying progressive teaching methods in British Columbia'.[23] Scarfe's comments largely went unheeded, and yet another return to basics was at hand.

In terms of reading and language arts instruction in the elementary schools, the Chant Commission cited several briefs by local district teachers' associations which argued that 'extensive research has established that a sound background in, and the continued use of phonics is essential to the highest reading and spelling achievement in children'.[24] Parents as well 'expressed dissatisfaction over the lack of progress their children in the primary grades were making in reading, and the majority attributed this to insufficient emphasis on phonics'.[25] Reflecting this popular view of phonics as an instructional panacea, the Commission found fault with the existing curriculum guide's qualified endorsement of phonics as neither 'sufficiently definite or informative'. The Commissioners recounted their observations:

> The observations and inquiries made by the members of the Commission while visiting schools indicated that the use of phonics varied from school to school and from classroom to classroom. In certain Grade I classes, by as late as the end of February, some of the pupils when questioned displayed little knowledge of how to sound out words. In other classes the commissioners observed that the pupils were being taught to sound the letters and syllables of words that were written on the blackboard. In a number of primary grades a common phonetic device was to have the pupils repeat words that rhyme, such as had, bad, dad, sad. Other groups were studying lists of words that commenced with the same letters and sounds, such as cat, cart, can, car, card, etc. However, in some classes these pupils were merely writing these in their exercise books rather than saying them aloud, and it is questionable if this method provides sufficient practice in phonics.[26]

Hence the Commission recommended 'that a more intensive use be made of phonics so that the pupils may be enabled thereby to extend their reading vocabularies by their own reading'. They did not argue for the shelving of the 'sight methods' advocated by Gray, Gates and Dickie, but rather maintained that the combination of both methods 'would give a balanced competence in reading that results neither in slow and stumbling readers nor in mere word pronouncers'.[27] But in a major recommendation which clearly diverged from existing Departmental curricular guidelines, the Commission argued that the formal teaching of phonics should be scheduled separately and that such instruction should be carried right through the elementary school grades.[28]

As for the status of the basics in literacy training, the Commission also recommended teaching a 'mastery of basic grammatical forms' and that teachers take 'greater care to correct mistakes in grammar and to indicate the correct usage in all written work'. Observing the teaching of spelling, the Commissioners toured the schools and 'chose words to be put to pupils', discovering that 'pupils are generally more proficient than they are ordinarily considered to be'.[29] Nonetheless, aspects of Quance's approach were criticized in several briefs, both as too rigid and as not sufficiently systematic and phonetically based. The Commission concluded that spelling lessons should 'include more sentence writing along with the learning of word lists', also noting that the rigid 'grade level assignment' of Quance's list was 'poor' and that 'material of a more challenging type is needed'.[30]

Another key aspect of reading and language arts curriculum was criticized: by 1960 American textbooks constituted 24 per cent of the elementary school materials.[31] While not singling out particular texts, the Commissioners noted that the 'Canadianization' undertaken by branch plant publishers of American texts 'appeared to have been carried out in a sketchy manner' and that 'the point of view from which the text-book has been written nearly always betrays itself in spite of the revisions'.[32] Hence, the Commission recommended 'that the possibility of procuring more Canadian and British textbooks be thoroughly canvassed'. The aim here, was to equalize perceived 'disadvantages in facilities' shared by both Canadian *and* British publishers against their American competitors.

Regarding the actual literary content of textbooks, the Commission noted 'evidence of careless preparation' by many textbook editors. Specifically, in terms of children's reading texts, the following was noted:

> The basic readers for the elementary grades were judged to be satisfactory by most of the teachers except for the Grade IV and VI readers, which were more often judged to be unsatisfactory, largely because of a lack of literary quality. The spellers in use in the elementary schools were criticized for poor organization and some discrepancies in spelling between the readers and spellers were pointed out.[33]

Hence, general recommendations were made 'against the use of abridgements of some well-known children's books'. The argument was made that 'such rewritings reduce the story to a form which destroys its literary value'. Similarly, the Commission maintained that textbooks should 'not be so copiously illustrated with pictures that the literary or informative value of the text is impaired'.

Two other aspects of basic approaches to elementary instruction were criticized: the progressive 'project method' and widespread IQ testing. The Commission noted that the enterprise approach 'should not be substituted for didactic instruction',[34] further cautioning teachers 'to avoid any project method that tends to draw the pupils' attention from the lesson as such'. Finally, the Commission noted that the use of IQ testing led to 'the common tendency to label pupils at an early age' and, moreover, that 'the Commissioners doubted the accuracy of some of the IQ's that appeared on pupils' records'.[35] Hence, they were sceptical of the 'overtendency to overemphasize IQ' in particular and psychological tests in general.

Scarfe's widely reported public judgment that the report was an assault on the foundation of progressivism was valid, at least in terms of the extent to which this particular return to the basics found fault with the very presuppositions, materials and methods of postwar literacy instruction. Many aspects of curriculum and instruction I have described here were scrutinized: the use of American textbooks, Gray and Dickie's emphasis on 'whole word' approaches, the paucity of literary quality in student reading materials, Deweyian 'project methods' of instruction, and the use of standardized testing for purposes of grouping and treatment.

The Chant Commission's findings on literacy instruction in elementary schools, however, were based largely on casual observation and the recommendations forwarded by parents' and teachers' groups. Several historical ironies resulted. First, the criticism of the literary content of upper primary readers contradicts Dickie's attempts to incorporate unabridged passages of literature into the prescribed Canadian Parade series. Despite teachers' apparent satisfaction with readers like the Curriculum Foundation series used in early primary grades, on the basis of the present study the general criticism of the irrelevance and literary poverty of textbooks applies most aptly to the latter series. The Commission's finding of spelling discrepancies between textbooks followed on no doubt from the differences between US, Canadian and UK versions.

Second, while the comments on Quance's approach to the teaching of spelling were defensible, the Commission's claim of the efficacy of phonics highlights its acquiescence to popular wisdom and commonsense about practice. In all, these and like problems throughout the document are the products of the very formulation of the Commission: the exclusion of acknowledged educational experts was intentional and led to a populist, consensus-based assessment.

In addition to Penner and Scarfe, many educators rushed to attack the findings of the Chant Commission. University of British Columbia reading researcher Geraldine Birkett argued that

> It should be emphasized that the recommendations of the Chant Commission do represent a point of view but much research still has to be done to find answers to unresolved questions in the teaching of phonics.[36]

She and others noted furthermore that such innovations as Glen McCracken's New Castle Reading Experiment — a Pennsylvania programme which used filmstrips, slides and pictures to aid the teaching of reading — and 'individualized reading programs' which allowed students to select their own reading materials were being introduced in British Columbia schools.[37] These innovations which led on from solid research foundations, Birkett maintained, were of perhaps more importance than the increased teaching of phonics and the return to the basics of grammar and spelling advocated by the Chant Commission.

As for the publishers, the Vice President of Gage Canada described his sense of the state of literacy and education in a speech delivered to faculty at the University of British Columbia in 1960. W.R. Wees was fully cognizant of the tensions within modern education between technicist and child-centred orientations:

> Thorndike assumed that the child was made up of bits and pieces which he called stimulus-response bonds, and having assumed his bits and pieces, he never could get the child together again. The organismic people have exactly the same trouble with their whole-child theory. Assuming that the child is indivisible, they can describe the child but they can never analyse him because how can they take him apart if he has no parts?[38]

Against the charge that the overemphasis on word recognition should be replaced with a renewed concern with phonics, Wees staunchly defended existing methods:

> In reading, we have achieved techniques in word recognition and pronunciation that we can be happy with — for a while, at least. I can illustrate the usefulness of our techniques in a rather dramatic way. Before the war, in the French areas of New Brunswick, illiteracy was common, in some pockets as high as 36%. At the time modern techniques in teaching French reading to French children were introduced, and today French literacy is almost equal to English literacy.[39]

Yet Wees, who ironically spoke on behalf of the publisher of both Gray and Arbuthnot's and Quance's series, concurred with the position forwarded by Chant, university academics and others regarding paucity of literary quality. He noted the post-McGuffey historical movement away from literary texts to purpose-built pedagogic texts.

> The present content of our reading programs is a hodge-podge, and this has been true ever since children learned to read from reading texts instead of the Bible. I would except McGuffey. Although one might question his concepts, the conceptual continuity in the McGuffey readers is more apparent than in any since. If learning proceeds, as I suspect it does, in patterns of conceptual development, how can we expect growth through reading when we teach a story about the love of God today and The Battle with the Ants tomorrow.[40]

His praise of existing approaches, then, was qualified by a scepticism of the skills orientation of the contemporary model. Wees observed that, too often, understanding of human interaction and concepts was overridden by a narrow preoccupation with teaching the mechanics of reading:

> In many classrooms we don't even teach the story because the course of study . . . talks about syllabification, or beauty of language, or grammatical relationships, and hardly ever mentions the human relationships, the understanding of character, that make the story.[41]

As a publisher, his primary concern was with the lack of identifiable Canadian content in textbook materials. Like the Chant commissioners, Wees felt that the mandates of the Massey Commission nearly a decade earlier largely had been ignored by educational officials. He argued that

> No wonder then our biggest import is other people's ideas. No wonder that the genius of the Canadian people is imitation and that since we probably secretly resent our position we don't even imitate very well. . . . Consider that half our manufacturing, three quarters of our mining and ninety per cent of our oil are controlled from the United States, and that our main exports are primary products. As a nation we are, literally, hewers of wood and drawers of water. And this control extends through the warp and woof of our economic life. Except for company unions, have we one labor union whose headquarters are in Canada?[42]

This economic dependency in turn was tied to the cultural impoverishment evidenced in Canadian textbooks:

> We have no song. We sing the folk songs of the Alabama negro, the Wyoming cowboy, and the heartaches of the Civil War. We read other nation's books. One large Canadian publisher says that he publishes one-half a book a year by a Canadian author. He may import nearly a thousand. Have we five prose writers in Canada for whom we can claim literary originality? Perhaps five. Of children's literature, we have none.[43]

In all, the Sputnik-era criticisms of existing curriculum for the teaching of literacy reflected the greater sense of crisis shared primarily by the public, some teachers, and university faculty in fields other than education. The general critique, framed by Royal Commissions and restated in the popular press and the pronouncements of academics in the humanities throughout Canada, concerned the moral poverty of progressive pedagogy and its inability to convey the basics while encouraging the educational excellence seen to be requisite for technological superiority. The tenor of this criticism was aptly paraphrased in a brief presented to the Chant Commission by a Duncan parents' group:

the noted resistance of local educational researchers and teacher educators to the Chant findings, it is apparent that the province's total educational establishment, whatever its periodic disputes with the Department, maintained a staunch defence of Weir and King's postwar version of progressivism throughout the 1950s and 60s.

A second factor which militated against change was that the paradigm itself, as has been indicated, was embodied in the total curricular packages successfully marketed by publishers. In spite of internal contradictions, the philosophic assumptions and attendant pedagogical practices of progressivism were built into series like the Curriculum Foundation and Canadian Parade readers. Hence the curricular packages themselves may have bred a familiarity with and allegiances towards particular approaches and materials, conveying and reinforcing commonsense conventions for the teaching and learning of literacy. Certainly, any contending text or subsequent replacement text had to compete as both philosophy and technological commodity: it would have to provide adjunct materials sufficient to bear favourable comparison with series like Gray's and Dickie's. The appeal of such complete packages to Departmental administrators, moreover, is understandable in light of the continuing shortage of qualified teachers in the early 1960s.

If Gray, Dickie, and Quance's texts are any indicator, the cycle of textbook obsolescence and replacement after the war was roughly fifteen to twenty years. This may seem like an extensive period, but it was a considerably briefer period than the forty to fifty years of use of the nineteenth-century British Columbia Readers, and the twenty-five years of the Highroads to Reading series. Nonetheless, few subsequent reading series have proved as durable in appeal to teachers and administrators as the Dick and Jane texts. The Chant report also provides evidence that, despite criticism dating back to the early 1950s of their ideological and literary content, the Dick and Jane variety of readers retained popularity among teachers into the early 1960s.

But these empirically verifiable factors alone cannot wholly account for the strength of this particular paradigm of literacy teaching. The legitimation potential of progressivism lay precisely with its ostensibly non-ideological character. For despite recurring accusations that progressivism was an incipient form of socialism, the public was assured continuously that the system had the best interests of *all* children in mind and that these interests were being maintained through the deployment of scientifically verified practices without the loss of educational excellence. The former coincided with the egalitarian, democratic goals of postwar societal development, while the latter ensured the efficiency of the system, in an era where scientific modernity was fast becoming the measure of all things.

Moreover, through the amassing of psychometric data on school achieve-ment, the Department was capable of defusing criticism, and drawing teachers into line with those pedagogical methods which yielded centrally verifiable results.

The battles about practice by and large could be waged in ideologically neutral terms: the stated purposes of the system never really came into ques-tion, for even the Sputnik-era critics of progressivism in jurisdictions like British Columbia, while criticial of secular amorality and rumoured permissiveness, could not fault 'scientific' approaches to education. Rather the debate, beginning from a human-capital argument, centred on the most efficacious methods to be used. The successful resistance to a phonics emphasis waged by Departmental officials and local teacher educators underlines the entrenchment of reigning pedagogical practice based on shared paradigmatic assumptions derived from long-standing research findings. Accordingly, reading experts like Gray, Dickie, and later Russell and Birkett could simply address the populist phonics issue — whether it had been raised by a Rudolf Flesh or a Royal Commission — and proceed to co-opt it, citing research findings for the justification of an eclectic method. Although the terms have changed, the debate continues to this day.

The staying power of the postwar model of literacy instruction, then, lay in its embrace of science and its promise of egalitarian results. The resultant (ideological) approach to the introduction of children into literate culture was self-legitimating, and its purported neutrality enabled it to deflect, or apparently ignore criticism within a socio-political debate centred on technological progress and competitiveness. Nonetheless, this very neutrality precluded it from addressing recurrent critiques of its overt ideological content: the decade-long calls for Canadian nationalism *and* the persistent attacks on its lack of moral and literary quality. Furthermore, as noted in the Chant Report, even subsequent attempts by Dickie and others to address the problem of national content and literary value were looked upon by teachers, scholars in the humanities, and even some publishers with a good deal of scepticism.

Apparently, in the estimation of many educators and public officials, the efforts of Dickie, Quance, Massey and others had not made substantial enough inroads into the neo-colonial hegemony of US curricular materials in the schools. Moreover, the prospects of additional Canadian content were not that great. For Wees and the Chant commissioners spoke in response to the post-Sputnik identity crisis which had beseiged American and Canadian educators in the late 1950s. If anything, because of the perceived Soviet threat to military security and technological superiority, Canada was enter-ing a period of closer economic, military and cultural ties with the US. And in the quest for technological expertise and academic excellence, in the production of trained human capital, in few fields would these renewed allegiances be more evident than in education.

Yet the criticisms of overt ideological bias, of literary poverty, of US influence remain today. The fact that they persist indicates the retention in current practice of significant aspects of the postwar teaching of reading and language arts: basal reading series with emphases on skills continue to coexist with a child-centred stress on thematic and integrated teaching and Monday-through-Friday spelling lists. Standardized reading achievement tests remain the benchmark of the early acquisition of literacy. Recalling Heath's comments that the history of literacy and literacy instruction has implications for current practice, it is with a speculative discussion on the possible educational effects of this particular historical ensemble of practices that the present study concludes.

Literacy and Ideology Reconsidered

> Education may well be, as of right, the instrument whereby every individual, in a society like our own, can gain access to any kind of discourse. But we well know that . . . every educational system is a political means of maintaining or of modifying the appropriation of discourse with the knowledge and powers it carries with it. . . . What is an educational system, after all, if not a ritualisation of the word; if not a qualification of some fixing of roles for speakers; if not the constitution of a (diffuse) doctrinal group; if not a distribution and appropriation of discourse, with all its learning and its powers? — Michel Foucault, *The Discourse on Language*[52]

Postwar literacy training in elementary schools entailed a systematic distribution of different kinds of discourse and competence at discursive practice to different kinds of children. This in itself constituted a mode of incorporation into a 'whole body of practices and expectations', an 'ordinary understanding of man and his world'.[53] In effect, interpretative communities were constructed by particular pedagogical practices. By tracing the discourse on and of literacy teaching, I have here depicted the complex historical linkages between the contexts of text generation, the structure and content of the texts themselves, and institutional contexts of readership. Yet to claim that literacy instruction is 'ideological' is to imply a value judgment on its role in the formation of the literate, and on the relationship of both that pedagogy and its subjects to the larger socio-cultural structures within which both exist.

The basal readers of the 1940s and '50s stood not simply to transmit ideological content but as well to convey and reinforce certain ideological schemata for human intersubjectivity: the mythology of Dick and Jane enshrined patterns of social relations, gender and race relations, hypothesis formation and problem-solving, categorization of the natural and social world, and so forth. Not incidentally, a schema for literacy was conveyed: children learned what was to count as appropriate reading, reader response, and writing and, for that matter, what was to count as a quality or interesting text. Reading is a rule-governed and boundaried process, and the production and reception of literature rely on the existence and possession of shared codes. If, as Eco insists, 'conditions for the necessity of the sign are socially determined', then the conditions for its reception also are stipulated and learned: one must crack the code of literacy, and within institutional literacy events this learning is circumscribed by a potentially ideological code of pedagogy.

Insofar as all school texts are modes for transmitting systematic bodies of ideas, attitudes, values and competences, they could be said to constitute a means of ideological incorporation, a selective tradition in action. However all encounters with pedagogically administered texts need not be 'biased' through and through. The reading of open and/or closed texts in an instructional context which encourages diversity of response does not entail this kind of imposition of meanings: texts and instructional events can generate unanticipated interpretations, the pursuit of text semantics by engaged and active readers. Then as now, a given pedagogic setting may have cultivated and encouraged readers to use their background knowledge to interpret *and* criticize texts. Hence the foregoing study has not been premised on a narrow ideological, textual, or pedagogical determinism which assumes that such texts were taught to the exclusion of all others in a singular, narrow mode. In every historical era, some teachers have encouraged independent selection and autonomous interpretation of texts, this in spite of attempts to standardize and control their thought and action. And yet in the era examined the quality of literacy learning and of learned literacy was constrained and delimited significantly by official norms for the acquisition of literacy.

Just as the interpretative codes for writing and reading/rewriting text are social and ideological constructions, not in any way innate or natural,[54] so too are the codes of pedagogical science and practice which stand to make and remake the 'literate' in any historical era. In accordance with the twentieth-century dominance of educational practice by the discourse of applied psychology, postwar educational scientists claimed that they merely were making textual and pedagogical practices on the basis of empirical study of the acquisition of literacy, that they were proceeding from 'truths' empirically derived from observation of that which was in the world (e.g., reading text, the literate). The resultant selective tradition of texts and pedagogical practices in fact constituted the aspiring literate in a finite range of roles and categories, from playful mischievous white male child in the community, to outdoorsy, tenacious Canadian youth, to 'slow learner' from a 'poor home environment'. The teacher of literacy likewise was reinvented as the unbiased empirical observer, the operator of scientific machinery, the institutionally observed worker, and the humane collaborative lover of children.

In comparison with other texts, pedagogical texts are more deliberate by degree in the kinds of cognitive and behavioural responses they mean to exact. Pedagogical texts written for the teaching of literacy are a special case of the teaching of paradigmatic knowledges and competences. For the serially disclosed meanings and relationships between meanings are indeed there to teach not only ideological content (selected values, ideas and meanings) but also teach attitudes towards, presuppositions about and procedures for contending with future texts (selected literate competences and 'skills'). Regarding the latter function of the literacy textbook, recall that Gray held what one read in early literacy instruction to matter less than how one learned to read. Defenders past and present of technicist approaches to the teaching of reading have argued, and continue to argue, that the particular methodological regime one learns to read under does not ultimately influence the character of mature literacy. And in passing, it is worth noting that cognitive, psycholinguistic and literary theories of intertextuality presuppose that the processing of a given text entails the invocation of prior readings of text. The constitutive effect of early literacy learning on one's mature literate tastes and competence therefore seems self-evident and undeniable.

Recognition of this special status of literacy textbooks in the ritual making the literate does not suggest that literary texts (e.g., novels, poetry) and functional texts (e.g., application forms, newspaper articles) do not also function on these dual didactic levels: indeed they too communicate messages, refer to the world and prescribe, in their textual form, the codes and conditions for their own reception and the reception of subsequent like and unlike texts. Effective writing of all types is rhetorical, setting out to achieve specific social purposes and psychological effects in the reader. And literacy events in everyday, non-pedagogical settings, too long ignored by researchers, can be significant moments in literate development.

But texts geared for the teaching of competence with text serve a particular social and political function: the differential and selective allocation of a competence which in modern Western cultures has been associated, if not always directly connected, with cultural, economic and political power.[55] And, a good deal of modern and historical educational research assures us, there is an inextricable correlation between competence with text, however construed and measured, total educational achievement, and ultimately, social status and economic attainment.[56] Regardless of the *actual* problematic relationship between literacy and cognitive development, between literacy and individual and national economic destiny, the *idée reçue* that institutionally defined, transmitted and verified literacy is somehow directly linked with cognitive prowess and sociocultural power makes the kinds of competence engendered in literacy training pivotal for the aspiring literate.

It goes without saying that any and all appraisals of the ideological and educational concomitants of literacy instruction must reflect, even if implicitly, a positive thesis regarding the sociocultural and individual power of literacy. Moreover, as noted at the outset of this study, current and historical definitions of literate competence and of the optimal conditions for its achievement are based upon concurrent presuppositions about the normative purposes of educational, social and cognitive development. Shared, however, by a range of theories of literacy are the notions that text has the potential to provide cognitive and social alternatives to readers and that interpretation can entail an active participation on the part of the reader. Presupposed in a variety of accounts of literate development is a belief in the potential of the text as a vehicle of individual development, whereby the reader is able (at least potentially and ideally) to use text actively to make meaning, and by means of which authors are able (at least potentially and ideally) to construct complex texts which invite inter-pretation and generate critique.

It is nonetheless quite possible to assess the ideological and educational effects of postwar mass literacy training without recourse to any particular positive thesis on the 'emancipatory' character of literacy. Certainly reading text and learning to read text can be an institutionally constrained experience, and textual semantic structure can preclude the presentation and apprehension of multiple possible worlds. Certain texts through overcoding, redundancy, and repetition do not serve the educational end of 'schema elaboration', of interpretation which entails the interactive extension of pre-viously experienced knowledges and understandings. Closed texts constrain the critical potential of literacy through an extensive ideological denotation both at the level of the sentence and the text grammar. Readers are rendered consumers rather than learners, and habitual encounters with the closed text may create further dependency:

> Each of these social types, the inmate, the spectator, the human commodity and the divided subject, has a different relation to knowledge. Each is adapted to a different text. To the veteran inmate, knowledge can only be read as a command. The habit of

acquiescence to instruction generalizes all information, and the inmate's social context, the asylum (whether mental hospital, school or society), is organized in ways that accommodate that need. The bureaucratic announcement/memo is the form of the closed text to which the inmate is accustomed. The spectator awaits excitement.[57]

How might this particular 'role of the reader' influence individuals' educational development? Richard C. Anderson argues that change and growth in the individual's schematic repertoire are linked to enhancement of the larger culture's 'interpretive schemes', its epistemological assumptions sutured together in daily perception into a '*Zeitgeist*'.[58] He claims that that 'dialectic' instruction, exemplified in Socratic dialogue, can 'cause a person to modify a world view, ideology or theory'.[59] Students and teachers possess and express distinct and often divergent schemata, varying kinds and levels of background knowledge brought to institutional literacy events. The resultant pedagogical interaction, Anderson maintains, can maximize 'schema change' when it shows that the person's 'difficulty' is resolved best through the utilization of a new, or different schema, or extension (that is, negation) of a previously held schema.

So seen, social and cognitive development for Anderson constitute a dialectical process, characterized by the elaboration and expansion, construction and criticism of schemata. Anderson's is a relativist position which views social change as change in the collective schemata, with little commentary on material or economic conditions. But he maintains that educational ends are not served by pedagogical techniques which engender 'schema assimilation': the uncritical acceptance of schemata, and the habitual usage of conventional schemata to account for and rationalize every new text, experience and historical phenomenon.[60]

This positive thesis on the dialectical potential of textual schemata in education parallels Eco's notion of open and closed readership. Eco's work implies that not all texts are monological transmissions, which would demand little more than pattern recognition and acknowledgment by the hungry reader. Here I do not mean to suggest that texts which are ambiguous are virtuous and 'non-violent', for as McLuhan and Olson remind us, textual language is 'high definition', it is biased towards explicitness, providing its own context for interpretation.[61] So read this not as a vindication of the vague and a condemnation of the textual explicitness. Some texts are explicit but by the very illocutionary force of that explicitness generate a range of possible interpretations.

As an ideal type, the open text provides the generative conditions for its own unexpected interpretation. While presuming compatibility between the author's and reader's interpretative codes, it expands and develops that schematic knowledge which the reader brings to the text, thus expressing possibility through the provision of open schematic patterns. In this manner, it not only conveys novelty but relies on that novelty to engage the reader. This 'openness' takes the form of unique, creative syntactic *and* semantic transformation. The unique use of lexicon and syntax, of language at the level of the sentence may contribute to novelty. The innovative use of commonly known and used terms and the construction of new lexical items characterize, for example, Tolkien sagas and Roald Dahl's reinterpretations of traditional fairy tales. Readers also may encounter particularly apt contextual uses of common grammatical structures and the wholescale invention/deconstruction of others. Even if readers limit the search for 'difference' to the level of the sentence, these texts challenge and dialectically threaten existing codes and taken-for-granted assumptions about text and about the world. This is, after all one of the powers of literature: the ability to generate novelty at the level of both textual micro- and macrostructure.

Contrapose against this readership engendered by the story schemata of adolescent romance novels,[62] basal series, or the passages from Ian Fleming noted by Eco, where the authors *appear* to be providing 'new' or 'novel' information, but in fact mechanically re-instantiate an already known schema. Dick needs help, goes to Father, Sally needs help, goes to Father. Bond walks into a room, Bond spots cigarette ashes, Bond notices woman's jewellery. Though the details may be different, the script — the ideational scaffold of the typical 007, or the typical Middletown possible world and plot — remains the same. The reader is asked by the text to recognize and slot information into an already high-definition schema. Ultimately her or his hunger, generated by a simple pattern of expectation and satisfaction, is sated momentarily by a predictable catharsis.

But are we to surmise, as Anderson implies, that phenomena like didactic teaching and closed textbooks are simply the result of ill-informed teachers and unenlightened textbook authors? What of the mass cultural causes, concomitants and consequences of this kind of literacy?

The parallels between the construction, structure and function of educational texts and the social texts of industrial and post-industrial culture are too obvious to ignore. Regarding the effects of this pedagogical and literary structuring of reality and competence and its degree of fit with postwar society, let us consider Eco's parallel analysis of the eighteenth-century 'feuilleton'. As consumer objects, closed texts follow the 'codes of the heavy industry of dreams in a capitalist society'. Offering neither subtle hypotheses, nor multifaceted characterizations, nor highly problematic story structures, closed texts simply reinforce existing beliefs:

> The feuilleton, founded on the triumph of information, represented the preferred fare of a society that lived in the midst of

messages loaded with redundance; the sense of tradition, the norms of associative living, moral principles, the valid rules of proper comportment in the environment of eighteenth century bourgeois society, of the typical public which represented the consumers of the feuilleton — all this constituted a system of foreseeable communication that the social system provided for its members and allowed life to flow smoothly without unexpected jolts and without upsets in its social system.[63]

Even given the possibility of pragmatic or pedagogical accidents resulting from active, though uninvited mediation by reader or teacher, closed texts, taught and read within highly circumscribed and rule-bound social contexts beget passive consumption and a hunger for redundance. Where this is the case, the very teaching of literacy becomes an ideological act, not the simple transmission of messages about a particular 'false consciousness' but rather the actual training in that consciousness. In this regard, previous studies of the ideological character of literacy training have perhaps concentrated too greatly on text content and not paid sufficient attention to how textual form and pedagogical context in unison can beget what Freire calls a 'disempowered' competence. Literally what is said in a text is of importance. But I have here tried to call attention to how and under what assumptions it is made (the social construction of school knowledge), how it is said (the semantic structure of the text) and how it is taught (the institutional conditions of reception) as interlocking parts which together constitute a selective tradition. The key here is a renewed focus on how text structure pragmatically stipulates the role of the reader and potentially renders reading itself an ideological act.

From this, we should not hastily conclude that putatively 'scientific' understandings of the processes of literacy acquisition are necessarily invalid bases for pedagogy. On the contrary, the present study has applied various social scientific perspectives to the reading of the aforementioned texts, rendering itself as guilty as any of the sins of hermeneutic science. But several larger considerations emerge. Following Habermas, it is important to recognize that the ascendancy of particular scientific truths to the status of educational common sense is based not only on empirical verification, canons of scientific validity and the like.[64] The applications of scientific theories in technical/practical domains like education are ideological and political selections. The case has been made that psychometrics itself is one such discourse[65] and the present study points to the need to examine further the ideological and economic grounds for paradigm shifts in reading research and other educational sciences. The greater danger for educators and researchers is the acritical acceptance of paradigmatic wisdom for, as

McHoul remarks, 'shared world commonsense background knowledge is the domain in which power [and ideology] operates most effectively simply by virtue of its taken-for-grantedness'.[66] These remain avenues for further investigation, but the present study indicates that particular historical discourses used to legitimate educational practices may have been selected for other than purely 'educational' reasons, and may have led to socio-cultural consequences unforeseen by their participants.

Reading the history of literacy, various historians, ethnographers and linguists have argued that literacy necessarily entails the standardization of language, and by extension, of thought. Indeed, text itself is a standardization of spoken language, and educators past and present have been concerned with the norming of the linguistic and literary corpus and the regulation of access to that corpus. In the 1950s, even in a colonial outpost like British Columbia, an industrial-style standardization of the quality of literate competence was occurring, fixing the roles of the reader and writer. Texts children learned to read with were ideologically coded in both axiomatic content and linguistic form; conditions of readership were similarly dictated via text. Even without presupposing the efficacy of this system, it is clear that ideological forms of literacy and attitudes towards the functions and values of literacy were engendered.

As for those who grew up, succeeded and failed within the machinery of the reading group, the standardized test and the weekly spelling test: most complied willingly. And those who could not or did not, readily accounted for by reference to the lower end of the institutional grid of specification, were diagnosed and treated accordingly. For a generation of Canadian students, school reading consisted of highly structured encounters with Dick and Jane, Petit Jean and Henri, Roger and Dutchy. Though Gray's basal readers ceased to be used in the late 1960s and early '70s, Dick and Jane remain in Canada — in the literate sensibilities of a particular interpretive community: the postwar 'baby-boom' generation.

Notes and References

1. Henry A. Giroux, 'Radical Pedagogy and the Politics of Student Voice', *Interchange* 17 (No. 1, 1986), 62.
2. See Walter J. Ong, *Orality and Literacy: The Technologizing of the Word* (London: Methuen, 1982).
3. Shirley B. Heath, 'Towards an Ethnohistory of Writing in American Education', in Marcia F. Whiteman (ed.), *Variation in Writing: Functional and Linguistic-Cultural Differences* (Hillsdale, N.J.: Erlbaum, 1981), p. 27.
4. Paul Dimaggio, 'Cultural Entrepreneurship in Nineteenth-Century Boston:

in Scientific Tradition and Change (Chicago: University of Chicago Press, 1977), esp. pp. 225–9.

61. Marshall McLuhan, *Understanding Media* (New York: McGraw-Hill, 1962); Olson, 'From Utterance to Text'.

62. Linda Christian-Smith, 'Power, Romance and Curriculum: Constructing Femininity in Adolescent Romance Novels', in Suzanne de Castell, Allan Luke and Carmen Luke (eds), *Language, Authority and Criticism: Readings on the School Textbook* (London: Falmer Press, forthcoming/1988); 'Gender, Popular Culture, and Curriculum: Adolescent Novels as Gender Text,' *Curriculum Inquiry* 17 (1987), 365–406.

63. Eco, *Role of the Reader*, p. 121.

64. See Jurgen Habermas, *Knowledge and Human Interests* (Boston: Beacon Press, 1971).

65. See Clarence J. Karier, 'Testing for Order and Control in the Corporate Liberal State', in Dale *et al.* (eds), *Schooling and Capitalism*, pp. 128–41; Steven Rose and Hilary Rose, 'The Politics of Neurobiology: Biologism in the Service of the State' in Dale *et al.* (eds), *Schooling and Capitalism*, pp. 120–7; cf. Ian Hacking, 'How Should we do the History of Statistics?', *Ideology and Consciousness* 8 (1981), 15–26.

66. Alec McHoul, 'Language and the Sociology of Mind: A Critical Introduction to the Work of Jeff Coulter', *Journal of Pragmatics* (forthcoming/1988).

Index

Note: The Index covers authors, subjects and titles mentioned in the text. It does not include matter from the Notes and References sections.